W9-AMZ-662

Brecht and Political Theatre:
The Mother on Stage

LAURA BRADLEY

CLARENDON PRESS · OXFORD

OXFORD
UNIVERSITY PRESS

Great Clarendon Street, Oxford OX2 6DP

Oxford University Press is a department of the University of Oxford.
It furthers the University's objective of excellence in research, scholarship,
and education by publishing worldwide in

Oxford New York

Auckland Cape Town Dar es Salaam Hong Kong Karachi
Kuala Lumpur Madrid Melbourne Mexico City Nairobi
New Delhi Shanghai Taipei Toronto

With offices in

Argentina Austria Brazil Chile Czech Republic France Greece
Guatemala Hungary Italy Japan Poland Portugal Singapore
South Korea Switzerland Thailand Turkey Ukraine Vietnam

Oxford is a registered trade mark of Oxford University Press
in the UK and in certain other countries

Published in the United States
by Oxford University Press Inc., New York

British Library Cataloguing in Publication Data

Data available

Library of Congress Cataloging in Publication Data

Data available

Typeset by Laserwords Private Limited, Chennai, India
Printed in Great Britain
on acid-free paper by
Biddles Ltd., King's Lynn, Norfolk

ISBN 0–19–928658–2   978–0–19–928658–4

1 3 5 7 9 10 8 6 4 2

Acknowledgements

I would like to thank all the people who have helped me during my work on this book, which is a revised version of a doctoral thesis submitted to the University of Oxford in 2003. I am particularly indebted to my supervisors, Tom Kuhn and Richard Sheppard, for their invaluable and unstinting advice, enthusiasm, and encouragement throughout the project. My thanks also go to those colleagues who provided thought-provoking comments on my work at various stages: Tony Phelan, Steve Giles, Karen Leeder, Katrin Kohl, Kevin Hilliard, and Ben Morgan.

I am extremely grateful to the Arts and Humanities Research Board for funding my doctoral research and to Merton College, Oxford, for enabling me to revise my thesis for publication during my Junior Research Fellowship. St Edmund Hall, Oxford, generously provided further academic and financial support, and the Modern Languages Faculty, Oxford, and Conference of University Teachers of German funded visits to German archives.

It is a pleasure to thank the people who have assisted me in archives and libraries, particularly Dr Wizisla and Dr Harder at the Brecht-Archiv, Frau Hübner at the Berliner Ensemble, Dr Ullrich at the Akademie der Künste, Dr Schirmer at the Stadtmuseum in Berlin, Frau Ganz at the Schaubühne, and Helen Buchanan and Jill Hughes at the Taylorian Library. I am equally grateful to the theatre practitioners who shared their experiences of staging *Die Mutter* with me: Wolf Bunge, Annie Castledine, Hans-Joachim Frank, Wera and Claus Küchenmeister, Jörg Mihan, Alexander Stillmark, Renate Richter, and Manfred Wekwerth.

I wish to thank the following for kind permission to publish archive material, quotations from personal interviews, and plates in this book: Barbara Brecht-Schall; Gudrun Bunge; Alice Eisler; Hans-Joachim Frank; Wera Küchenmeister; Michael Mayhew; Jörg Mihan; Beate Nelken; Daniel Pozner; Monika Rittershaus; Maria Steinfeldt; Alexander Stillmark; Ulrike Stoll-Neher; Vera Tenschert; Holger Tesch-ke; Sebastian Weisenborn; Manfred Wekwerth; Berliner Ensemble; Bertolt-Brecht-Archiv; henschel SCHAUSPIEL; Landesarchiv Berlin; Schaubühne am Lehniner Platz; Scottish Theatre Archive, Glasgow

University Library, Department of Special Collections; Stadtmuseum Berlin; Stiftung Archiv der Akademie der Künste; Stiftung Archiv der Parteien und Massenorganisationen der DDR im Bundesarchiv.

Finally, I would like to thank my family for their encouragement and interest, and for even coming to see one of the productions.

L B

Contents

List of Illustrations

List of Abbreviations

AdK	Akademie der Künste
AP	Associated Press
APO	Außerparlamentarische Opposition
BArch	Bundesarchiv
BBA	Bertolt-Brecht-Archiv
BE	Berliner Ensemble
BEA	Berliner Ensemble Archive
BFA	*Große kommentierte Berliner und Frankfurter Ausgabe*
CDU	Christlich Demokratische Union
cond.	conducted by
CPR	Centre for Performance Research
DDR	Deutsche Demokratische Republik
dir.	directed by
EHA	Elisabeth-Hauptmann-Archiv
FAZ	*Frankfurter Allgemeine Zeitung*
FBI	Federal Bureau of Investigation
FDJ	Freie Deutsche Jugend
FRG	Federal Republic of Germany
GDP	Gross Domestic Product
GDR	German Democratic Republic
GLL	*German Life and Letters*
GWA	Günther-Weisenborn-Archiv
HEA	Hanns-Eisler-Archiv
IRA	Irish Republican Army
KPD	Kommunistische Partei Deutschlands
NATO	North Atlantic Treaty Organization
ND	*Neues Deutschland*
n.d.	date of publication unknown
n.p.	no pagination
NT	National Theatre

NTA	National Theatre Archive
PDS	Partei des Demokratischen Sozialismus
RAF	Rote Armee Fraktion
RBA	Ruth-Berlau-Archiv
RDA	République Démocratique Allemande
RF	*Die Rote Fahne*
RKP	Robert-Koch-Platz, Berlin
RUC	Royal Ulster Constabulary
SA	Schaubühne am Lehniner Platz Archive
SAPMO	Stiftung Archiv der Parteien und Massenorganisationen der DDR
SB	Stadtmuseum Berlin
SED	Sozialistische Einheitspartei Deutschlands
SEW	Sozialistische Einheitspartei Westberlins
SPD	Sozialdemokratische Partei Deutschlands
STA	Scottish Theatre Archive
SW	Schloß Wahn Theatersammlung, Cologne
TDR	*The Drama Review*
USSR	Union of Soviet Socialist Republics
ZK	Zentralkomitee

Introduction

1. BRECHT, PERFORMANCE, AND *DIE MUTTER* (*THE MOTHER*)

Bertolt Brecht argued that performance was the true test of any dramatic text.[1] Ever the writer-director, he revised his plays during rehearsals and then evaluated their reception by the audience. He often incorporated the changes into subsequent editions of the published texts, which then functioned as the starting-point for his future productions. This practice enabled Brecht to tailor plays to his target audience and to address the political and social issues of the day. His development as a writer, director, and theorist of theatre can therefore be fully understood only in relation to performance.

The importance that Brecht attached to performance reflects the fact that a dramatic text can only ever be provisional. This is because its interpretation is always contingent on the manner of its performance, when the set design, costumes, movement, gesture, and line delivery all interact with the words to produce meaning. Interpretations of a dramatic text also change in response to the performance context, which affects the theatre's approach and the audience's reactions. By examining the different ways in which a play has been staged, performance history foregrounds the impact of theatre aesthetics and context on the text's interpretation.

Die Mutter is an ideal subject for a production history of one of Brecht's plays, both in its own right and in relation to his theatrical practice. The play's confrontational politics and distinctive aesthetic pose particular challenges to directors seeking to transfer it to new contexts and audiences, as Brecht himself discovered. *Die Mutter* is

---

[1] e.g. Bertolt Brecht, *Große kommentierte Berliner und Frankfurter Ausgabe* (henceforth *BFA*), ed. Werner Hecht *et al.*, 30 vols (Frankfurt/Main and Berlin: Suhrkamp and Aufbau, 1988–2000), xxvi (1994), 395.

actually the only text that he staged in the Weimar Republic, in exile, and in the GDR, and Brecht also advised his co-worker Ruth Berlau on her productions in Copenhagen in 1935 and in Leipzig in 1950. Brecht's productions of *Die Mutter* show how his theatrical practice developed, how he responded to different political, cultural and institutional contexts, and how the experience of staging and evaluating plays contributed to the development of his theories. They also reveal how, and how far, Brecht's theories articulated and influenced his practice at different points in time. This is important because he often formulated his theoretical writings as polemical contributions to context-specific debates.

Since Brecht's death in 1956, *Die Mutter* has been staged by another four leading German directors, Peter Stein, Ruth Berghaus, Manfred Wekwerth, and Claus Peymann, and by theatre practitioners in most European countries and the Americas, Australia, Japan, India, and Afghanistan. In the 1970s and 1980s, it became a seminal text for politicized theatres in Britain and Scandinavia. These postwar productions demonstrate how directors have developed and exploited Brecht's theories and techniques for new purposes and audiences, and how Brecht has influenced twentieth-century theatre in Germany and abroad.

As an overtly Communist play, *Die Mutter* divided critics along political lines at the première and has continued to do so ever since. During the Cold War, East German critics like Werner Hecht, Werner Mittenzwei, and Ernst Schumacher presented it as an important step forward in Brecht's work.[2] In contrast, many Western critics regarded *Die Mutter* as an aberration and rejected it, sometimes in polemical terms. Bjørn Ekmann, for instance, called it '[eine] blutrünstige Hetze' ('bloodthirsty rabble-rousing'), and Jan Needle and Peter Thomson argued that 'it is hard to find much merit in *The Mother* except as a sop to the converted'.[3] Since the collapse of state Socialism in the Eastern bloc, Brecht's call for revolution has been criticized as out of date. *Die Mutter* thus exemplifies the challenges facing left-wing literature in

---

[2] Werner Hecht, *Sieben Studien über Brecht* (Frankfurt/Main: Suhrkamp, 1972), 68; Werner Mittenzwei, *Bertolt Brecht: Von der 'Maßnahme' zu 'Leben des Galilei'*, 4th edn (East Berlin: Aufbau, 1977), 98; Ernst Schumacher, *Die dramatischen Versuche Bertolt Brechts 1918–1933* (East Berlin: Rütten & Loening, 1955), 432.

[3] Bjørn Ekmann, *Gesellschaft und Gewissen: Die sozialen und moralischen Anschauungen Bertolt Brechts und ihre Bedeutung für seine Dichtung* (Copenhagen: Munksgaard, 1969), 189; Jan Needle and Peter Thomson, *Brecht* (Oxford: Blackwell, 1981), 77.

general, and Brecht's work in particular, before, during, and after the Cold War.

Although literary critics have often regarded *Die Mutter* as simplistic, its performance history reveals a wide variety of theatrical interpretations. These in turn shed new perspectives on the text, showing it to be far more subtle and sophisticated than many critical accounts suggest. This book examines how directors have constructed fresh interpretations for new contexts and new audiences; how stagings of the play have changed; and what these stagings reveal, both about the text itself and about broader developments in twentieth-century German theatre, politics, and culture.

2. BRECHT'S POLITICAL THEATRE: METHODS AND CONCEPTS

Brecht defined political theatre in terms of form, not just content. He argued that new theatrical forms were needed to deal with modern socio-economic reality: 'Schon die Erfassung der neuen Stoffgebiete kostet eine neue dramatische und theatralische Form. Können wir in der Form des Jambus über Geld sprechen? ... Das Petroleum sträubt sich gegen die fünf Akte, die Katastrophen von heute verlaufen nicht geradlinig, sondern in der Form von Krisenzyklen.'[4] In Brecht's view, existing theatrical forms promoted conservative interests. This was partly because they encouraged the spectator to receive productions passively, so that '[er] gibt seine Vernunft mit dem Mantel in der Garderobe ab'.[5] But it was also because they suggested that spectators were powerless to change society: 'Das Theater, wie wir es vorfinden, zeigt die Struktur der Gesellschaft (abgebildet auf der Bühne) nicht als beeinflußbar durch die Gesellschaft (im Zuschauerraum).'[6] According to Brecht, even Naturalist drama, which dealt with

---

[4] 'Even just to tackle the new areas of subject-matter, we need a new dramatic and theatrical form. Can we talk about money in iambic form? ... Petroleum resists any division into five acts; today's catastrophes do not run in a straight line, but in the form of cyclical crises.' 'Über Stoffe und Form', *BFA*, xxi (1992), 302–4 (303). Unless otherwise indicated, all quotations from the *BFA* are by Brecht and translations are my own.

[5] '[He] hands the cloakroom attendant his brain along with his coat.' 'Dialog über Schauspielkunst', *BFA*, xxi. 279–82 (280).

[6] 'Theatre, as we know it, shows the structure of society (depicted on stage) as incapable of being influenced by society (in the auditorium).' 'Kleines Organon für das Theater', *BFA*, xxiii (1993), 65–97 (78).

social and political issues, encouraged spectators to resign themselves to the status quo by presenting workers as powerless victims of their heredity and environment.[7] Brecht was not alone in viewing Naturalist drama as an inadequate vehicle for the problems facing modern society; the Communist director Erwin Piscator criticized the genre on the grounds that it presented only outbursts of desperation, not solutions.[8]

In the 1920s, Brecht and Piscator pioneered new forms of representation in German theatre. But whereas Piscator relied primarily on modern stage technology, including film, to provide a political commentary and extend the scope of his productions, Brecht developed new dramatic as well as theatrical forms. Through his dramatic techniques, acting methods, and staging devices, Brecht created a dialectical theatre that would expose the contradictions in social reality and depict society as an ever-changing process, not a fixed state. By replacing the 'Vortäuschung der Harmonie' ('feigned harmony') of bourgeois aesthetics with the Hegelian clash of thesis and antithesis, he sought to confront his spectators with real alternatives and show that their decisions would shape the future.[9] Although Brecht would not consider using the name 'dialectical theatre' until 1954, dialectics were already central to his theatrical practice in the late Weimar Republic.[10]

Brecht's theatre transforms the spectators' relationship with the stage action in order to change not just what they think, but how they think: 'Bemüht, ihren Zuschauer ein ganz bestimmtes praktisches, die Änderung der Welt bezweckendes Verhalten zu lehren, verleiht [Brechts Dramatik] ihm schon im Theater eine grundsätzlich andere Haltung, als er gewohnt ist. Er wird in die Lage versetzt, eine kritische, kontrollierende Haltung einzunehmen.'[11] In order to cultivate this critical attitude, Brecht's theatre destroys the illusory 'fourth wall'—the convention that the audience is eavesdropping on the action, unbeknown

---

[7] e.g. 'Die dialektische Dramatik', *BFA*, xxi. 431–43 (433–4).

[8] Erwin Piscator, *Das politische Theater* (Berlin: Adalbert Schultz, 1929), 30.

[9] '[Nachträge zum *Kleinen Organon*]', *BFA*, xxiii. 289–95 (294).

[10] e.g. '[Vom epischen zum dialektischen Theater I]', *BFA*, xxiii. 299. See also Brecht's 1930–1 essay 'Die dialektische Dramatik', *BFA*, xxi. 431–43.

[11] 'In its efforts to teach its spectator a very specific practical type of behaviour, aimed at changing the world, [Brecht's drama] already grants him a fundamentally different attitude in the theatre from the one to which he is accustomed. He is enabled to adopt a critical attitude and to monitor the performance.' '[Das deutsche Drama vor Hitler]', *BFA*, xxii.1 (1993), 164–8 (166).

to the characters. It displays the stage apparatus, such as the lights, in full view of the audience and introduces narrative elements into the performance. Songs interrupt the dramatic action; projected images provide a visual commentary, as in Piscator's productions; and captions summarize the play's political arguments and the content of individual scenes. The juxtaposition of these narrative or 'epic' elements with the dramatic action forces the spectator to adopt an active, critical role by comparing and evaluating the different pieces of information. So whereas the epic and the dramatic constitute separate genres in Aristotle's *Poetics*, Brecht combined them to form his 'epic' or 'non-Aristotelian' theatre.

Epic theatre requires its actors, like its spectators, to retain their critical and political awareness. Instead of immersing themselves in their roles, the actors present their characters to the audience: 'die Schauspieler [vollziehen] die Verwandlung nicht vollständig, sondern [halten] Abstand zu der von ihnen dargestellten Figur, ja, [fordern] deutlich zur Kritik auf.'[12] The final clause shows that the actors are to remain detached in order to invite criticism of the character—in this context, sociopolitical criticism. By emphasizing the decisions that inform the actions of the characters, the performers encourage spectators to see how alternative courses of action could have provoked different outcomes. Brecht called this technique the *Nicht, Sondern Prinzip*, the 'not, but principle': 'Der Schauspieler soll bei allen wesentlichen Punkten zu dem, was er macht, noch etwas ausfindig, namhaft und ahnbar machen, was er nicht macht. Er sagt z.B. nicht: ich verzeihe dir, sondern: das wirst du mir bezahlen.'[13] So when, in Scene 3 of the 1951 production of *Die Mutter*, the factory police asked the worker Smilgin where he had found an illegal pamphlet, Smilgin hesitated and looked at the real culprit, the Mother, before deciding not to betray her—a class comrade—and claiming instead that it had lain on the floor.

Brecht also promoted self-conscious, stylized acting through his technique of *Gestus*. This is a problematic and complex term which

[12] 'The actors [do] not [transform] themselves completely, but [retain] a distance from the character they are presenting; indeed, they clearly [invite] criticism.' 'Vergnügungstheater oder Lehrtheater', *BFA*, xxii.1. 106–16 (108).
[13] 'At every essential point, the actor should, in addition to what he does, make the audience discover, note, and sense what he does not do. For example, he does not say: I forgive you, but: you'll pay for this.' 'Anweisungen an die Schauspieler', *BFA*, xxii.2. 667–8 (667).

Brecht used in a variety of contexts, but in relation to acting it is best understood as a physical action or spatial configuration which reveals the ideological, social and economic relations between two or more characters.[14] In Scene 8 of the 1951 production, for example, Brecht placed his Communist heroine at the opposite side of the stage to the nationalistic strikebreakers, so that this physical distance illustrated the ideological gulf between them. And in Scene 6, the teacher stood right underneath the Tsar's portrait while declaring that it would be senseless to educate the masses. This configuration exposed the teacher and, by extension, the Russian education system as a mouthpiece for the Tsar's ideology and a bulwark against political change. By thus drawing the spectators' attention to ideological and socio-economic factors, gestic acting suggests that human behaviour is not the inevitable result of innate psychology. Together, *Gestus* and the *Nicht, Sondern Prinzip* show that there is a dynamic relationship between humans and society: humans influence, and are influenced by, society.

The most famous, and most frequently misunderstood, of Brecht's techniques is *Verfremdung*, a term which entered his theoretical writings in 1936.[15] It is best translated as 'estrangement' or 'defamiliarization', and it aims to make spectators see familiar phenomena and people from fresh angles—just as acquiring a stepfather forces a man to view his mother in a new light: as another man's husband.[16] Brecht explains:

Einen Vorgang oder einen Charakter verfremden heißt zunächst einfach, dem Vorgang oder dem Charakter das Selbstverständliche, Bekannte, Einleuchtende zu nehmen und über ihn Staunen und Neugierde zu erzeugen…. Damit ist gewonnen, daß der Zuschauer die Menschen auf der Bühne nicht mehr als ganz unänderbare, unbeeinflußbare, ihrem Schicksal hilflos ausgelieferte dargestellt sieht…. Damit ist gewonnen, daß der Zuschauer im Theater eine neue Haltung bekommt.[17]

---

[14] Cf. 'Gestik', *BFA*, xxiii. 187–8. For a detailed analysis of *Gestus*, see Meg Mumford, 'Showing the Gestus: A Study of Acting in Brecht's Theatre' (unpublished doctoral thesis, University of Bristol, 1997).

[15] See Jan Knopf, 'Verfremdung', in *Brechts Theorie des Theaters*, ed. Werner Hecht (Frankfurt/Main: Suhrkamp, 1986), 93–141.

[16] 'Kurze Beschreibung einer neuen Technik der Schauspielkunst, die einen Verfremdungseffekt hervorbringt', *BFA*, xxii.2. 641–59 (656).

[17] 'Estranging an event or a character simply means, in the first instance, divesting the event or the character of all its self-explanatory, familiar, strikingly clear qualities, and arousing astonishment and curiosity about it…. It ensures that the spectator no

The *Verfremdungseffekt* (estrangement effect) is thus another method of provoking critical reflection and prompting spectators to question phenomena which they usually take for granted. As such, it is an important tool for promoting political consciousness.

Although *Verfremdung* is often translated misleadingly as 'alienation', it does not imply any rejection of emotion. The characters in epic theatre experience the full range of emotions, and Brecht simply wants the spectator to retain sufficient critical detachment to analyse these emotions: 'Das epische Theater bekämpft nicht die Emotionen, sondern untersucht sie und macht nicht halt bei ihrer Erzeugung.'[18] By preventing total identification, epic theatre gives the spectator the freedom to experience different emotions from the characters: 'Er kann Zorn empfinden, wo die Bühnenfigur Freude empfindet usw.'[19]

Despite common preconceptions, Brecht's theatre actually combines his radical claims for the epic form with more traditional dramatic techniques. Even though *Die Mutter* features epic devices prominently, it still relies on a complex interplay of the dramatic and the epic. In Chapter 1, I compare the play to Brecht's own contrasts between dramatic and epic theatre, which were first included in his notes on *Mahagonny* and then reprinted in the programme for the 1932 première of *Die Mutter*. My analysis reveals that the play's dramaturgy is far subtler than Brecht's polemical statements about epic theatre, or indeed most literary critics' interpretations, suggest.

Brecht also strove to transform the theatre apparatus. His most radical experiments occurred between 1929 and 1932, when he developed the *Lehrstück* (learning play), as a pedagogical exercise for performers.[20] By transferring the emphasis from the performance to the staging

---

longer sees the human beings on stage as completely unchangeable, incapable of being influenced, helplessly exposed to their fate.... It ensures that the spectator experiences a new attitude in the theatre.' 'Über experimentelles Theater', *BFA*, xxii.1. 540–57 (554–5).

[18] 'Epic theatre does not combat emotions, but investigates them and does not stop short at producing them.' 'Kleine Liste der beliebtesten, landläufigsten und banalsten Irrtümer über das epische Theater', *BFA*, xxii.1. 315–16 (315).

[19] 'He can experience anger when the character on stage experiences joy, etc.' 'Nachtrag zur Theorie des *Messingkaufs*', *BFA*, xxii.2. 701–2 (701).

[20] Although *Lehrstück* has often been translated as 'teaching play' or 'didactic play', Brecht preferred the term 'learning play'. This term emphasizes that the performers are active participants, rather than the passive recipients of pre-fabricated lessons. See 'The German Drama: pre-Hitler', *BFA*, xxii.2. 939–44 (941).

process, Brecht challenged the dominant concept of theatre as the supplier of a product. Indeed, he even argued that the *Lehrstück* did not need an audience: performance was only a possible by-product, not an essential end-product, of rehearsals.[21] These experiments with the theatre apparatus stalled during Brecht's exile when, as I show in Chapter 4, his plays were staged relatively infrequently and in conditions over which he had little control. Nevertheless, when Brecht established his own company in the GDR, he placed in-house political and theatrical education at the heart of his project to transform professional theatre from within. In order to understand the nature and significance of his theatrical practice and the reasons why it became a model for subsequent practitioners of political theatre, we therefore need to devote as much attention to the staging process as to the finished productions.

3. *DIE MUTTER*: THE TEXT AND PLOT

Brecht wrote *Die Mutter* in 1931–2 in collaboration with the writer Elisabeth Hauptmann, the composer Hanns Eisler, the Bulgarian director Slatan Dudow, and the playwright Günther Weisenborn. The team's literary sources were Gorky's 1907 novel 'Мать' (*Mother*), in Adolf Hess's German translation, and a dramatization completed in 1931 by Weisenborn and Günther Stark, a dramaturge from the Volksbühne.[22]

Although most literary critics interpret *Die Mutter* as if it existed as a single text, directors actually have to choose between five versions, only two of which are included in the new edition of Brecht's collected works, the *Berliner und Frankfurter Ausgabe*.[23] This diversity exists because Brecht revised the text after each of his three productions and fed the changes into the 1933, 1938 and 1957 editions. In 1951, the Berliner Ensemble's version was published for the exclusive use of theatres, and in 1970, the dramaturge and director Joachim

---

[21] 'Zur Theorie des Lehrstücks', *BFA*, xxii.1. 351–2.

[22] Maxim Gorky, *Die Mutter*, trans. Adolf Hess (Berlin: Malik, 1927); Günther Stark and Günther Weisenborn, 'Die Mutter', ed. Emma Lewis Thomas, *Brecht heute*, 3 (1973), 64–105.

[23] A rare exception is John Fuegi, who notes that 'a major difficulty in discussing *The Mother* is the fact that there really is no single definitive text'. Fuegi, *The Essential Brecht* (Los Angeles: Hennessey & Ingalls, 1972), 51.

Tenschert published another version that incorporated some of the changes that had been made during the production's long run.[24] Far from presenting any edition as definitive, Brecht actually encouraged directors to experiment with the text. For instance, in 1933 he suggested that they might place choruses in the audience to comment on the action, and in 1938 he published an optional scene set in a railway carriage, which was based on an idea by Paul Peters, the American translator of the 1935 production.[25] The following outline is based on the 1933 edition.

Brecht's play charts the transformation of an apolitical Russian widow, Pelagea Wlassowa, into an active revolutionary. Scene 1 presents her desperate plight: the wages of her son, Pawel, have been cut, and she can see no way to make ends meet. But even as she resigns herself to her fate, Pawel is already actively seeking redress: in Scene 2, he and his comrades print leaflets calling for a strike. Wlassowa is deeply sceptical of this political activity and hostile towards Pawel's comrades, but she volunteers to deliver the leaflets in order to protect him from danger. In Scene 3, she skilfully smuggles the leaflets into the factory and watches the police arrest an innocent bystander simply for reading one. This arbitrary arrest sparks Wlassowa's curiosity: in Scene 4, she engages the revolutionaries in debate, learns about their motivation, and overcomes her suspicion. In Scene 5, she joins the strikers' May Day demonstration. When Smilgin, the worker bearing the flag, is shot dead by the police, Wlassowa carries it in his place. The contradiction between her apolitical outlook and her political activity is thus resolved in favour of revolutionary commitment.

The next phase sees Wlassowa become an independent revolutionary as she takes over from Pawel, who is now in prison. In Scene 6, she goes to live with the bourgeois teacher Nikolai Wessowtschikow, the brother of Pawel's comrade Iwan, because she has been evicted from her own home. Wlassowa converts her new neighbours to Communism and cajoles Nikolai into teaching them how to read and write so that they can print their own leaflets. In Scene 7, Wlassowa visits Pawel in prison to discover which peasants support the strikes in the countryside. She delivers propaganda to them in Scene 8 and convinces the local butcher to join the strike.

[24] Brecht, *Die Mutter* (East Berlin: Henschel, [1951]), Berliner Ensemble Archive (henceforth BEA), box file 132; *idem*, *Die Mutter: Bühnenfassung des Berliner Ensembles*, ed. Joachim Tenschert (East Berlin: Henschel, 1970).

[25] *BFA*, iii (1988), 391–8.

The final phase presents pivotal episodes from Wlassowa's biography and typical examples of her revolutionary activity. In Scene 9, Wlassowa is reunited with Pawel for the last time. Their previous roles are reversed: Wlassowa prints political leaflets while Pawel prepares his own food. In Scene 10, she tries to win over customers in a shop; however, this scene was written after the 1932 première and was omitted from the 1938 edition, Brecht's own productions, and all the major stagings covered in this book. This omission allowed Brecht and his successors to move straight from the joyful reunion in Scene 9 to Scene 11, in which Wlassowa learns of Pawel's death. Despite her grief, she continues her political struggle by agitating against rent prices and superstition, turning down her landlady's offer of the loan of a Bible. When the First World War breaks out, Wlassowa campaigns against it: unsuccessfully at the street corner in Scene 12 and with better results at the copper collection point in Scene 14. She battles against personal illness and injury, struggling from her sickbed in Scene 13, and is rewarded in Scene 15, in which she leads a demonstration in the 1917 Revolution.

Brecht's selective adaptation of Gorky's novel emphasized the parallels between the situation in pre-revolutionary Russia and the Weimar Republic, focusing on the topical issues of wage cuts, strikes, and police brutality. By extending the action to 1917, Brecht reminded his spectators that Communism had already triumphed in Russia and challenged them to fight for a revolutionary solution to Germany's political and economic crisis. Eisler's music heightened the play's political impact: the songs distilled the play's arguments and were performed separately at concerts and rallies in 1932.

Brecht's version of *Die Mutter* combined different genres, like agitprop, the biography play, *Lehrstück*, and historical drama. In fact, he assigned different generic labels to it on separate occasions, depending on his theatrical interpretation as a director. In the 1933 edition, he wrote that the play was 'im Stil der Lehrstücke geschrieben' ('written in the style of the *Lehrstücke*'), and four years later the Russian writer Sergey Tretyakov argued that 'it would be wrong to regard it as a historical play about a Russian working woman'.[26] Yet in 1951 Brecht

---

[26] *BFA*, xxiv (1991), 115; Sergey Tretyakov, 'Bert Brecht', in *Brecht: A Collection of Critical Essays*, ed. Peter Demetz (Englewood Cliffs, NJ: Prentice-Hall, 1962), 16–29 (25).

did precisely this when he called *Die Mutter* 'eigentlich einfach ein historisches Stück' ('really just a historical drama').[27] Ernst Schumacher and Klaus Völker follow Brecht's first statement by arguing that *Die Mutter* is a *Lehrstück*, whereas Henning Rischbieter calls it a *Chronik* (chronicle), and Werner Mittenzwei and Karl-Heinz Schoeps see it as a transitional work influenced by, but distinct from, the *Lehrstück*.[28] In contrast, Petermichael von Bawey argues that *Die Mutter* should be seen as a tragicomedy because the optimistic promise of a Communist victory relieves the tragedy of the deaths of Smilgin and Pawel.[29]

By attempting to pin down *Die Mutter* to a single genre, these literary critics have overlooked one of the text's major features: its complex combination of a variety of genres and forms, which directors have exploited in different ways in performance—as Brecht's own comments indicate. This generic interplay is complicated further because the effect of the play's ending depends on the spectator's knowledge of the outcome of the Russian Revolution—an outcome that changed between 1932 and the most recent production in 2003. So although the left-wing spectators of 1932 could celebrate the final demonstration as a Russian triumph and a promise of future German success, audiences aware of Stalin's Purges and the collapse of the Soviet Union were unlikely to share their optimism.

4. RE-INTERPRETING *DIE MUTTER* FOR NEW AUDIENCES

Although the play's initial topicality might suggest that it would be difficult to transfer to other historical and cultural contexts, it has since

[27] Werner Hecht (ed.), *Materialien zu Bertolt Brechts 'Die Mutter'* (Frankfurt/Main: Suhrkamp, 1976), 125.

[28] Schumacher, 381; Klaus Völker, *Bertolt Brecht: Eine Biographie* (Munich: DTV, 1978), 219; Henning Rischbieter, *Brecht*, 2 vols (Velber: Friedrich, 1966), i. 117; Mittenzwei, 94; Karl-Heinz Schoeps, 'Brecht's *Lehrstücke*: A Laboratory for Epic and Dialectic Theatre', in *A Bertolt Brecht Reference Companion*, ed. Siegfried Mews (Westport, Conn.: Greenwood Press, 1997), 70–87 (70–1).

[29] Petermichael von Bawey, 'Dramatic Structure of Revolutionary Language: Tragicomedy in Brecht's *The Mother*', in *Critical Essays on Bertolt Brecht*, ed. Siegfried Mews (Boston, Mass.: G. K. Hall, 1989), 96–106.

sustained a remarkable variety of interpretations and weathered political and cultural change even into the twenty-first century. These new interpretations include Brecht's own staging at the Berliner Ensemble (BE) in 1951, when he transformed the play into a historical drama, altered the balance between the epic and dramatic devices, and made major concessions to the political and cultural sensibilities of the GDR authorities and audience.

In liberally revising and re-interpreting texts for the stage, Brecht displayed his flagrant disregard for *Werktreue*, the concept of fidelity to the original work, which conservatives have cited in defence of dominant literary interpretations and traditional modes of performance. In his theoretical writings, Brecht argued consistently that directors should adopt a fresh approach towards the classics. For example, in an essay of 1929, he wrote:

Diese ehrerbietige Haltung hat sich an den Klassikern sehr gerächt, sie wurden durch Ehrerbietung ramponiert und durch Weihrauch geschwärzt. Es wäre ihnen besser bekommen, wenn man ihnen gegenüber eine freiere Haltung eingenommen hätte, wie die Wissenschaft sie zu den Entdeckungen, auch zu großen, eingenommen hat, die sie doch immerfort korrigierte oder sogar wieder verwarf, nicht aus Oppositionslust, sondern der Notwendigkeit entsprechend.[30]

Brecht's view is now widely accepted by performance theorists as well as directors. Whereas *Werktreue* assumes that a work has a stable and accessible essence, reception theorists emphasize that a work can be perceived only by individual subjects whose readings will differ. As Richard Sheppard comments: 'a text's signified is not some kind of Gnostic essence that has been trapped within a fleshly prison of words and awaits its redemption there by a soteriological literary critic'—or, indeed, by a director.[31]

---

[30] 'This reverential attitude has taken a terrible toll on the classics; they have been knocked about by reverence and blackened by incense. They would have fared better if people had adopted a freer attitude towards them, just as science has adopted towards discoveries, even to great ones, which it has constantly corrected or even refuted, not from sheer cussedness but from necessity.' 'Gespräch über Klassiker', *BFA*, xxi. 309–15 (310–11).

[31] Richard Sheppard, *Tankred Dorst's 'Toller': A Case-Study in Reception* (New Alyth: Lochee, 1989), 8. For two of the most influential contributions to reception theory, see Wolfgang Iser, *Der Akt des Lesens: Theorie ästhetischer Wirkung* (Munich: Wilhelm Fink, 1976); Hans Robert Jauß, *Literaturgeschichte als Provokation der Literaturwissenschaft* (Konstanz: Universitätsverlag, 1967).

Even so, Brecht tacitly re-asserted *Werktreue* when he presented his postwar stagings as definitive and required other theatres to copy them, a policy which his heirs continued. By ignoring the many political and aesthetic compromises that Brecht had made in his 1951 production of *Die Mutter*, this policy obscured one of the central principles of his theatrical practice: his insistence on tailoring plays to the context in which they were performed. The imposition of the 1951 *Modellinszenierung* (model production) caused stagings of *Die Mutter* to stagnate in the 1950s and 1960s, and it was only in the 1970s that directors began to re-interpret the play for their own times.

Although directors rarely copy Brecht's postwar productions today, these stagings are still widely regarded as authoritative interpretations of his plays and definitive statements of his theatrical practice. For example, in *Brecht and the West German Theatre* John Rouse extrapolates Brecht's staging methods exclusively from his work at the BE.[32] This approach replicates the teleological assumptions of literary critics like Martin Esslin and Ernst Schumacher who interpret Brecht's career as a progression towards the 'mature' plays.[33] Moreover, it ignores the fact that Brecht's postwar productions were designed for a unique and delicate situation, when epic theatre was under sustained attack from conservative aestheticians in the GDR. Instead of continuing to regard Brecht's postwar productions as authoritative, scholars now need to examine them critically in their historical, political and cultural context.

The BE faced particular challenges in dealing with the model, as the company experienced conflicting pressures after Brecht's death: on the one hand, to preserve his achievements, and on the other, to continue the process of innovation. My analysis of the BE's four productions of *Die Mutter* reveals how, and how far, the company's priorities shifted between 1951 and 2003 in response to changes in internal management, external state controls, and the broader theatrical, cultural and political context. These new insights are important, because no authoritative history of the company has yet been published.

The question of Brecht's influence on twentieth-century theatre is crucial, because so many postwar practitioners use him as a reference point,

---

[32] John Rouse, *Brecht and the West German Theatre: The Practice and Politics of Interpretation*, Theatre and Dramatic Studies, 62 (London: UMI, 1989).

[33] e.g. Martin Esslin, *Brecht: A Choice of Evils* (London: Mercury, 1965), esp. 61, 102.

whether positively or negatively. His name has become synonymous with political theatre: after 1968, Western left-wing practitioners—like Peter Stein—explicitly invoked Brecht as their model, whereas in the 1990s postmodern directors—like Frank Castorf—presented their work as a reaction against Brecht's political theatre of reason. Even so, Sarah Bryant-Bertail and Meg Mumford have both suggested that postmodern performance actually exploits the radical potential of Brecht's experiments.[34] By examining contrasting productions since Brecht's death, this book assesses the different ways in which directors have responded to his legacy.

5. METHODOLOGY: RECONSTRUCTING PAST PRODUCTIONS

Reconstructing past productions is, in the first instance, a historical task. Indeed, once performance is viewed as a social and historical event as well as an aesthetic phenomenon, then it is clear that there is no difference in principle between performance analysis and any other form of historical investigation. Even though the theatre historian has no direct access to the production, she or he can use a wide range of evidence to reconstruct the participants' textual and aesthetic choices.

This study exploits an immense range of archive material from Germany, Britain, and the USA. It relies chiefly on archives in Berlin: the BE Archive, Brecht Archive, Bundesarchiv (Federal Archive), Schaubühne Archive, and Stiftung Archiv der Akademie der Künste (Academy of Arts Archive). The BE Archive is a particularly rich resource because Brecht insisted that copies of all correspondence, rehearsal notes, prompt scripts, and set designs be deposited there, a policy which his successors have continued. Even so, scholars have only recently begun to exploit its vast holdings: Bryant-Bertail has analysed the use of space and time in Brecht's stagings of *Der Hofmeister* (*The Tutor*) and *Mutter Courage* (*Mother Courage*), and Mumford has examined the role of *Gestus* across several productions.

Prompt scripts are central to my investigation, for they contain the edited text, together with notes on the actors' movements, lighting,

---

[34] Sarah Bryant-Bertail, *Space and Time in Epic Theater: The Brechtian Legacy* (Rochester, NY: Camden House, 2000), 153–207; Mumford, 204–6, 237–57.

music, and sound. I have collected prompt scripts of twelve productions of *Die Mutter*. Even after directors have chosen which edition to use, they may make changes for entirely pragmatic reasons, deleting lines to shorten the production, doubling up roles, and cutting minor characters to fit their available cast: after all, Brecht's 1951 production lasted three hours and required a cast of forty-four actors. Such pragmatic changes already interpret the text by deciding what is expendable, even before directors add or rewrite lines in order to emphasize their own production concept—a tendency which became increasingly common and important during the twentieth century.

Video recordings are the best visual and aural guide to past productions, and I have collected recordings of four stagings of *Die Mutter*.[35] Such recordings are still far from ideal, for they transpose the live theatrical performance into a different aesthetic medium, presenting viewers with virtual images rather than a physical presence, distorting the lighting effects, and forcing the camera's perspective on the viewer.[36] Consequently, even where video recordings are available, I have also consulted photographs and set designs. I have obtained audio recordings of a further two productions, which supply valuable information about the music, line delivery, and audience response.[37]

Whilst these sources provide evidence about the finished productions, it is also important to analyse the staging process and reception. I trace each production from the initial discussions through to the final performances, using notes made by the director and his or her assistants, correspondence and records of discussions between the participants, and nightly reports on performances (*Abendberichte*), wherever these are available. I examine how each company presented its production to the audience through the programme, posters, press releases, and interviews, and then assess how theatre critics and other spectators responded, using newspaper reviews, questionnaires, and records of post-show discussions. Where appropriate, I examine how the authorities reacted

---

[35] *Die Mutter*, dir. Bertolt Brecht, film dir. Manfred Wekwerth, DEFA, 1958 (Goethe-Institut, London); *Die Mutter*, dir. Wolfgang Schwiedrzik, Patrick Steckel, Peter Stein, film dir. Uwe Reuter (Akademie der Künste am Robert-Koch-Platz, henceforth AdK RKP); *Die Mutter*, dir. Hans-Joachim Frank, 1998 (Centre for Performance Research, Aberystwyth, henceforth CPR); *La Mère*, dir. Jacques Delcuvellerie Groupov, film dir. Michel Jakar, Wallonie Image Production, 1997 (AdK RKP).

[36] Cf. Marco de Marinis, ' "A Faithful Betrayal of Performance": Notes on the Use of Video in Theatre', *New Theatre Quarterly*, 1.4 (Nov. 1985), 383–9.

[37] Audio recordings of the BE's 1974 production (BEA) and 1988 production (Manfred Wekwerth's personal copy).

to productions, using censorship reports and, in the case of the GDR, internal government records which have been made available since reunification. This close attention to the changing reception of *Die Mutter*, by the authorities, theatre critics, and audiences, complements Brecht's own interest in *Zuschaukunst* (the art of spectating).[38]

The range and depth of this study far exceed those of most production histories. Indeed, one of the book's central tenets is that production histories should be far more ambitious in their source material and scope. Like many production histories, Peter Thomson's *Mother Courage and her Children*—the only other production history of a Brecht play—relies primarily on newspaper reviews, discusses none of the textual changes made for productions, and pays surprisingly little attention to music, aesthetics, and set design.[39] Whilst reviews can be valuable, they provide evidence of professional reception and inevitably reflect the critics' pre-existing views of the writer, director, genre, or play. In this study, they are therefore treated as just one among many other forms of evidence. The scope and detail of this evidence enable me to comment not only on theatrical interpretations of *Die Mutter*, but also on the process of staging and reception, and on broader issues of cultural, political and institutional history.

6. STRUCTURAL OUTLINE

This production history focuses on the development of Brecht's polit-ical theatre, the dissemination and reception of his staging methods, the institutional development of the BE, and Brecht's influence on twentieth-century political theatre in and beyond Germany. Accord-ingly, it concentrates on productions by Brecht and subsequent leading German directors, Peter Stein, Ruth Berghaus, Manfred Wekwerth, and Claus Peymann, all of whom were committed to political theatre but practised it in different ways. After Brecht's own stagings, those by Stein, Berghaus, and Peymann stand out because the directors inter-preted *Die Mutter* in new ways and produced high-quality stagings

---

[38] e.g. '[Die Schauspielkunst wird für gewöhnlich nicht in Büchern gelehrt]', *BFA*, xxii.2. 618–20.

[39] Peter Thomson, *Brecht: Mother Courage and her Children* (Cambridge: Cambridge University Press, 1997). Cf. Douglas A. Joyce, *Hugo von Hofmannsthal's 'Der Schwierige': A Fifty-Year Theater History* (Columbia, SC: Camden House, 1993); Egil Törnqvist, *Ibsen: A Doll's House* (Cambridge: Cambridge University Press, 1995).

that challenged the 1951 model. My broadly chronological approach allows me to identify lines of development, continuity, and change in German political theatre, but I interrupt this account with a thematic chapter on translation and transference in order to compare what productions in different countries and continents reveal about these issues.

In Chapters 1 and 2, I analyse Brecht's two contrasting Berlin productions. In Chapter 1, I investigate the play's genesis and 1932 première, exploring how Brecht collaborated with other artists and how he responded to contemporary events through the text and its staging. Then, in Chapter 2, I turn to Brecht's 1951 staging at the BE and show how he transformed *Die Mutter* into an uncontroversial historical drama in order to overcome his audience's hostility to the Russian subject-matter, make the play conform broadly to the principles of Socialist Realism, and comply with the official line that the German 'Revolution' had been completed in 1949.

The rest of the book examines how later directors have related *Die Mutter* to the experiences of new audiences. In Chapter 3, I compare two productions in West and East Berlin, by Peter Stein at the Schaubühne am Halleschen Ufer in 1970 and by Ruth Berghaus at the BE in 1974. These stagings are particularly significant because Stein and Berghaus developed Brecht's staging methods selectively and subversively to serve their own political and artistic purposes. I examine how the broader context and internal theatre politics influenced these productions and their reception before considering what the case studies reveal about cultural and political developments in both states. Next, in Chapter 4, I examine foreign-language productions in Europe and the USA. After providing an overview of the play's international performance history and explaining the patterns that emerge, I explore the different ways in which directors have negotiated the cultural difference between the text and their audiences. I have deferred Brecht's 1935 staging at the Theatre Union to this chapter because it is a clear example of failed cultural transference.

In Chapter 5, I consider four German productions between 1988 and 2003, two of which were staged at the BE by Wekwerth and Peymann, and two of which were staged at smaller theatres, theater 89 in Berlin and the Stadttheater in Konstanz. Although the two latter productions attracted less interest from theatre critics at the time, they are historically and politically significant because they provide contrasting perspectives on *Die Mutter* after German reunification and on East Germany's attempts to come to terms with its recent past. The comparison of these four productions reveals how directors have thus far enabled *Die Mutter* to survive the political system that it came to uphold. This is one of the most pressing challenges now facing not only this particular Communist text but Brecht's entire *œuvre*.

1

From Nizhni-Novgorod to Moabit: The Genesis and Première of *Die Mutter*, 1931–2

1. INTRODUCTION

1.1 The Analytical Focus

The genesis and première of *Die Mutter* provide significant insights into Brecht's authorial and theatrical practice in the Weimar Republic, engagement with Communist ideas, and responses to contemporary events. He and his co-workers addressed topical, far left-wing debates, using dramatic, musical and aesthetic techniques that were strongly influenced both by more widely practised recent experiments and by his own ideas on epic theatre. In turn, the production and its reception helped Brecht to develop and articulate his aesthetic theories still further.

In political and aesthetic terms, *Die Mutter* is more complex than Brecht's presentation of it in 1932 suggests. Although he conceived the play as a contribution to the political struggle of the German Communist Party (KPD), certain aspects contravened the Party line and offended Communist commentators. These differences indicate the limits of Brecht's political grasp in 1932 and explain the Party's ambivalence towards him. In the programme, meanwhile, his polemical claims for epic theatre obscured the substantial interplay between the epic and the dramatic techniques in the text and its staging.[1] In addition to exploring the political and aesthetic complexities of *Die Mutter*, my contextual analysis of the première provides a central point of comparison with Brecht's postwar practice at the BE and productions in other historical and cultural contexts.

---

[1] 1932 programme, Bertolt-Brecht-Archiv (henceforth BBA) SBbba 1797.

1.2 Source Material

Although the 1932 script has not survived, I have discovered substantial evidence about the staging in Brecht's published and unpublished notes, his collaborators' testimonies, the set designs, photographs, newspaper reviews, censorship reports, and programme. By comparing the 1933 edition of the text with these sources, I have established that it corresponded closely to most of the 1932 script.

Scholars agree that Brecht made two changes for the 1933 edition: he added a new scene, set in a shop, after Scene 9 and introduced a new character, Smilgin, to Scene 5.[2] However, he probably made another two major changes after the première. Astonishingly, in over seventy reviews, not one theatre critic mentioned either Pawel's death or the Bible scene (Scene 11 of the 1933 edition)—not even Paul Brand, who devoted over 900 words to summarizing the action.[3] The fact that no critics mentioned Pawel's death is remarkable, not just because of the event's intrinsic significance in the plot, but also because it is revealed in an epic report—the 'Grabrede' ('Funeral Oration')—that departs from the 'dramatic' tradition just as strikingly as the demonstration scenes, which did elicit considerable critical comment.[4] The Bible scene is the only scene of which no known photographs exist, and—with the obvious exception of Wlassowa—the cast list in the programme does not mention its characters, the landlady, her niece, and the female worker, whereas it does list the secondary characters from other scenes. Moreover, even though the reviewer in the *Katholisches Kirchenblatt* (Catholic Church News) strongly objected that Wlassowa relinquishes her private life, delivers agitational leaflets, and joins demonstrations, she or he made no reference to Brecht's anti-religious propaganda.[5] So, in contrast to every other scene in the play, there is absolutely no evidence that either the 'Grabrede' or the Bible scene were performed at the première, or indeed

[2] e.g. *BFA*, iii. 482; Albrecht Dümling, 'Die Mutter', in *Brecht Handbuch*, ed. Jan Knopf, 5 vols (Stuttgart: J. B. Metzler, 2001), i. 294–309 (297).

[3] Paul Brand, 'Brechts Lehrstück ein großer Erfolg', *Die Rote Fahne* (henceforth *RF*; Berlin), 19 Jan. 1932.

[4] e.g. Herbert Jhering, 'Komödienhaus: Gorki, Pudowkin, Brecht', *Berliner Börsen-Courier*, 18 Jan. 1932; Florian Kienzl, 'Veraltetes Zeittheater', *Dresdner Anzeiger*, 26 Jan. 1932; Heinz Lüdecke, 'Die Mutter', *Illustrierte Rote Post*, 4/1932; P[aul] W[iegler], 'Gorkis *Mutter*', *Berliner Zeitung*, 18 Jan. 1932.

[5] H. B. [possibly H. Bachmann], 'Im Komödienhaus hat sich wieder einmal die Gruppe Junger Schauspieler breit gemacht', *Katholisches Kirchenblatt* (Berlin), 7 Feb. 1932.

that Pawel died while attempting to escape in this version. It is possible that Brecht introduced these sections later in the run, after the reviews had been published, for his essay and notes on the production mention Wlassowa's anti-religious propaganda and a poem that reported Pawel's death.[6] In any case, the fact that scholars have overlooked the reviewers' omissions indicates how far, in the 1933 edition, Brecht's 'Grabrede' departed from 'dramatic' convention: in epic theatre the death of the heroine's son no longer provided the all-important climax and catharsis.

2. THE GENESIS OF THE TEXT

2.1 'Of Course, Brecht has Always had his Collaborators ...'

Although Brecht always presented *Die Mutter* as a collaborative project,[7] he was characteristically lax about crediting his co-workers; at the première, the programme acknowledged just Brecht, Eisler, and Weisenborn. We can only speculate why Brecht failed to cite his two other collaborators, Hauptmann and Dudow. Perhaps the play's genesis already seemed unusually complicated, given his acknowledgement of the team's sources. As it was, Ferdinand Junghans commented in a leading nationalist newspaper: 'Die Entstehung ist diesmal so kompliziert, daß man nicht genauer davon berichten kann.'[8]

The discrepancies between the acknowledgements in different editions of *Die Mutter* have subsequently created further confusion. Since the 1933 edition followed the credits in the 1932 programme, Dudow was first acknowledged in the 1938 Malik edition.[9] In 1949, Brecht explained that he had ordered his publisher to remove references to Weisenborn and the earlier adaptation from the 1938 edition, as they could have exposed Weisenborn to danger: unlike Brecht's other collaborators, he was still in Germany in 1938.[10] After the War, Brecht

[6] '[Das Stück *Die Mutter*]', *BFA*, xxiv. 110–14 (112), 121.

[7] 'Er [Brecht] hat ja immer seine Mitarbeiter gehabt ...' (trans. in subheading 2.1). H. Bachmann, 'Die kommunistische Mutter', *Germania* (Berlin), 19 Jan. 1932. On Brecht's collaborative working practices and the genesis of *Die Mutter*, see also Bradley, 'Collaboration and Cultural Practice: The "Brecht" Version of *Die Mutter*', *Brecht Yearbook*, 28 (2003), 189–208.

[8] 'The genesis is so complicated this time that we cannot go into it in any detail.' Ferdinand Junghans, 'Man sieht nur noch die Trümmer rauchen', *Neue Preußische Kreuzzeitung* (Berlin), 18 Jan. 1932.

[9] Brecht, *Die Mutter; Geschichten aus der Revolution*, Versuche 15–16 (Berlin: Kiepenheuer, 1933), 64; *idem*, *Gesammelte Werke*, 2 vols (London: Malik, 1938), ii. 150.

[10] *BFA*, xxix (1998), 563.

credited Weisenborn alongside Dudow and Eisler in the programmes for the Leipzig production in 1950 and the Berlin staging in 1951, and the 1957 edition also acknowledged all three collaborators.[11] Even so, Brecht repeatedly failed to acknowledge Hauptmann, which suggests that she may not have been credited for her work on other projects, either.

News of Hauptmann's involvement in *Die Mutter* was not published until 1964, in Weisenborn's autobiography.[12] But even though her contributions were acknowledged again by Fuegi in 1972, Jan Knopf in 1980, and Heinz-Dieter Tschörtner in 1986, many critics have remained unaware of them.[13] For example, in 1983 John Willett asserted that she 'was not among the principal collaborators on [Brecht's] most openly Communist works', whilst Astrid Horst's 1992 biography of Hauptmann does not even mention the play, and volume iii of the *BFA* (1988) does not acknowledge Hauptmann's involvement.[14] Indeed, although Paula Hanssen's 1994 biography notes Fuegi's claims about her contributions, they were not corroborated until 1997, by Sabine Kebir.[15]

The persistence of this confusion owes as much to the often parochial nature of (auto-)biography as to Brecht's inconsistent and insufficient acknowledgements. Weisenborn's biographers have tended to focus exclusively on his testimony, whilst Hanssen mistakenly thought that Brecht and perhaps Hauptmann worked with a dramatist called 'Eisenborn'.[16] Some critics even seem to have overlooked key published primary sources: for instance, Emma Lewis Thomas's ignorance of Dudow's and Hauptmann's involvement suggests that she was unfamiliar with Weisenborn's autobiography and the 1938 and

---

[11] Programmes from the Stadtgeschichtliches Museum Leipzig and the BEA; Brecht, *Stücke*, ed. Elisabeth Hauptmann, 14 vols (Frankfurt/Main: Suhrkamp, 1953–67), v (1957), 6.

[12] Günther Weisenborn, *Memorial: Der gespaltene Horizont: Niederschriften eines Außenseiters* (East Berlin: Aufbau, 1982), 415, 540.

[13] Fuegi, *Essential Brecht*, 228 n. 20; Jan Knopf, *Brecht-Handbuch: Theater* (Stuttgart: J. B. Metzler, 1980), 119; Heinz-Dieter Tschörtner, '*Die Mutter* für das Theater', *Neue Deutsche Literatur*, 34 (1986), 168–72 (170).

[14] John Willett, 'Bacon ohne Shakespeare? The Problem of Mitarbeit', *Brecht Yearbook*, 12 (1983), 121–37 (128); Astrid Horst, *Prima inter pares: Elisabeth Hauptmann: Die Mitarbeiterin Bertolt Brechts* (Würzburg: Königshausen & Neumann, 1992); *BFA*, iii. 479.

[15] Paula Hanssen, *Elisabeth Hauptmann: Brecht's Silent Collaborator* (Frankfurt/Main: Peter Lang, 1994), 10; Sabine Kebir, *Ich fragte nicht nach meinem Anteil: Elisabeth Hauptmanns Arbeit mit Bertolt Brecht* (Berlin: Aufbau, 1997), 236–7.

[16] Tschörtner, 168–9; Roswita Schwarz, *Vom expressionistischen Aufbruch zur Inneren Emigration: Günther Weisenborns weltanschauliche und künstlerische Entwicklung in der Weimarer Republik und im Dritten Reich* (Frankfurt/Main: Peter Lang, 1995), 204–7; Hanssen, 70.

1957 editions, despite having undertaken a detailed comparison of *Die Mutter* and its sources. Because of this basic oversight, one of her conclusions is based on an entirely false premise: 'Weisenborn remained the only playwright on the list apart from Brecht; therefore, he had the opportunity to exert more influence on this version than he has perhaps been given credit for.'[17] In the absence of drafts of *Die Mutter*, other critics have made even bolder, largely unsubstantiated claims. Thus in 1986 Tschörtner declared that 'Günther Weisenborn ist von den Koautoren mit Abstand der wichtigste', whereas in 1994 Fuegi called *Die Mutter* 'the Hauptmann–Brecht adaptation'.[18] The first significant attempt to synthesize some of the published evidence was made only in 2001, by Albrecht Dümling in the *Brecht-Handbuch*.[19]

2.2 Contributions Towards the Text

All the available evidence suggests that Brecht was ultimately in charge of *Die Mutter*, which was written during the summer and autumn of 1931. On 23 August 1962 Weisenborn told Hans Bunge, then head of the Brecht Archive: 'Kurz und gut: er übernahm bei diesem Stück die Führung—aufgrund viel besserer Einsichten in die ganze Problematik des Klassenkampfes.'[20] Indeed, an entry in one of Brecht's notebooks even suggests that his interest in Gorky's novel preceded the Stark–Weisenborn adaptation. Dated to 1929, it reads: '1) Lob des Wissens / 2) Unausrottbarkeit des Kommunismus / 3) Lingen / 4) Begrüßung der Wlassowa.'[21] Evidence from Eisler's and Hauptmann's papers confirms that the collective comprised four core members besides Brecht. For example, Weisenborn told Bunge: 'Zuerst war ich mit

---

[17] Emma Lewis Thomas, 'The Stark–Weisenborn Adaptation of Gorky's *Mutter*: Its Influence on Brecht's Version', *Brecht heute*, 3 (1973), 57–63 (62). See also *idem*, 'Bertolt Brecht's Drama *Die Mutter*: A Case of Double Adaptation' (unpublished doctoral thesis, Indiana University, 1972).

[18] 'Günther Weisenborn is by far the most important of the co-authors.' Tschörtner, 172; John Fuegi, *Brecht & Co.: Sex, Politics, and the Making of the Modern Drama* (New York: Grove, 1994), 269.

[19] Dümling, 'Die Mutter', i. 295–7.

[20] 'In short: he took charge of this play—because he had far better insights into all the problems of class struggle.' Conversation between Weisenborn and Bunge, 23 Aug. 1962, Hanns-Eisler-Archiv (henceforth HEA) 2875/2, AdK RKP.

[21] '1) In Praise of Knowledge / 2) Inexterminability of Communism / 3) Lingen / 4) Wlassowa's Welcome.' BBA 804/35, also quoted by Dümling, 'Die Mutter', i. 295. The orthography of quotations from Brecht's manuscripts has been standardized.

Brecht allein—dann kam Eisler dazu, dann Dudow, Elisabeth Hauptmann.'[22] This testimony is corroborated by a letter that Hauptmann
wrote to Weisenborn on 6 July 1967 in which she recalled: '[ich traf Sie
erst wieder], als Brecht ... *Die Mutter* dramatisierte.... Eisler war dabei
und Dudow.'[23]

The testimonies of Brecht's collaborators also offer significant clues
about the nature and extent of their respective contributions. Despite the
evidence in Brecht's notebook, Hauptmann's letter indicates that Weisenborn initiated work on the new dramatization: 'Das war Ihr Vorschlag,
und es wurde von Ihrer ersten Fassung ausgegangen.'[24] On two separate
occasions, Weisenborn himself laid claim to the copper collection scene.
In 1962, he told Bunge 'daß ich die Szene mit der Kupfersammelstelle
in [Brechts] Abwesenheit ... schrieb, und er hat sehr wenig daran
geändert'.[25] Three years later, in the GDR weekly newspaper *Sonntag*,
Weisenborn recalled: 'Ich brachte eines Morgens die Kupferkesselszene
mit, die von den beiden zurechtgezupft und gebilligt wurde.'[26] In a subsequent interview with Joseph-Hermann Sauter, Weisenborn stated that
Eisler had contributed significantly towards the text, not just the music:

Als Dramaturgen schätze ich ihn darum, weil er das tat, was einen guten
Dramaturgen ausmacht, er hilft einem bei der Arbeit, er hilft dichten ....
Eisler fragte: Warum denn diese Szene? Dieser Charakter hat ja nur drei
Eigenschaften, warum hat er nicht vier? Ein Mensch ist doch reicher, als nur
drei Eigenschaften aussagen. Und in der vierten Eigenschaft kann man doch
diese und diese Szene dann verstärken.[27]

Eisler's own testimony supports Weisenborn's statement: on 18 Septem-
ber 1961, he told Nathan Notowicz how much the characterization

[22] 'At first Brecht and I were on our own—then Eisler joined us, followed by Dudow,
Elisabeth Hauptmann.' HEA 2875/2.
[23] '[I did not meet you again], until Brecht ... was dramatizing *The Mother*.... Eisler
was present and so was Dudow.' Hauptmann to Weisenborn, Berlin, 6 July 1967,
Elisabeth-Hauptmann-Archiv (henceforth EHA) 627, AdK RKP.
[24] 'It was your suggestion, and we proceeded from your first draft.'
[25] 'I wrote the scene with the copper collection point in [Brecht's] absence, and he
altered very little of it.' HEA 2875/2.
[26] 'One morning I brought along the copper kettle scene, which they both straightened
out and approved.' Weisenborn, 'Hanns Eisler', *Sonntag* (East Berlin), 10 Jan. 1965.
[27] 'I rate him as a dramaturge because he lived up to the definition of a good
dramaturge: he helps you with your work, he helps to write literature .... Eisler would
ask: What is the point of this scene? This character has only three qualities, why doesn't
he have four? After all, a human being is richer than only three qualities suggest. And we
can then use the fourth quality to strengthen these particular scenes.' Joseph-Hermann
Sauter, 'Gespräch mit Günther Weisenborn', *Sinn und Form*, 20 (1968), 714–25 (718).

of the teacher owed to his memories of his father, a neo-Kantian philosopher 'der sich seine Lebzeit bemüht[,] Idealismus mit Materialismus zu *versöhnen*. (Er ist das Urbild des Lehrers aus der *Mutter*. Ich gab Brecht diesen Bericht über meinen Vater.')[28] Significantly, Brecht acknowledged Eisler's contribution to the text, crediting him both as a collaborator and as the composer in the programmes for the 1932 and 1951 Berlin productions and in the 1933 and 1938 editions.[29]

Although Brecht never credited Hauptmann's contributions, Weisenborn considered them invaluable. In his conversation with Sauter he spoke of her as someone 'die man nie vergessen sollte, wenn von unserer Arbeit die Rede ist, da sie durch ihre sehr konkrete Klugheit das literarische Gewissen darstellte'.[30] Similarly, when interviewed in 1972 for the documentary *Die Mitarbeiterin* (*The Collaborator*), Hauptmann argued that her political experience had been crucial and that her name had been omitted purely by chance:

Mein Beitrag zur Bearbeitung von Gorkis *Die Mutter* bedarf einer kleinen Erläuterung, denn mein Name steht nicht (das war purer Zufall) bei diesem Stück. Der Beitrag war hier ein besonderer. Und kam bei mir auch aus einer ganz anderen Ecke. Ich hatte etwas Neues kennengelernt und war voll davon. Ich meine damit, daß ich politisch etwas mehr wusste, was natürlich sehr wichtig war, und in die Partei eingetreten war und ziemlich bald mit Funktionen betraut wurde. Sonst hätte ich mich garnicht ernsthaft mit der *Heiligen Johanna*, mit der *Ausnahme und die Regel* und vor allem mit der *Mutter* befassen können.[31]

Interestingly, Hauptmann's claim was not included when the documentary was broadcast—perhaps another pure coincidence—with the result that critics have overlooked these comments. As this omission

---

[28] 'Who strives his whole life to *reconcile* idealism and materialism. (He is the prototype of the teacher from *The Mother*. I gave Brecht this report about my father.)' Hanns Eisler, 'Briefe an Nathan Notowicz', in *Sinn und Form* (*Sonderheft Hanns Eisler*), ed. Deutsche Akademie der Künste (East Berlin: Rütten & Loening, 1964), 278–81 (280).

[29] Cf. nn. 1, 9, 11.

[30] 'Whom one should never forget when talking about our work, since her intelligence and common sense enabled her to act as our literary conscience.' Sauter, 718.

[31] 'My contribution to the adaptation of Gorky's *Mother* requires a short explanation, as the play does not bear my name (this was a pure coincidence). Here I made a special contribution, drawing on a completely different part of my life. I had become acquainted with something new and was full of it. What I mean is that I knew more politically, which was naturally very important, and that I had joined the Party and been entrusted, fairly quickly, with responsibilities. Otherwise I certainly would not have been able to deal seriously with *Saint Joan, The Exception and the Rule*, and above all *The Mother*.' Interview for *Die Mitarbeiterin*, EHA 354.

suggests, Brecht does not bear sole responsibility for the long delay in acknowledging her input.

On at least three occasions Hauptmann made more precise claims about her contributions. According to Fuegi, she told him in 1966–7 that she had suggested opening *Die Mutter* with a direct address to the audience.[32] This claim has recently been corroborated by Kebir's discovery of a will which Hauptmann had drawn up in 1962, stating: 'Dabei sei vermerkt, daß bei einigen Stücken, in die ich auch eine ganze Menge (fast erkennbar) hineingesteckt habe (*Mann ist Mann, Der Jasager, Die Mutter*, vor allem hier die 1. Szene—der 1. Mai—die Bibelszene) ich nicht beteiligt bin'—a reference to royalties.[33] Hauptmann's letter to Weisenborn contains a similar claim: 'Ich selber durfte zur Eingangsszene (die zuletzt geschrieben wurde), zum Bericht vom 1. Mai und zur Bibelszene etwas beisteuern.'[34] These claims are entirely plausible, for the 'epic' reports in the opening scene and May Day demonstration were influenced by Japanese Noh drama, which Hauptmann knew well from her work on Arthur Waley's translations. Finally, the fact that Hauptmann subsequently wrote a commentary on the Bible scene suggests that she may well have had a vested interest in it.[35]

The above evidence casts serious doubt on speculation by Thomas and Tschörtner that Weisenborn was Brecht's most significant collaborator on this project. Eisler's recollections undermine their claims even further, since he told Bunge that Weisenborn 'hatte keine Ahnung' and 'machte die komischsten Vorschläge', 'weil er einfach den Arbeitsstil Brechts

---

[32] Fuegi, *Essential Brecht*, 227 n. 15, and 228 n. 20.

[33] 'Here it should be noted that I do not have a stake in several plays, into which I (almost recognizably) put a great deal (*A Man's a Man, He Who Says Yes, The Mother*, in this case above all Scene 1—1 May—the Bible scene).' EHA 462, quoted by Kebir, 236–7.

[34] 'I myself was able to make a contribution to the opening scene (which was written last), to the report of 1 May and to the Bible scene.' EHA 627. In the short autobiographical story 'Gedanken am Sonntagmorgen' ('Thoughts on Sunday Morning'), Hauptmann's narrator recalls: 'Wir [Brecht und ich] haben auch oft bis spät gearbeitet. Die Vielfraßszene usw. aus *Mahagonny*, die Bibelszene aus der *Mutter*, viele Gedichte—alle wurden spät am Abend, manches noch später geschrieben.' ('We [Brecht and I] often worked late too. The glutton scene etc. from *Mahagonny*, the Bible scene from *The Mother*, many of the poems—they were all written late in the evening, some later still.') Elisabeth Hauptmann, *Julia ohne Romeo: Geschichten, Stücke, Aufsätze, Erinnerungen*, ed. Rosemarie Eggert and Rosemarie Hill (East Berlin: Aufbau, 1977), 226–32 (230).

[35] Bertolt Brecht *et al.*, *Theaterarbeit: Sechs Aufführungen des Berliner Ensembles*, ed. Berliner Ensemble and Helene Weigel, 3rd rev. edn (East Berlin: Henschel, [1966]), 144–6.

noch gar nicht zur Kenntnis nehmen konnte'.[36] It thus seems likely that both Thomas and Tschörtner fell prey to Weisenborn's occasional tendency to distort the facts. For example, in *Sonntag* he referred only to his work with Brecht and Eisler, whereas we know that Dudow and Hauptmann—'die man nie vergessen sollte' ('whom one should never forget')—were also involved. Likewise, in a lecture given on a Russian cruise in 1968, Weisenborn told his listeners:

Vor 35 Jahren haben drei Theaterleute aus Berlin durch ihre Arbeit an der *Mutter* ein wenig dazu beigetragen, die Gedanken Gorkis in der Welt zu verbreiten. Als allein noch Lebender von ihnen erlaube ich mir, den Dank von Brecht, Eisler und von mir dieser neuen, veränderten Welt gegenüber auszusprechen, die uns hier höchst lebendig umgibt.[37]

Although the above evidence suggests that some critics have underestimated Hauptmann's involvement, it still does not justify Fuegi's description of *Die Mutter* as 'the Hauptmann–Brecht adaptation' since, besides implying—wrongly—that Hauptmann was in ultimate control, this description marginalizes the contributions of Dudow, Eisler, and Weisenborn. Moreover, in the absence of any evidence about the nature and extent of Dudow's involvement, it would be unwise to claim that any one of Brecht's collaborators was more important than the others.

2.3 Brecht's Practice of Collaboration

Despite their limitations, Weisenborn's accounts offer a fascinating insight into Brecht's working methods, which closely resembled the collaborative approach commonly found in theatre. In fact, the *ad hoc* improvisation that Weisenborn describes suited the project well, for it allowed Brecht and his collaborators to create dramatic dialogue collectively, through dialogue with each other. In an unpublished section of the manuscript for *Memorial* Weisenborn reveals: 'Wir

[36] 'Didn't have a clue', 'made the most bizarre suggestions', 'simply because he was not yet able to take Brecht's way of working on board'. Hans Bunge (ed.), *Gespräche mit Hans Bunge: Fragen Sie mehr über Brecht: Hanns Eisler im Gespräch* (Leipzig: Deutscher Verlag für Musik, 1975), 38.

[37] '35 years ago, three theatre practitioners from Berlin played a small part in spreading Gorky's ideas around the world, through their work on *The Mother*. As the only one of them alive today, I would like to express the thanks of Brecht, Eisler, and myself towards this new, changed world which surrounds us here, brimming with life.' Weisenborn, 'Wie wir Gorkis *Mutter* dramatisierten', Günther-Weisenborn-Archiv (henceforth GWA) 107, AdK RKP.

spielten einander auch die Szenen vor in verschiedenen Fassungen, wie sie jeder von uns dachte.'[38] He recalls that Brecht often invited his collaborators to discuss scenes that he had written in advance, whilst on other occasions the group wrote completely new ones or sketched out the dialogue together.[39] Weisenborn also remembers that Brecht had a blackboard in his studio and that they would each write a line or a scene on it, an account which accords with a photograph of Brecht, Dudow, and Eisler using a blackboard to map out their ideas for *Kuhle Wampe*.[40]

Ever the pragmatist, Brecht sought advice on *Die Mutter* from all quarters. For instance, Weisenborn recalls that occasional visitors to Brecht's apartment, including the critic Herbert Jhering, the director Erich Engel, and the actors Theo Lingen and Peter Lorre, were invited to express their opinions.[41] During rehearsals, Brecht listened to suggestions from the cast and crew, and the technician Helmuth Morbach claims that his comments prompted Brecht to alter one line:

In der *Mutter* war ein Vers über die Polizisten und Soldaten, 'die *viel* Geld bekommen und zu allem bereit sind'. Ich sagte, daß ich nicht der Meinung sei, daß sie viel Geld bekommen, ein Arbeiter verdient doch mehr als ein Polizist. Brecht hat geändert, 'die wenig Geld bekommen, doch zu allem bereit sind'. Ich wußte doch: im Arbeitsnachweis in der Gormannstraße lief der Luxemburgmörder rum. Viel kann er nicht bekommen haben für seinen Mord.[42]

These examples support the impression given by Brecht's more theoretical writings: that his overriding concern was the quality of the play, not the proprietary authorship of each line. As Weisenborn commented:

---

[38] 'We performed the scenes to each other in different versions, as we each imagined them.' Weisenborn, draft manuscript of *Memorial*, GWA 306/151.

[39] HEA 2875/2 and 5; *Memorial*, 415.

[40] HEA 2875/2; Werner Hecht, *Brecht Chronik* (Frankfurt/Main: Suhrkamp, 1997), 311.

[41] Weisenborn, *Memorial*, 415.

[42] 'In *The Mother* there was a line about policemen and soldiers, "who receive a *lot* of money and will go to any lengths". I said that in my opinion they didn't receive a lot of money; after all, a worker earns more than a policeman. Brecht changed it to: "who receive little money, but will go to any lengths". After all, I knew that [Rosa] Luxemburg's murderer was hanging about in the job centre on Gormannstraße. He can't have received much for his murder.' Käthe Rülicke, 'Dreizehn Bühnentechniker erzählen', in *Sinn und Form (Sonderheft Bertolt Brecht)*, ed. Deutsche Akademie der Künste (East Berlin: Rütten & Loening, 1957), 465–77 (471).

'Brecht kannte überhaupt keinen Besitz-Instinkt; Szenen, die gut waren, nahm er.'[43]

3. PREPARATIONS FOR THE PREMIÈRE

The rehearsals for the première highlight the contradictions in Brecht's theatrical practice towards the end of the Weimar Republic. Although accounts of Brecht's development often imply a chronological shift from the operas *Die Dreigroschenoper* (*The Threepenny Opera*) and *Mahagonny* to the more austere *Lehrstücke* and the overtly Communist works, the rehearsals for *Die Mutter* and the revised version of *Aufstieg und Fall der Stadt Mahagonny* (*The Rise and Fall of the City of Mahagonny*) actually took place at the same time and in the same building, the Theater am Kurfürstendamm. They were even financed by the same businessman, Ernst Josef Aufricht, who had backed *Die Dreigroschenoper* and *Happy End*. Although Aufricht had no sympathy for the political aims of *Die Mutter*, he considered his investment a small price to pay for Brecht's absence from the rehearsals for *Mahagonny*, where his constant arguments with Kurt Weill were threatening to ruin the production.[44]

Most of the actors for *Die Mutter* came from the *Gruppe Junger Schauspieler* (Group of Young Actors), a collective that had adapted to the economic crisis by renting out empty theatres and dividing profits amongst its members. Although the group had lower overheads than permanent companies, it was still short of funds: Gerhard Bienert, who played the teacher in *Die Mutter*, received only ten marks for the entire run.[45] As many of the members had previously worked with Piscator and acted in *Kuhle Wampe*, they were familiar with recent, far left-wing cultural experiments. Their social commitment was evident from their repertoire, which included plays by Peter Martin Lampel, Friedrich Wolf, and Theodor Plivier.[46] Since the production of *Die Mutter* also involved lay actors, including Brecht's future collaborator Margarete Steffin, it bridged the gap between professional and amateur theatre.

[43] 'Brecht had absolutely no proprietary instincts; he took scenes which were good.' HEA 2875/2.

[44] Ernst Josef Aufricht, *Erzähle, damit du dein Recht erweist* (West Berlin: Propyläen, 1966), 126–7.

[45] Gerhard Bienert, *Ein Leben in tausend Rollen*, ed. Dieter Reimer (East Berlin: Henschel, 1989), 80.

[46] Ibid. 57–80.

Like the genesis of the text, the production demonstrated Brecht's skill in gathering together talented co-workers, many of whom would subsequently collaborate on his postwar productions at the BE. Most notably, the *Gruppe Junger Schauspieler* was joined by the actors Ernst Busch, Theo Lingen, and Helene Weigel. Busch had already acted in *Die Dreigroschenoper*, *Die Maßnahme* (*The Decision*), and *Kuhle Wampe*, whilst Lingen—who was married to Brecht's former wife Marianne Zoff—had played the clown at the controversial première of *Das Badener Lehrstück vom Einverständnis* (*The Baden-Baden Learning Play on Consent*). Although Weigel had also performed in several of Brecht's productions, including *Mann ist Mann* (*A Man's a Man*) and *Die Maßnahme*, he still doubted her suitability for the part of Wlassowa, a wonderful irony given her success in the role between 1932 and 1971.[47] Brecht also appointed his long-standing collaborator Caspar Neher as the set designer and Emil Burri as the director. A keen amateur boxer and aspiring playwright, Burri had collaborated with Brecht and Hauptmann on *Die heilige Johanna der Schlachthöfe* (*Saint Joan of the Slaughterhouses*) and assisted with the 1931 production of *Mann ist Mann*.[48] Even though Brecht attended all rehearsals from 22 December onwards,[49] the programme credited Burri as sole director and did not mention Brecht's involvement. Since this omission contradicts the thesis that Brecht systematically exploited his co-workers, Fuegi ingeniously suggests that he lacked the courage to assume responsibility for a Communist production.[50] Nevertheless, the fact that he was already responsible as co-author suggests that the omission more probably resulted from his lack of 'Besitz-Instinkt' ('proprietary instincts').

Starting on 12 January, four closed performances of *Die Mutter* were held in the Wallner-Theater, which was situated near the Jannowitzbrücke, seated 1,300 and had recently housed the third Piscatorbühne. Then, on 17 January, the production opened to the public in the Komödienhaus am Schiffbauerdamm, which had a capacity of 1,100, before transferring on 25 January to the Lustspielhaus, which had 633 seats and was located on Friedrichstraße near Hallesches Tor.[51] Although the production closed on 10 February, Weigel recalls that one

[47] Werner Hecht, *Helene Weigel: Eine große Frau des zwanzigsten Jahrhunderts* (Frankfurt/Main: Suhrkamp, 2000), 65.

[48] Hecht, *Brecht Chronik*, 182, 195, 303, 340.   [49] Ibid. 316.

[50] Fuegi, *Brecht & Co.*, 283.

[51] Karl Baedeker, *Berlin und Umgebung*, 20th edn (Leipzig: Karl Baedeker, 1927), 15–16.

further performance took place on 29 February in a community hall in the working-class district of Moabit.[52] Since the collective capacity of these venues suggests that nearly 25,000 tickets were probably available over the whole run, Brecht's claim that some 15,000 working-class women saw the production is just about plausible.[53]

4. POLITICS

Die Mutter addressed topical political issues and advocated revolution as the solution to Germany's socio-economic problems. Its Russian historical setting served to rally convinced Communists by reminding them that revolution was possible, and had the additional advantage that indirect political criticism of Germany was more likely to escape censorship at a time when the emergency decrees of 28 March 1931 had been used to impose a near-total ban on agitprop performance in Berlin.[54] But the Russian setting was also designed to force unaligned spectators to recognize the similarities between the Weimar Republic and Tsarist Russia and to encourage them to see the Russian Revolution as a model for Germany. It thus functioned as a *Verfremdungseffekt*, even though Brecht would not use this term until 1936.

Brecht's textual changes shifted the political focus from Nizhni-Novgorod in 1902 to Berlin in 1932, so that *Die Mutter* engaged closely with the revolutionary discourse of the German Left. The link between wage cuts and the subsistence crisis dominates the opening scene:

> DIE MUTTER ... ich kann kein Fett mehr hineintun, nicht einen halben Löffel voll. Denn erst vorige Woche ist ihm von seinem Lohn eine Kopeke pro Stunde abgezogen worden, und das kann ich durch keine Mühe mehr hereinbringen.[55]

In the next scene, Mascha argues that only revolution can solve domestic hardship:

---

[52] *RF*, 9 Feb. 1932; Hecht, *Helene Weigel*, 61.   [53] *BFA*, xxiv. 110.

[54] Peter Jelavich, *Berlin Cabaret* (Cambridge, Mass.: Harvard University Press, 1993), 220.

[55] 'THE MOTHER ... I cannot put any more fat in it, not half a spoonful. For only last week one kopeck per hour was cut from his wages, and nothing I do can make up for it.' *BFA*, iii. 263.

MASCHA   Da mußt du den ganzen Staat
                Von unten nach oben umkehren
                Bis du deine Suppe hast.[56]

Even the police inspector acknowledges the link between hunger and politics, calling the almost empty dripping-pot political.[57] Brecht's treatment of the subject corresponded closely to the coverage in the KPD newspaper *Die Rote Fahne* (*The Red Flag*), which reported regularly on falling wages and rising prices, emphasizing their impact on domestic life in articles aimed at women, whom the KPD was particularly keen to recruit.[58]

Brecht broadened Gorky's discussion of industrial action in two key respects. In Scene 8, he included strikes by agricultural labourers, which were more likely to interest his urban spectators than Gorky's description of the difficulties of winning over peasants. In 1930–2, *Die Rote Fahne* reported in similar vein on strikes in the countryside and the problems facing farm labourers.[59] Furthermore, in Scene 3 Brecht substituted a reformist, Karpow, for Gorky's factory director in the confrontation with the revolutionaries. This enabled him to depict the fight against reformism, another major concern of the KPD, which regarded the reformist Social Democratic Party (SPD) as its chief adversary. Communist reviewers like Paul Brand recognized gleefully that Karpow represented the SPD Trade Unionist Fritz Tarnow, whom the KPD regularly vilified. Pawel's jibe 'Also der Kapitalismus ist krank, und du bist der Arzt'[60] alluded to a speech at the SPD conference in June 1931, in which Tarnow had claimed that the SPD stood at capitalism's sickbed: 'Wir sind … dazu verdammt, sowohl Arzt zu sein, der ernsthaft heilen will, und dennoch das Gefühl aufrechtzuerhalten, daß wir Erben sind, die lieber heute als morgen die ganze Hinterlassenschaft des kapitalistischen Systems in Empfang nehmen wollen.'[61] This statement

---

[56] 'MASCHA You must overturn the whole state/From top to bottom/Until you have your soup.' Ibid. 267.

[57] Ibid. 268.

[58] e.g. anon., 'Was sollen wir essen?', *RF*, 15 Aug. 1929; anon., 'Teuerung, Teuerung!', *RF*, 24 Nov. 1929.

[59] e.g. anon., 'Landarbeiterstreiks dehnen sich aus', *RF*, 14 Jan. 1932.

[60] 'So capitalism is sick, and you are the doctor.' *BFA*, iii. 275.

[61] 'We are condemned both to be the doctor, who has a serious desire to heal, and none the less to feel that we are heirs who would prefer to take possession of the entire legacy of the capitalist system today rather than tomorrow.' Sozialdemokratische Partei Deutschlands, *Protokoll über die Verhandlungen des Parteitages* (Berlin: J. H. W. Dietz Nachfolger, 1931), 45.

had outraged the KPD because it renounced Marx's view of the proletariat as the gravedigger of the bourgeoisie and, with it, the commitment to revolution. Thus far, then, Brecht's changes accorded entirely with Party policy.

It soon became clear, however, that Brecht viewed reformists differently from the KPD. Instead of characterizing Karpow as irredeemably selfish and opportunistic, Brecht presented him as basically decent and capable of change. Thus, in Scene 3 of the version that was performed at the première, Karpow was arrested because he refused to betray Wlassowa to the factory police.[62] In a complete volte-face, he then recognized that the system could not be changed from within, joined the revolutionaries' demonstration, and was shot by the police—a solution which portrayed one of the Communists' arch enemies as a revolutionary martyr. This understandably outraged the KPD, which had adamantly refused to unite with the SPD, even against the Nazis. Accordingly, 'S. M.' argued in the Communist *Illustrierte Neue Welt*: 'hier werden falschen Auffassungen über die brennende Tagesfrage "Einheitsfront mit wem?" Tür und Tor geöffnet',[63] and in *Die Rote Fahne* Brand objected to the speed and ease of Karpow's conversion: 'Einen richtigen alten Reformisten schmeißt das bißchen Mißtrauen der Belegschaft nicht um.'[64] Following these criticisms, Brecht changed the text for the 1933 edition, replacing Karpow at the end of Scene 3 and in Scene 5 with a new character, Smilgin. Unlike Karpow, Smilgin is a former revolutionary who opposes the strike but then realizes his mistake, a conversion which was acceptable to the KPD. Brecht's willingness to make this change suggests that he may not have appreciated that his original version would inevitably offend the Party.[65]

State oppression and brutality feature prominently in Gorky's novel and the Stark–Weisenborn adaptation, but these themes had a particular resonance for Brecht's audience. In Scene 5, Karpow's death recalled the events of 1 May 1929 when the Berlin police had fired

---

[62] *BFA*, iii. 277; Brand, *RF*, 19 Jan. 1932.

[63] 'This opens the floodgates to wrong opinions about the burning issue of the day: "a united front with whom?".' S. M., '"Ast" oder "Klassenkampf"', *Illustrierte Neue Welt*, 1/1932.

[64] 'A little bit of mistrust from the workforce doesn't make a real old reformist cave in.' Brand, *RF*, 19 Jan. 1932.

[65] The controversy over the original version entirely escapes Richard Bodek, who assumes that the published version of Scene 3 was performed at the première. Bodek, *Proletarian Performance in Weimar Berlin: Agitprop, Chorus, and Brecht* (Columbia, SC: Camden House, 1997), 145.

on workers in the streets. Tensions had been running high in the weeks before the May Day demonstration because the SPD police chief, Karl Zörgiebel, had refused to rescind his ban on demonstrations. Understandably, Communist organizations perceived his decision as provocative, particularly because 1929 marked the May Day demonstration's fortieth anniversary. The scenes of police brutality made a strong impression on Brecht, who watched events unfold from Fritz Sternberg's flat near the Karl-Liebknecht-Haus, the KPD's headquarters.[66] Since an SPD official had sanctioned the use of force, it is remarkable that Brecht did not foresee the KPD's objections to Karpow's martyrdom.

'Blutmai 1929' ('the bloodbath of May 1929') quickly entered Communist mythology and was commemorated in poems and songs by writers including Johannes R. Becher and Erich Weinert.[67] Like the reports in *Die Rote Fahne*, Brecht's description stressed the demonstrators' solidarity and discipline and the police's unprovoked aggression:

IWAN   Wir marschierten ruhig und in Ordnung ...
PAWEL   ... Als die ersten Leute umschlugen, erfolgte nichts weiter als eine Verwirrung. Viele konnten nicht glauben, daß das, was sie sahen, wirklich geschehen war. Dann setzten sich die Polizisten in Bewegung auf die Menge zu.[68]

Significantly, Brecht did not identify the demonstration with the failed Russian Revolution of 1905, as he subsequently did in 1951.[69] In 1932, dating the demonstration to 1905 would have suggested parallels with the German uprisings of 1918–19 and 1923, whose failure still provoked bitter recriminations within the KPD. Instead, Pawel's prison song encouraged the audience to see the 1929 demonstration as the start of capitalism's final and most desperate phase.[70]

Brecht's use of Russia as a model for Germany encountered difficulties where the two situations differed and the German allusions were not

---

[66] Fritz Sternberg, *Der Dichter und die Ratio: Erinnerungen an Bertolt Brecht* (Göttingen: Sachse & Pohl, 1963), 25.

[67] Thomas Kurz, *'Blutmai': Sozialdemokraten und Kommunisten im Brennpunkt der Berliner Ereignisse von 1929* (Bonn: J. H. W. Dietz Nachfolger, 1988), 129.

[68] 'IWAN We marched in a calm and disciplined manner ... PAWEL ... When the first people collapsed, only confusion followed. Many could not believe that what they were seeing really had happened. Then the police started moving towards the crowd.' *BFA*, iii. 281–2; cf. anon., 'Der 1. Mai des roten Berlin', *RF*, 3 May 1930.

[69] 'Bühnenmanuskript' of the 1951 production, BBA 637/30.

[70] *BFA*, iii. 296.

explicit, since the critics then interpreted them solely as references to Russia. For example, Brecht's depiction of the collapse of Russian anti-war opposition alluded to the SPD's 1914 vote in favour of war credits, but Brand and 'S. M.' missed this allusion and accused Brecht of ignoring the Bolsheviks' exemplary conduct.[71] Again, Brecht's failure to foresee the KPD's predictable objections indicates the limits of his political grasp.

Although Communist reviewers had significant reservations about Brecht's ideological stance, they still deemed his treatment of contemporary socio-economic problems valuable. Consequently, they encouraged their readers to see the production: *Berlin am Morgen* declared that every woman and every mother must see Brecht's lively new Marxist play.[72] Several Communist organizations, including the *Internationale Arbeiterhilfe* (International Workers' Relief) and the *Interessengemeinschaft für Arbeiterkultur* (Interest Group for Workers' Culture), signed a declaration supporting the production, and *Die Rote Post* even subsidized six performances for its readers.[73] The final accolade came when the actors were asked to perform a scene at an election rally for Ernst Thälmann on 26 February 1932.[74]

5. DRAMATURGY AND AESTHETICS

In the programme, Weisenborn reprinted the table contrasting 'epic' and 'dramatic' theatre from Brecht's 'Anmerkungen zur Oper' ('Notes on the Opera', 1930) and thereby presented *Die Mutter* as the antithesis of conventional theatre. Fuegi rejects the programme's claims for the 'epic' entirely, arguing instead that *Die Mutter* is 'a largely traditional, highly conservative ... example of the dramatic mode'.[75] But Brecht had originally presented his contrasts as 'Gewichtsverschiebungen', 'keine absoluten Gegensätze, sondern lediglich Akzentverschiebungen'.[76] We can only speculate why the programme omitted these crucial qualifications: perhaps Weisenborn overlooked their importance, or perhaps

---

[71] Brand, *RF*, 19 Jan. 1932; S. M., *Illustrierte Neue Welt*, 1/1932.
[72] Anon., 'Kennen Sie schon das Lehrstück *Die Mutter?*', *Berlin am Morgen*, 24 Jan. 1932.
[73] Lüdecke, *Illustrierte Rote Post*, 4/1932.
[74] Jürgen Schebera, *Hanns Eisler: Eine Bildbiografie* (East Berlin: Henschel, 1981), 63.
[75] Fuegi, *Essential Brecht*, 60.
[76] 'Shifts of emphasis', 'not absolute contrasts, but just shifts of stress'. *BFA*, xxiv. 78.

Brecht wanted to generate maximum publicity. Either way, the original 'Gewichtsverschiebungen' suggest that epic theatre relies on a complex combination of 'epic' and 'dramatic' techniques. This is particularly true of *Die Mutter*.

5.1 Dramatic Structure

The programme contrasted *Montage* with the organic plot development, or *Wachstum*, of dramatic theatre, where each scene exists for the next. In Scenes 1 and 2, for instance, the songs interrupt the flow of the action and provide an overt political commentary. Even so, the plot of the first eight scenes still clearly exhibits *Wachstum*: Scenes 1–5 follow the preparations for the demonstration through to the reported event itself, and then Scenes 6–8 depict the immediate aftermath, as Wlassowa moves to the teacher, visits Pawel in prison, and delivers leaflets to agricultural workers on his behalf. It is only after Scene 8 that the action develops *in Sprüngen* (in leaps), when Brecht presents pivotal episodes from Wlassowa's biography: her brief reunion with Pawel, the outbreak of war, and the revolution. Chronologically, a similar shift occurs from *Wachstum* towards *Montage*, for whilst the action in Scenes 1–4 takes place within twenty-four hours, that in Scenes 5–8 occurs over a longer period of weeks or months, and the gaps between the later scenes extend to several years. This suggests that although *Wachstum* is the dominant structural principle until Scene 8, it is strongest in the first four scenes.

Further 'dramatic' cohesion can be discerned in the historical chronology and learning narrative, which link the individual episodes. This cohesion is increased by Wlassowa's presence in every scene and the structural parallels between the episodes. For example, the situation in which Wlassowa watches Pawel print leaflets in Scene 2 is reversed in Scene 9, and the final demonstration parallels the demonstration in Scene 5.[77] Similarly, the learning journeys of the teacher, butcher, and maid parallel the master-narrative of Wlassowa's development. Politically, these learning journeys indicate Brecht's interest in how class-consciousness is generated and his concern not to preach exclusively to the converted. But in structural terms they also demonstrate that *Die Mutter* combines traditional 'dramatic' techniques with Brecht's more radical claims for the 'epic' form.

---

[77] *BFA*, iii. 266–7, 305–6, 323–4, 281–4.

5.2 Narrative in Theatre

Although the programme contrasted *erzählend* (narrating) with *handelnd* (acting), the narrative techniques in *Die Mutter* actually achieve their effect through the interplay with the dramatic action. Wlassowa's stylized opening monologue contains strong epic elements: it replaces the traditional 'dramatic' exposition through dialogue, introducing the heroine's name, age, social position, and plight directly. Even so, it also retains a strong dramatic dimension: the character narrates her own plight in the first person, within the dramatic setting of her home, and treats the audience as her collective *confidante*, asking: 'Was kann ich, Pelagea Wlassowa, 42 Jahre alt, Witwe eines Arbeiters und Mutter eines Arbeiters, tun?'[78] The combination of these epic and dramatic elements means that the monologue's impact depends on the spectators' political beliefs and the actress's approach. Whilst unaligned spectators might identify uncritically with Wlassowa, Communists might criticize her defeatism. And whereas an 'Aristotelian' actress might use the direct address to encourage the spectators to identify with Wlassowa, an epic actress would invite them to criticize her. It is only after the monologue, when the chorus sings 'Wie die Krähe' ('Like the Crow'), that Brecht's text unequivocally forces the audience to analyse Wlassowa's plight and see her 'als Mitmensch, dem ich begegne, nicht als Ich oder Auchich'.[79]

Brecht's narrative techniques challenged contemporary dramatic convention only in the demonstration scenes. Although many playwrights use narrative description to avoid scenes that would be difficult to stage, they traditionally supply a naturalistic motivation for reports in the main body of the action. In Scene 22 of Kleist's *Penthesilea*, for instance, an onlooker reports the heroine's struggle with Achilles from the vantage-point of a hilltop as the action unfolds. Even in *Die Maßnahme* the young comrade's death is reported and re-enacted for the benefit of the Party tribunal. In contrast, Wlassowa's comrades report events directly to the audience in the past tense. This technique heightens the spectators' awareness of the demonstration's importance, for Pawel announces Karpow as though to a historical tribunal, recording his service to the movement, his social class, and the exact time of

[78] 'What can I, Pelagea Wlassowa, 42 years old, the widow of a worker and mother of a worker, do?' Ibid. 263.
[79] 'As a fellow human being whom I meet, not as myself or my alter-ego.' 'Die Mutter: Anmerkungen I', BBA 444/83.

his martyrdom, which—appropriately—occurs on the *Erlöserboulevard* (Saviour's Boulevard):

> PAWEL   15 Jahre in der Bewegung, Arbeiter, Revolutionär, am 1. Mai 1900, vormittags 11 Uhr an der Ecke des Erlöserboulevards, im entscheidenden Augenblick.[80]

Brecht shifts to the present tense in order to signal the start of a flashback, a popular cinematic technique:

> [KARPOW]   Jetzt stehe ich hier, hinter mir sind es schon viele Tausende, aber vor uns steht wieder die Gewalt. Sollen wir die Fahne weggeben?[81]

The transference of this technique to the stage significantly modifies its impact, since the actor playing Karpow is present throughout the past-tense report, whereas the flashback reveals that this character died during the event. Furthermore, whilst Karpow speaks solely in the present tense during the flashback, his comrades combine present-tense direct speech with past-tense narration, alternating between the second and third persons:

> ANTON   Gib sie nicht weg, [Karpow]! Es geht nicht durch Verhandeln, sagten wir, und die Mutter sagte ihm ...[82]

By combining the flashback with the report, this part of the scene operates on two levels of dramatic time and space, which occupy the same real time and space on stage. Consequently, Scene 5 relies on a far more complex and subtle interplay of techniques than the programme's opposition of *handelnd* and *erzählend* suggests.

5.3 Agitational Strategies

The agitational strategies in the text and the première were strongly influenced by recent experiments in far left-wing theatre, particularly agitprop and Piscator's stagings. Slogans and pictures were projected on

[80] 'PAWEL 15 years in the movement, worker, revolutionary, on 1 May 1900, at 11 o'clock in the morning on the corner of the Saviour's Boulevard, at the decisive moment.' *BFA*, iii. 283.

[81] '[KARPOW] Now I stand here, behind me there are already many thousands, but in front of us stand the armed forces once more. Should we surrender the flag?' Ibid. Cf. Wolfgang Gersch, *Film bei Brecht: Bertolt Brechts praktische und theoretische Auseinandersetzung mit dem Film* (East Berlin: Henschel, 1975), 169.

[82] 'ANTON Don't surrender it, [Karpow]! Negotiations don't work, we told him, and the Mother told him ...' *BFA*, iii. 283.

to a screen, reminding viewers of the broader historical and political context of the action.[83] Although most of the captions in the 1933 text simply set the scene like a stage direction, those in Brecht's 'Anmerkungen' supply a clear sociopolitical commentary on the action. For instance, the 1933 caption for Scene 1 reads: 'Früh am Morgen kocht die Mutter dem Sohn, der auf Arbeit geht, die Suppe', whereas Brecht's 'Anmerkungen' suggest: 'Die Wlassowas aller Länder'—a caption that recalls the appeal by Marx and Engels to the 'Proletarier aller Länder'.[84] Other slogans in the 'Anmerkungen' quote Marx and Lenin directly:

Im Zuschauerraum als Transparent:
'OHNE DIE FRAUEN GIBT ES KEINE WIRKLICHE MASSENBEWEGUNG.' (LENIN)[85]

But Brecht's 'Anmerkungen' again overstated his case, this time when he responded to criticisms that the captions were simply aids for naïve listeners: 'Die Projektionen sind keineswegs einfache mechanische Hilfs-mittel im Sinne von Ergänzungen, keine Eselsbrücken; sie nehmen keine Hilfsstellung für den Zuschauer ein, sondern Gegenstellung: sie vereiteln seine totale Einfühlung, unterbrechen sein mechanisches Mitgehen.'[86] In fact, by communicating the play's political arguments, the captions both functioned as aids and disrupted spectators' involvement in the action.

Like the captions, the projected images encouraged the spectators to relate the action to broader political issues. Piscator had pioneered this technique in Germany by replacing the traditional illustrative backcloth with a geo-political map in *Rußlands Tag* (*Russia's Day*, 1920), and since then such techniques had featured regularly in far left-wing performances, like *Die Mausefalle* (*The Mousetrap*, 1931) by Truppe 1931. In Scene 8 of *Die Mutter*, separate images of the hammer and sickle commented on Luschin's scepticism about Lenin's proposed worker–peasant alliance. This unorthodox use of the Soviet emblem functioned as another early *Verfremdungseffekt* by showing that the alliance was both essential and achievable. Accordingly, after Wlassowa

---

[83] *BFA*, xxiv. 116.
[84] 'Early in the morning Pelagea Wlassowa cooks soup for her son, who is going to work', 'the Wlassowas of all countries', 'workers of all countries'. *BFA*, iii. 263; xxiv. 116.
[85] 'In the auditorium as a banner: "WITHOUT WOMEN THERE IS NO TRUE MASS MOVEMENT." (Lenin).' *BFA*, xxiv. 117.
[86] 'The projections are by no means simple mechanical aids in the sense of amplifica-tions; they are not crutches; they do not support the spectator, but rather oppose him: they frustrate his total identification, interrupt him when he goes along with the action mechanically.' Ibid. 116.

had secured the butcher's co-operation, the hammer and sickle were reunited in the familiar emblem.[87]

5.4 Reason and Emotion

Although the programme contrasted *Gefühl* (feeling) with *Ratio* (reason), *Die Mutter* does use emotion for agitational purposes. Both the house search in Scene 2 and Karpow's death in Scene 5 aroused spectators' anger, as Kurt Kersten reported in the left-wing *Welt am Abend*: 'das Blut steigt einem in den Schädel'.[88] Furthermore, when workers refuse Wlassowa's leaflets at the street corner, Brecht invites the spectators' sympathy in order to ensure that they, unlike the workers, respond positively to Wlassowa's arguments.[89] Brecht subsequently modified the misleading opposition of *Gefühl* and *Ratio* by implying in his 'Anmerkungen' that a calculated use of empathy was acceptable: '[die nichtaristotelische Dramatik] bedient sich der *hingebenden Einfühlung* des Zuschauers keineswegs so unbedenklich wie die aristotelische'.[90] This comment conceded that the text works in a more complex way than the earlier, schematic opposition had suggested.

None the less, Brecht's selective use of emotion was far removed from the sentimentality of Gorky's novel and the Stark–Weisenborn adaptation—much to the disappointment of Gorky's admirers. For instance, writing in *Der Abend*, the evening edition of the SPD newspaper *Vorwärts*, Max Hochdorf lamented the loss of Gorky's heart-warming psychology.[91] The humour, energy, and obstinacy of Brecht's heroine all contrast strikingly with Gorky's characterization of Wlassowa as 'weich, schwermütig, demütig' ('soft, melancholy, humble').[92] Where Gorky's Wlassowa resigns herself to incomprehension, Brecht's character asks probing questions and refuses to take any nonsense from the revolutionaries.[93] In the Stark–Weisenborn version, Wlassowa's halting language reflects her diffidence:

---

[87] Ibid. 117.

[88] 'It makes your blood boil.' K[urt] K[erste]n, 'Die Mutter', *Die Welt am Abend*, 18 Jan. 1932.

[89] *BFA*, iii. 316–17.

[90] '[Non-Aristotelian drama] does not rely nearly so unthinkingly on the spectator *surrendering himself over to empathy* as Aristotelian drama.' *BFA*, xxiv. 115.

[91] Max Hochdorf, 'Bert Brechts Episches Theater', *Der Abend*, [18] Jan. 1932.

[92] Gorky, *Die Mutter*, 17.   [93] *BFA*, iii. 270–1, 277–81.

MUTTER (*leise*) Marja sagt, ich soll morgen ... in der Mittagspause auf dem Fabrikhof ... Essen verkaufen. Ich könnte morgen ... auf dem Fabrikhof ... (*atemlose Stille*) die Flugblätter ... auch ... nämlich ... vielleicht ... mein ich ...[94]

Again, this contrasts with the brisk, businesslike approach of Brecht's Wlassowa: 'Gebt die Flugblätter her, ich, nicht Pawel, werde gehen und sie verteilen.'[95] Besides preserving Gorky's sentimentality, the Stark–Weisenborn adaptation also includes sensationalist episodes: in Scene 2, for example, the bloodstained victim of an industrial accident is carried across the stage.[96] By rejecting this strategy, Brecht indicated his preference for the 'lange Zündung' ('long smouldering fuse') over the short-term shock effect.[97]

5.5 The Set and Costumes

At the première, the set and costumes defied the conventions of illusionist theatre. As Brecht explained, Neher's minimalist set merely delineated the acting space and did not pretend to be a real location.[98] It consisted of white sheets stretched between the poles of a metal frame, with wooden doors that could be opened and closed—a feature that already pointed towards the crafted aesthetic and authentic materials that Neher would subsequently employ at the BE. Besides restricting the props to the bare essentials, Brecht and Neher made no attempt to disguise their improvised nature. For instance, Morbach recalls: 'in der Fleischerszene hatten wir eine Margarinetonne als Hackklotz, ein paar Beine darunter... Das Publikum hat es natürlich gesehen, aber Brecht fand, das mache nichts.'[99] This pragmatic approach suited the team's tight budget: Aufricht had limited his stake to 3,000 marks, and low entrance prices were the key to attracting a working-class audience; most tickets cost ninety pfennigs, and some were even available at sixty.[100] Furthermore, if the production was to be transferred

---

[94] 'MOTHER (*softly*) Marja says, tomorrow I am to sell ... food ... in the factory yard at lunchtime. Tomorrow in the factory yard I could ... also ... (*breathless silence*) deliver the leaflets ... well ... perhaps ... I mean ...' Stark and Weisenborn, 70.

[95] 'Give me the leaflets: I, not Pawel, will go and distribute them.' *BFA*, iii. 271.

[96] Stark and Weisenborn, 72.   [97] GWA 107.   [98] *BFA*, xxiv. 115.

[99] 'In the butcher's scene we had a margarine barrel as a chopping block, with a couple of legs underneath... The audience saw, of course, but in Brecht's opinion that didn't matter.' Rülicke, 470.

[100] Aufricht, 127; *RF*, 19 and 28 Jan., 9 Feb. 1932.

to other theatres, it needed a set that could be easily dismantled and transported.

Neher's austere aesthetic also matched the economy of the play's language and setting. In an unpublished note, Brecht explained: 'Die nichtaristotelische Dramatik bedient sich auf einer Reihe von Gebieten, die das Theater für gewöhnlich möglichst reich ausstattet, (Charakterisierung der Personen, der Milieuschilderungen, der Lagebeschreibungen usw.) einiger Vereinfachungen.'[101] The absence of local colour, in both the set and the costumes, also served Brecht's aim of using the Russian Revolution as a model for Germany. Yet right- and even left-wing critics perceived these simplifications as evidence that Neher's aesthetic was primitive. In *Der Westen*, 'H. A.' declared: 'Schmutzige Bettlaken herauszuhängen hat nichts mit Kunst zu tun!'[102] Similarly 'S. M.' wrote in the *Illustrierte Neue Welt*: 'Das Bühnenbild ist schmucklos—primitiv. Ohne Notwendigkeit... Das Proletariat lebt in primitiven Verhältnissen. Es war noch nie übersättigt und hat deshalb auch keine Sehnsucht nach Primitivität.'[103] These last comments indicate the growing hostility in the KPD towards the agitprop aesthetic, hostility that would have major consequences for artistic policy and epic theatre in the early GDR.

5.6 Blocking the *Fabel*

As John White points out, it was not until the *Kleines Organon* that the *Fabel* occupied a central place in Brecht's theatrical theories.[104] Brecht used this concept to refer to the sociopolitical story which the director wanted to tell through the production; his assistant Käthe Rülicke-Weiler explains that the *Fabel* is told 'vom Standpunkt der Gesellschaft aus' ('from the perspective of society').[105] So although White argues that Brecht's poetic rendering of the *Fabel* of *Die Mutter*

---

[101] 'Non-Aristotelian drama uses certain simplifications in a series of areas which theatre usually presents as richly as possible (characterization, descriptions of the milieu and situation, etc.).' BBA 444/62.

[102] 'Hanging out dirty sheets has nothing to do with art!' H. A., 'Uraufführung: Die Mutter', *Der Westen*, 19 Jan. 1932.

[103] 'The set is unadorned—primitive. Unnecessarily so... The proletariat lives in primitive conditions. It has never been over-sated and therefore has no longing for the primitive.' S. M., *Illustrierte Neue Welt*, 1/1932.

[104] John J. White, *Bertolt Brecht's Dramatic Theory* (Rochester, NY: Camden House, 2004), 225.

[105] Käthe Rülicke-Weiler, *Die Dramaturgie Brechts: Theater als Mittel der Veränderung* (East Berlin: Henschel, 1968), 92.

in *Theaterarbeit* offers 'a far more positive valorization of the plot material than the neutral noun "Fabel" suggests',[106] in Brecht's usage the *Fabel* was not neutral. The BE's records show that, when preparing a new production, Brecht and his assistants would summarize the *Fabel* and identify the developments in each scene which contributed towards it.[107] They would then foreground these developments through the blocking: that is to say, the movement and configuration of the actors on stage.

Brecht's 'Anmerkungen' and the photographs of the 1932 production reveal that analysis of the *Fabel* was already integral to his theatrical practice in the late Weimar Republic. In section IV of the 'Anmerkungen', for example, Brecht divided Scene 2 into seven discrete processes which should be shown through the blocking. Unlike naturalistic directors, Brecht eliminated superfluous movement so that every grouping expressed the meaning of the *Fabel* clearly and simply: 'Das epische Theater bedient sich denkbar einfachster, den Sinn der Vorgänge übersichtlich ausdrückender Gruppierungen. Die "zufällige", "Leben vortäuschende", "zwanglose" Gruppierung ist aufgegeben.'[108] Brecht acknowledged that his approach was influenced by silent film: 'Schon der stumme Film hat die Schauspieler darin geschult, so zu spielen, daß auch der nur Schauende oder der der Sprache nicht Mächtige den Sinn der Szene erfassen kann.'[109]

In 1932, the blocking clearly depicted the characters' relationships and attitudes. At the start of Scene 2, for example, the physical distance between Wlassowa and the revolutionaries reflected her disapproval of their activities and emotional distance from Pawel. During the police house search, however, the configuration changed, and Mascha joined Wlassowa in a *Gestus* of solidarity. After the police's departure Wlassowa confronted the revolutionaries, and in Scene 4 she sat amongst them, as if in a family circle. Thus, the blocking showed how Wlassowa's hostility towards the revolutionaries gradually changed into trust—a change that was a crucial part of the larger story of her political

---

[106] White, 148.

[107] e.g. 'MUTTER-Fabel', in 'Die Mutter 1951', file 5, MN29, BEA.

[108] 'Epic theatre uses the simplest possible groupings, which clearly express the meaning of the events. It renounces the "chance", "unforced" grouping that gives "an illusion of real life".' *BFA*, xxiv. 118.

[109] 'Silent film has already trained actors to perform in such a way that even someone who is only watching, or who is unable to understand the language, can grasp the point of a scene.' 'Die Mutter: Anmerkungen II', BBA 445/01.

development. Brecht's lengthy, unpolemical explanation of his approach in the 1933 edition indicates that he was already attempting to influence theatrical practice in general, and future productions of his plays in particular.[110] These considerations would become central to his work at the BE.

6. MUSIC

6.1 Eisler's Collaboration with Brecht and Busch

Die Mutter was Eisler's third major project with Brecht, following *Die Maßnahme* (1930) and *Kuhle Wampe* (1931). Unlike Brecht's earlier musical collaborators Kurt Weill and Paul Hindemith, Eisler possessed valuable experience of the workers' movement. He had collaborated with the agitprop troupe *Das Rote Sprachrohr* (The Red Megaphone), lectured at the *Marxistische Arbeiterschule* (Marxist Workers' School), and contributed regularly to *Die Rote Fahne*.[111] Through his agitprop and choral work, Eisler strove to place music in the service of social progress, activating the emotion and understanding of both singers and listeners. He thus shared Brecht's interest in *Gebrauchskunst* (utilitarian art) and concern to communicate clearly with his audience; in his 1932 essay 'Unsere Kampfmusik' ('Our Music for the Struggle'), he explained: 'Die erste Forderung, die der Klassenkampf an Kampflieder stellt, ist eine große Faßlichkeit, leichte Verständlichkeit und energische präzise Haltung.'[112] Eisler found his ideal interpreter in Ernst Busch, and from 1929 they collaborated on political ballads and songs. Busch played Pawel in the 1932 production of *Die Mutter*, and advertisements displayed his name prominently alongside Eisler's, promising to attract a large working-class audience.

6.2 The Different Versions of Eisler's Score

Eisler collaborated on Brecht's three productions of *Die Mutter* and produced three stage versions of the score, plus three concert versions.

[110] Brecht, *Die Mutter; Geschichten*, 66–7.   [111] Schebera, 34–9.
[112] 'The first demand that the class struggle makes of its battle songs is that they are readily intelligible, easy to understand, energetic, and precise.' Hanns Eisler, *Materialien zu einer Dialektik der Musik* (Leipzig: Reclam, 1976), 81–2 (81).

1. Solidarity when under pressure: the *Gruppe Junger Schauspieler*, 1932. Helene Weigel as Wlassowa, second from left.

The first concert version was completed in 1932; the second was written in 1935 for the American New Singers; and the third—a cantata—was premièred by Österreichischer Rundfunk in 1949. The genesis of the stage and concert versions has been discussed by Manfred Grabs, Joachim Lucchesi and Ronald Shull, and in greater detail by Albrecht Dümling.[113] I refer to their findings in section 6.3, where I examine the content, style, and function of the 1932 stage version and show how the interaction between the text and music contributed to the première's success. I discuss the changes that Eisler made for subsequent stage versions in Chapters 2 and 4.

6.3 The 1932 Stage Version

6.3.1 Content

Although the score of the 1932 stage version has not survived, the programme and reviews offer some clues about its content. As Dümling notes, the programme lists nine musical pieces in a sequence that differs slightly from the 1933 edition: the programme lists the 'Lob des Kommunismus' ('In Praise of Communism') seventh, before 'Die Partei ist in Gefahr' ('The Party is in Danger'), whereas in the 1933 edition it comes third, before the 'Lob des Lernens' ('In Praise of Learning').[114] So although Brecht's essay 'Das Stück *Die Mutter*' ('The Play *The Mother*') suggests that the songs in the 1932 production prefigured the 1933 sequence, it is entirely possible that the 'Lob des Kommunismus' was performed later in the play on the first night. Whilst the programme contains two unfamiliar titles, 'Über die Unzerstörbarkeit des Kommunismus' ('On the Indestructibility of Communism') and 'Schlußmusik' ('Finale'), reviews corroborate the conventional assumption that the former was actually the 'Lied im Gefängnis' ('Song in Prison'): several reviewers complimented Busch on his prison solo, and Junghans even quoted the refrain: 'Ehe sie verschwinden, und das wird bald sein, werden sie gemerkt haben, das ihnen das alles nichts mehr

[113] Manfred Grabs, *Hanns Eisler: Kompositionen—Schriften—Literatur: Ein Handbuch* (Leipzig: Deutscher Verlag für Musik, 1984), 65–8; Joachim Lucchesi and Ronald K. Shull, *Musik bei Brecht* (Frankfurt/Main: Suhrkamp, 1988), 540–5; Albrecht Dümling, ' "Im Stil der Lehrstücke": Zu Entstehung und Edition von Eislers Musik für Brechts Gorki-Bearbeitung *Die Mutter*', in *Der Text im musikalischen Werk: Editionsprobleme aus musikwissenschaftlicher und literaturwissenschaftlicher Sicht*, ed. Walther Dürr *et al.* (Berlin: Erich Schmidt, 1998), 361–81.
[114] Dümling, ' "Im Stil" ', 376.

nützt.'[115] Even more significantly, reviews prove that Lucchesi, Shull, and Dümling were wrong to conclude that the 'Lied von der Suppe' ('Song of the Soup') was cut before the première.[116] Three reviewers actually quoted from this song: for example, 'E. Kr.' complained about Eisler's 'radikale Songs, ... etwa: "Wenn du keine Suppe hast, mußt du den Staat umkehren"'.[117] The programme did, however, omit the 'Lob des Revolutionärs' ('In Praise of the Revolutionary') and 'Grabrede', which Eisler subsequently added to the first concert version.

6.3.2 Orchestration

The programme shows that the 1932 stage version was orchestrated for a small ensemble, using instruments traditionally associated with *Kampfmusik*: trumpet, trombone, percussion, and piano. This contrasted with the richer orchestration of *Die Maßnahme*, which was modelled on Bach's Passions and required three trumpets, two horns, two trombones, percussion, and piano.[118] The sparse orchestration of *Die Mutter* points again to the collective's limited resources, which were stretched further when the musicians insisted on their full tariff, unlike the actors and technicians.[119] It also suited the austere performance aesthetic and enabled the listeners to pick out the melody's different strands more easily. In 1939 Eisler elaborated on this latter aspect in his essay 'Moderne Instrumentation' ('Modern Instrumentation'): 'Wir bevorzugen heute ... eine Instrumentation, in der die Instrumente ihren Solocharakter behalten, anstatt ihn wie im vorigen Jahrhundert zu einem Brei zu vermengen.'[120] This preference corresponded to Eisler's and Brecht's more global views on the function of music in performance. In his notes on *Mahagonny*, for example, Brecht advocates 'die Trennung der Elemente' ('the separation of the elements') and argues

---

[115] 'Before they disappear, as they will do soon, they will have realized that all this can no longer save them.' Junghans, *Neue Preußische Kreuzzeitung*, 18 Jan. 1932; cf. S. M., *Illustrierte Neue Welt*, 1/1932.

[116] Lucchesi and Shull, 547; Dümling, '"Im Stil"', 366.

[117] 'Radical songs, ... such as: "If you don't have any soup, you must overturn the state."' E. Kr., 'Bühnen-Versuche', *Der Montag* (Berlin), 18 Jan. 1932. Cf. B. P., 'Kommunistisches Theater', *Berliner Morgen-Zeitung*, 18 Jan. 1932; anon., 'Brechts bolschewistische *Mutter*-Propaganda', *Völkischer Beobachter* (Munich), [n. d.], BBA 404/33.

[118] Lucchesi and Shull, 489.   [119] Hecht, *Helene Weigel*, 65.

[120] 'Nowadays we prefer ... an instrumentation in which the instruments retain their solo character, instead of being mixed into porridge as in the previous century.' Eisler, *Materialien*, 163–5 (164).

that music should comment on the text and develop its arguments, rather than simply illustrating it.[121] Eisler incorporated this idea into an essay written in 1936, where he contrasts the old use of music as illustration with its new function as commentary.[122] Significantly, this essay uses the same format as Brecht's notes on *Mahagonny*, demonstrating the inspiration that Eisler, like Brecht, drew from their two-way partnership.

6.3.3 Styles and Techniques

The songs that were designed to rouse the audience employed the style and techniques of *Kampfmusik*. For instance, 'Wie die Krähe', 'Lob des Lernens', and 'Die Partei ist in Gefahr' each contain a chorus with a stirring march rhythm. To emphasize the urgency of Brecht's commands, Eisler often placed the first syllable on the upbeat so that the rhythm drives the singer forward into the next bar; he used this technique in 'Lob des Lernens'.[123] Aggressive rhythms are equally important in 'Die Partei', where a repeated pattern of accented quavers in the harmony emphasizes the urgency of the Party's summons.[124] By including such rhythms in the final bars of these two songs, Eisler hoped that their energy would not be dissipated at the conclusion but would continue to activate the listeners.[125]

Just as Brecht used different dramaturgical techniques, so Eisler employed styles that contrasted completely with *Kampfmusik*. Since the 'Lob des Kommunismus' seeks to dispel prejudice against Communism, Eisler set the lyrics to an innocuous lullaby which, according to Brecht, '[verschafft] durch ihren freundlich beratenden Gestus sozusagen der Stimme der Vernunft Gehör'.[126] This piece also contrasted stylistically with the recitation against music in 'Lob der Wlassowas' ('In Praise of Those Like Wlassowa'), 'Lob der dritten Sache' ('In Praise of the Third Cause'), and the verses of 'Wie die Krähe', where the music disciplines

---

[121] *BFA*, xxiv. 74–84 (79).

[122] Eisler, '[Gesellschaftliche Umfunktionierung der Musik]', in *Materialien*, 122–8 (126).

[123] Hanns Eisler, *Neun Balladen aus 'Die Mutter'*, ed. Manfred Grabs (Leipzig: Deutscher Verlag für Musik, 1977), 16, bars 10–11. This edition is based on the manuscripts of the 1932 concert version (HEA 70/1–52; C115; 17/82–128; 154/1–138).

[124] Ibid. 63, bars 1–4.   [125] Ibid. 21, bars 53–4, and 68, bars 41–2.

[126] 'Whose *Gestus* of friendly advice [ensures], as it were, that the voice of reason is heard.' 'Über die Verwendung von Musik für ein episches Theater', *BFA*, xxii.1. 155–64 (161).

the speaker into reciting 'in einer bestimmten, musikalisch fixierten Weise'.[127]

The aggressive rhythms of 'Die Partei' and the lullaby of 'Lob des Kommunismus' serve the same function as Brecht's lyrics, as Ekmann has argued with regard to the agitational songs.[128] Nevertheless, Eisler also used the melody and harmony to comment on Brecht's lyrics, in accordance with Brecht's claims for 'die Trennung der Elemente'. In 'Die Partei', for instance, the Party sings 'Du bist krank, aber die Partei stirbt' to the melody of 'er ist vernünftig, jeder versteht ihn' from 'Lob des Kommunismus'.[129] This indicates that the Party understands Wlassowa's plight but still needs her—and the spectators—to understand the urgency of its summons.

A similar effect was achieved through the interaction of the melody and harmony in 'Lob des Lernens'. As Georg Knepler has shown, Eisler combined two different motifs to demonstrate the link between knowledge and power, associating one motif with learning ('Lerne das Einfachste') and the other with seizing power ('Du mußt die Führung übernehmen!').[130] Whereas Brecht's lyrics can voice these ideas only in succession, Eisler's music expresses them simultaneously. Thus, the lyrics of the refrain are sung to the melody of the power motif, whilst the harmony in the accompaniment follows the rhythm of the learning motif.[131] This evidence suggests that the music performs a more independent role than Ekmann concedes, even though it never contradicts the lyrics entirely—unlike, for example, Weill's mock-religious setting of Peachum's blasphemous hymn in *Die Dreigroschenoper*.

6.3.4 The 'Grabrede auf den Tod eines Genossen' ('Funeral Oration on the Death of a Comrade')

Although the 'Grabrede' was probably first included in Eisler's 1932 concert version, it still merits consideration here because its function and style are so distinctive. Far from rejecting feeling in favour of reason, Eisler's poignant music actually heightens the tragedy of Pawel's death.

[127] 'In a particular manner determined by the music.' 1932 programme.
[128] Ekmann, 190.
[129] 'You are sick, but the Party is dying'; 'it is logical, everyone understands it'. Eisler, *Neun Balladen*, 11, bars 2–3, and 63–4, bars 7–8.
[130] 'Learn the basics', 'You must seize power'. Ibid. 15, bar 2, and 16, bars 13–14; Georg Knepler, 'Was des Eislers ist …', *Beiträge zur Musikwissenschaft*, 15 (1973), 29–47 (34–9).
[131] Eisler, *Neun Balladen*, 18, bars 25–6.

Yet at the same time, Brecht's lyrics channel the listeners' emotional response towards the tragedy and their sympathy for Wlassowa towards a political goal, thus dispensing with catharsis. Brecht achieves this in two steps: first, he places Wlassowa's private grief in a social context by showing that Pawel was shot by men from his own class; and second, he offers grounds for hope by revealing that the soldiers are 'nicht ewig auch unbelehrbar' ('not eternally unteachable').[132] Thus, the song uses the spectators' emotion to fuel their intellectual will to change reality.

Eisler's setting recalls the style of Bach's Passions and presents Pawel as a Christ-like martyr, thus commemorating his sacrifice and implying that Communism is the route to secular salvation. After the first two bars a basso continuo accompanies the solo alto, suggesting a funeral march. The regular chords support the melody and ensure that the tempo is maintained, in accordance with Eisler's instructions. In the third verse, however, the accompaniment's rhythm changes to a repeated pattern of one minim followed by two crotchets. This rhythm, which Eisler uses in the melody of '[er] ging noch gefesselt in [Ketten]' ('[he] walked still bound in [chains]'),[133] continues throughout the verse, as if describing Pawel's walk from prison to the wall, a situation which recalls the Via Dolorosa. In bar 74 the rhythm slows in preparation for the impassioned climax which is accompanied only by long chords and sung *fortissimo*: 'Ihn aber führten seinesgleichen zur Wand jetzt'.[134] Significantly, bars 76–8 again recall the melody of 'er ist vernünftig, jeder versteht ihn', even though the lyrics have described the soldiers' *failure*—thus far—to understand Communism. The motif therefore reminds listeners of the paradox that Communism is 'das Einfache/Das schwer zu machen ist' and shows how Pawel's initially intellectual commitment to Communist teachings is being put to the ultimate test.[135] Thus, Eisler's music comments independently on Brecht's lyrics and appeals to both reason and emotion.

6.3.5 Audiences

Besides showing Eisler's skill at tailoring his settings to each song's function, the score's contrasting styles indicate the range of audiences

---

[132] *BFA*, iii. 310.   [133] Eisler, *Neun Balladen*, 57, bars 43–5.

[134] 'Right now, however, men like him were leading him to his execution'. Ibid. 61, bars 75–9.

[135] 'The simple thing/That is hard to do.' *BFA*, iii. 286. Cf. Fred Fischbach, 'Pour une nouvelle lecture des pièces de Brecht à la lumière de la musique de scène de Hanns Eisler', *Recherches germaniques*, 13 (1983), 137–66 (151).

for whom it was written. The music appealed so strongly to Eisler's proletarian audience that the agitational songs were performed at political meetings, and the lyrics of 'Lob des Lernens' and 'Die Partei' were published in Communist newspapers.[136] Indeed, the House Committee on Un-American Activities even cited 'Lob des Lernens' as evidence against Brecht and Eisler in 1947.[137] None the less, the complex variations in the melody and harmony suggest that Eisler's score was also conceived for a musically literate public. This is particularly evident from the versions that were designed for concert performance. For example, Dümling notes that Eisler even cited Bach's Magnificat in the 1949 cantata by setting the line 'Arbeite, arbeite, arbeite mehr, spare, teile besser ein, rechne, rechne, rechne genauer!' to the melody of 'Deposuit, deposuit potentes'.[138] This provides the clearest example of Eisler's musical commentary, for the lyrics ask 'was ist der Ausweg' ('what is the answer?'), and the music answers 'deposuit potentes' ('he has put down the mighty from their seats'). The function of this musical quotation was admittedly ambivalent: whilst it made a political point, the incongruous spectre of revolutionary workers singing to the Magnificat also invited humour. Even so, the stylistic variety and complexity of Eisler's score demonstrate his commitment to producing high-quality, anti-élitist art for a hybrid audience, like the première itself.

7. THE POLARIZED RECEPTION AND BRECHT'S RESPONSE

7.1 Opposition and Censorship

Die Mutter was designed to polarize spectators by rallying the KPD's supporters, winning over unaligned workers, and antagonizing bourgeois and right-wing opponents. Brecht emphasized this point in the 'Lob des Revolutionärs': 'Viele sind zu viel / Wenn sie fort sind, ist es besser.'[139]

---

[136] Friedrich Wolfgang Knellessen, *Agitation auf der Bühne: Das politische Theater der Weimarer Republik* (Emsdetten: Lechte, 1970), 201; 'Lob des Lernens', *Illustrierte Rote Post*, 3/1932; 'Wie die Krähe', *Welt am Abend* (Berlin), 29 Jan. 1932.

[137] Albrecht Dümling, *Laßt euch nicht verführen: Brecht und die Musik* (Munich: Kindler, 1985), 535.

[138] 'Work, work, work harder, scrimp, save more effectively, count, count, count more precisely!' Ibid. 550.

[139] 'Many people get in the way. / It's better when they're gone.' *BFA*, iii. 291.

Although this text was probably first included in the 1933 edition, Weigel recalls that some spectators did indeed walk out, slamming the door behind them.[140] In the *Neue Preußische Kreuzzeitung* Junghans called the production 'Grob, aufreizend, propagandistisch gemacht. Ein Pfingstfest für die Gesinnungsgenossen, wirksamer als Reden und Zeitungen. Ein Irrsinn für den Außenstehenden. Eine Frechheit für den Gegner.'[141] Several other right-wing newspapers, including *Der Montag* and the Nazi *Völkischer Beobachter*, criticized the authorities for allowing the production to proceed, and the Catholic Centre Party's *Germania* even campaigned for a ban.

Germania's case centred on the play's opposition to the state and support for Communism. On 19 January H. Bachmann declared: 'Das Stück opponiert hundertprozentig gegen das bei uns herrschende Staatssystem und plädiert für Moskau. *Also—muß es verboten werden.*'[142] Ten days later, another article complained of the authorities' intolerable inaction. *Germania* claimed to have received a series of letters from outraged spectators and quoted one letter which argued that the play incited workers to take up arms against the state: 'Als einziger Ausweg für den Arbeiter aus seiner heutigen bedrängten Lage wird ihm gründlichst eingehämmert: Nimm die Waffe in die Hand und beseitige mit Gewalt die heutige Ordnung!'[143] Such criticism was exaggerated, for the 1932 production did not explicitly endorse violence: none of the revolutionaries were armed in the final demonstration.[144] Nevertheless, *Germania*'s next objection was more pertinent, because the writer of the aforementioned letter argued that Russian history was simply a veil for Brecht's real target, the German state: 'Gewiß breitet man zart einen Schleier historischer Erinnerungen über das Stück, aber ohne jeden Zweifel wird klar und deutlich gegen die heutige Staatsform gehetzt, die

---

[140] Hecht, *Helene Weigel*, 63.

[141] 'Crude, provocative propaganda. An absolute joy for those who share its views, more effective than speeches and newspapers. Lunacy for outsiders. A piece of cheek for opponents.' Junghans, *Neue Preußische Kreuzzeitung*, 18 Jan. 1932.

[142] 'The play is one hundred per cent opposed to our system of government and makes the case for Moscow. *Therefore—it must be banned!*' Bachmann, *Germania*, 19 Jan. 1932.

[143] 'As the only way for workers to escape their current hard-pressed situation, the message is hammered into them as hard as possible: take your weapons in your hand and remove the current authorities with force!' Anon., 'Unhaltbare Passivität', *Germania*, 29 Jan. 1932.

[144] Ludwig Hoffmann and Klaus Pfützner (eds), *Theater der Kollektive: Proletarisch-revolutionäres Berufstheater in Deutschland 1928–1933: Stücke, Dokumente, Studien*, 2 vols (East Berlin: Henschel, 1980), i, no. 49.

heutige Polizei beschimpft, die heutige Justiz verächtlich gemacht.'[145] If this allegation had been upheld, the police could have banned the production under the 1931 decrees or charged the participants under § 110 of the penal code. This paragraph made anyone who incited the public to disobey laws or decrees liable for a fine or a two-year prison sentence and, according to case history, included attempts to undermine the authority of the law.[146] On 6 February, *Germania* asked its readers indignantly how long the police intended to expose the state to these activities.[147]

Although an investigation was launched into *Germania*'s allegations, the police saw no grounds for prosecution and reported on 29 February: 'Zu Störungen der öffentlichen Sicherheit und Ordnung ist es bei diesen Aufführungen, die von hier aus laufend überwacht worden sind, nicht gekommen.'[148] In this report, the police acknowledged that *Die Mutter* was a Communist play but argued that it depicted naïve and improbable activities and therefore posed no serious threat. For example, they claimed that the lesson in reading and writing occupied a large proportion of the play, was relevant only to circumstances in Russia, and had no topical value. Besides exaggerating the scene's length, this assessment overlooked its real function: to demonstrate the political link between knowledge and power, and to incite workers to appropriate both. But the naïve interpretation instead led the police to conclude: 'Eine unmittelbare Beschimpfung oder Hetze gegen die *deutsche* Justiz, Polizei und Staatsform wird vermieden. Die Vertreter der Polizei werden als russisch-zaristische Typen dargestellt.'[149] Whilst the play does avoid openly criticizing the German system, tacitly encouraging spectators to identify the German police with their Tsarist counterparts was a popular Communist propaganda device.[150] Nevertheless, a second report endorsed the preliminary findings.[151] Both reports indicate that

---

[145] 'It is true that the play is lightly veiled in historical memories, but there can be no doubt that it agitates quite clearly against the current state, abuses the current police force, disparages the current judicial system.' Anon., *Germania*, 29 Jan. 1932.

[146] Reinhard Frank (ed.), *Das Strafgesetzbuch für das Deutsche Reich*, 18th edn (Tübingen: J. C. B. Mohr, 1931), 280–5 (280, 282).

[147] Anon., 'Eine Anfrage. Nochmals: *Die Mutter*', *Germania*, 6 Feb. 1932.

[148] 'These performances, which have been under our constant surveillance, have not led to any breaches of public law and order.' Landesarchiv Berlin, 1046.

[149] 'Direct abuse of, or agitation against, the *German* judiciary, police, and state is avoided. The representatives of the police are portrayed as Russian Tsarists.' Ibid.

[150] e.g. anon., 'In eigener Sache!', *RF*, 24 May 1929.

[151] Landesarchiv Berlin, 1046.

Brecht's tactical use of Russian history was surprisingly successful in fooling his literal-minded censors.

Although the police decided not to prosecute Brecht, an attempt to transfer the production to the working-class district of Moabit on 29 February still encountered official resistance. After a licence had been granted for the performance in the community hall on Wiclefstraße, the Theatre Department of the Building Police intervened on 28 February, arguing that there was no need for the performance and that it constituted an unacceptable fire risk.[152] Since performances were regularly held in the hall and the question of a performance's necessity mattered only in applications for a compulsory licence, both objections were clearly pretexts. Indeed, Jhering alleged that the issue of necessity was raised only 'wenn es um Experimente geht, um Versuche, dem Theater ein neues Publikum zu erobern'.[153] But even though the actors decided to perform the text without the set and costumes, officials intervened during the performance, ordering the actors not to use the curtain and eventually permitting them only to sit in a row and read out their lines.[154] Nevertheless, Weigel remembers the performance as 'eine unserer erfolgreichsten Aufführungen, weil die Leute herrlich fanden, daß wir uns nicht kleinkriegen ließen und weitermachten unter immer schwierigeren Bedingungen'.[155] Or, in other words, the progressive elimination of many of the ancillary aspects of the production actually intensified its effect because the authorities' interventions confirmed Brecht's political arguments—as *Die Rote Fahne* concluded.

The difficulties encountered in Moabit almost certainly explain why the production did not tour working-class districts extensively.[156] According to Jhering, the police banned one further performance, this time in Spandau, after three-quarters of the tickets had been sold.[157]

[152] Anon., 'Die feuergefährliche *Mutter*', *RF*, 1 Mar. 1932.
[153] 'When experiments are at stake, attempts to conquer a new audience for the theatre.' Herbert Jhering, 'Die Bedürfnisfrage', *Berliner Börsen-Courier*, 5 Mar. 1932.
[154] Anon., *RF*, 1 Mar. 1932.
[155] 'One of our most successful performances because people thought it was wonderful that we refused to be beaten and continued under increasingly difficult conditions.' Hecht, *Helene Weigel*, 62–3.
[156] Weigel told Hecht that no further performances took place in working-class districts, but the actor Alfred Dreifuß remembers a performance in a factory in Priesteritz. Ibid. 62; Alfred Dreifuß, *Ensemblespiel des Lebens: Erinnerungen eines Theatermannes* (East Berlin: Der Morgen, 1985), 118.
[157] Jhering, *Berliner Börsen-Courier*, 5 Mar. 1932; this performance had been advertised in *Die Rote Fahne* on 4 Mar. 1932. See also ' "Junge Volksbühne" im Wedding', *RF*, 20 Mar. 1932.

Several months later, when Weigel performed songs from the play at a political meeting, she was arrested and released only after proving that she belonged to the respectable bourgeois Staatstheater.[158] These isolated instances of censorship suggest that *Die Mutter* was perceived as a political threat only when it left the theatre for less institutionalized venues where the proletarian spectators were less likely to react with the decorum expected of a theatre audience that also included Communist intellectuals and bourgeois theatre-goers.

7.2 Brecht's Evaluation

The polarized reception of *Die Mutter* stimulated Brecht's theoretical reflections on *Gebrauchskunst*, the social function of education, and the interpretive role of spectators. In his 'Anmerkungen' Brecht defended the production's direct political arguments and austere aesthetic, arguing that the simple dialogue and staging gave the arguments 'die Primitivität von Handwerkzeugen' ('the primitiveness of tools') so that they could easily be used for a political purpose.[159] Brecht then attributed criticism of Neher's aesthetic to bourgeois prejudices.[160] Many bourgeois critics had indeed voiced such criticism: for instance, in the *Heidelberger Tageblatt* an anonymous reviewer had protested that *Die Mutter* was designed for simpletons, 'als säßen nur geistig Obdachlose im Theater', a view shared by Franz Köppen in the *Berliner Börsen-Zeitung*.[161] But Brecht omitted to mention that, as we saw in section 5, some Communist reviewers had actually sided with the bourgeois critics. This omission points to his failure or unwillingness to confront the aesthetic differences within the German Left—differences which would become even more serious in 1934, when the Union of Soviet Writers adopted Socialist Realism as its orthodox aesthetic.

In the 'Anmerkungen', Brecht also interpreted critics' prejudice against didacticism as evidence of a false opposition between learning and entertainment in bourgeois society, where education is treated as a commodity that the individual must purchase in order to enter the production process. Consequently, in Brecht's view, learning becomes so associated with immaturity that people are discouraged from learning

---

[158] Knellessen, 201.   [159] BBA 445/04.   [160] *BFA*, xxiv. 125.
[161] 'As if only intellectually homeless people were sitting in the theatre.' Anon., 'Berliner Theaterbrief', *Heidelberger Tageblatt*, 26 Jan. 1932; Franz Köppen, 'Die Mutter', *Berliner Börsen-Zeitung*, 18 Jan. 1932.

in later life.[162] He subsequently incorporated these ideas into his essay 'Vergnügungstheater oder Lehrtheater' ('Theatre for Pleasure or Theatre for Instruction', 1935), which foregrounds the same link between learning and fighting as 'Lob des Lernens': 'dennoch gibt es lustvolles Lernen, fröhliches und kämpferisches Lernen'.[163] Both in this essay and in the 'Anmerkungen', Brecht's emphasis on workers' hunger for knowledge echoes Wlassowa's words to the teacher: 'Gib es nur her, dein Wissen, wenn du es nicht brauchst.'[164]

Brecht's impatience with the reviewers' prejudice against didacticism also led him to consider the interpretive role of spectators. He saw the reviews as proof that 'jene[n], die dem schwer beherrschbaren "Stoff" keine Interessen entgegenbrachten und keinen Anlass sahen, ihn beherrschen zu wollen, war mit den Vereinfachungen nicht gedient'.[165] Consequently, he concluded, political theatre can activate only those who are predisposed to share its interests: 'es können auch solche Interessen nicht so leicht geweckt werden, denn damit müssen sie wenigstens in den Zuhörern "schlummern"'.[166] Even though Brecht *had* intended to split his audience, his private recognition of the limits of political art was tinged with frustration. Perhaps this was because he was not aiming exclusively at reaching a proletarian audience, but also at securing his literary reputation with the cultural establishment.

8. CONCLUSION

Die Mutter marked the next important stage in Brecht's political and artistic development after *Die Maßnahme* and showed his strong commitment to Communism and *Gebrauchskunst*. At the première, Brecht was already employing techniques and approaches that would characterize his work at the BE, displaying projected images and conveying the *Fabel* through the blocking. Furthermore, by documenting these techniques in his 'Anmerkungen' and then publishing these notes with

---

[162] *BFA*, xxiv. 134–5.
[163] 'None the less there is fun-filled learning, cheerful and combative learning.' *BFA*, xxii.1. 106–16 (112); iii. 290.
[164] 'Hand it over, your knowledge, if you don't need it.' *BFA*, iii. 290.
[165] 'Those who brought no interests to the challenging "material" and saw no reason to master its challenge, did not benefit from the simplifications.' BBA 445/52.
[166] 'Such interests cannot be awoken very easily since, for this to happen, they at least need to be "slumbering" in the listeners.' BBA 445/21.

a photograph of the set and three of Neher's designs in the 1933 edition, he was already trying to influence future productions of *Die Mutter*.[167] But Brecht was not always his own best critic, for the 'Anmerkungen'—like the programme—obscured the way in which his text and Eisler's music combined traditional techniques with his more radical claims for the 'epic' form. Indeed, *Die Mutter* relies on a more complex interplay between the 'epic' and the 'dramatic' than even the comparatively moderate term 'Gewichtsverschiebungen' implies.

Both Brecht's text and the 'Anmerkungen' also reveal significant limitations in his political grasp of the situation in 1931–2. Although Brecht was eager to comply with the KPD's political line, he failed to foresee that some aspects of *Die Mutter* would inevitably offend Communist reviewers. Understandably, the KPD regarded him and his co-workers with suspicion, and this uneasy relationship would continue during the GDR period, when the young Party functionaries of 1932 wielded political power. More immediate consequences, however, resulted from Brecht's flawed assessment of the production's appeal to working-class spectators. By assuming that the play's directness and simplicity appealed to such spectators because of their class, he ignored the fact that agitprop theatre had prepared them for his techniques. Ironically, then, the positive German working-class response gave Brecht a false sense of security when he tried to replicate Neher's aesthetic at the New York Theatre Union in 1935. After the disastrous failure of this production, Brecht adopted a new aesthetic approach in his 1951 production at the BE, to which I shall now turn.

[167] Brecht, *Die Mutter; Geschichten*, facing 64–5.

2

Model or Museum Exhibit? *Die Mutter* at the Berliner Ensemble, 1951–71

1. INTRODUCTION

1.1 The 1951 Model Production

The 1951 production of *Die Mutter* reveals Brecht's willingness to re-invent his work in the early GDR, even at the cost of sacrificing some of his principles. He made significant textual and aesthetic changes in order to transform his agitational play into a deceptively innocuous piece of family history. In the short term, these strategic concessions, both to official cultural policy and to the audience, helped Brecht to propagate his anti-war argument successfully. In the longer term, however, they had major consequences for the East German reception of *Die Mutter*. This was because Brecht encouraged subsequent directors to study and copy the 1951 production, even though he had tailored it to a unique and delicate situation.

In 1951, Brecht was strongly committed to the overall political goals of the Socialist project but was under pressure to conform to the cultural policy of the SED (Socialist Unity Party). During his years in exile, the conservatives had gained the ascendancy in the long-running debate on left-wing aesthetics, and after the War the new East German authorities had endorsed Socialist Realism as the orthodox aesthetic.[1] Art was required to adhere to nineteenth-century standards of realism and to project a positive view of society's progress towards Socialism. Since Brecht drew prominently on the anti-illusionist techniques associated with Piscator and agitprop, he was particularly vulnerable to accusations

---

[1] For cultural politics in the early GDR, cf. Manfred Jäger, *Kultur und Politik in der DDR 1945–1990* (Cologne: Nottbeck, 1995), 5–86; Stephen Parker, Matthew Philpotts, and Peter Davies, 'Introduction to Part Five', in *Brecht on Art and Politics*, ed. Steve Giles and Tom Kuhn (London: Methuen, 2003), 273–81.

of Formalism. Although this term, strictly defined, referred to works which experimented with form for its own sake, conservatives increasingly used it to describe anything that deviated from Socialist Realism. In 1949, for example, the critics Susanne Altermann and Fritz Erpenbeck discerned signs of Formalism in the BE's production of *Mutter Courage*.[2] Such accusations were highly damaging because they jeopardized the BE's state funding and Brecht's negotiations for a permanent home for the Ensemble. Until 1954, the BE was forced to share the Deutsches Theater with Wolfgang Langhoff's resident company, an arrangement that created considerable logistical difficulties: the first rehearsal for *Die Mutter* had to be postponed for eleven days because no rehearsal space was available.[3] Brecht's desire to resolve this frustrating situation gave him a strong incentive not to antagonize his opponents in the Central Committee.

Making *Die Mutter* appear aesthetically acceptable to the SED was not Brecht's only challenge in 1951. During the Third Reich, sustained propaganda had whipped up fears of Bolshevism, which the subsequent Soviet invasion and occupation of East Germany seemed to confirm. Consequently, the play's uncompromising support for Communism was unlikely to appeal to more than a minority of German spectators. Within this context, Brecht's 1932 strategy of antagonizing anti-Communists and activating the Party faithful was no longer appropriate. Instead, his new production courted the audience's sympathy for the Russian occupiers and their revolutionary history.

Although this production was designed specifically for Brecht's 1951 audience, it actually remained in the BE's repertoire until Weigel's death in 1971. This was never Brecht's intention, and it is questionable whether the production was suited to such a long run precisely because it had been tailored so successfully to the situation in 1951. So in my analysis of the 1967 revival, I identify the changes made by Brecht's successors and assess how far they addressed the needs and aspirations of new spectators. This question is crucial, for many directors have treated Brecht's productions at the BE as universally valid interpretations of his

---

[2] Susanne Altermann, 'Wo beginnt die Dekadenz? Bemerkungen zur Polemik um Brechts *Mutter Courage*', *Tägliche Rundschau* (East Berlin), 12 Mar. 1949; Fritz Erpenbeck, 'Einige Bemerkungen zu Brechts *Mutter Courage*', *Die Weltbühne*, 4 (1949), 101–3; both reprinted in Helmut Kreuzer and Karl-Wilhelm Schmidt (eds), *Dramaturgie in der DDR (1945–1990)*, 2 vols (Heidelberg: C. Winter, 1998), i. 54–8, 45–7.

[3] Peter Palitzsch, 'Von der Leseprobe zur Premiere', BBA 1969/84; 'Die Mutter 1951', file 5, sect. 2.13, BEA.

plays. In section 6, I examine how far such treatment represents an abuse of the model production, as Brecht's theoretical statements suggest, and how far it reflects an inherent contradiction in the concept.

1.2 The Critical Debate

Despite its significance and renown, the 1951 production has attracted little critical attention, partly because of the play's Communist politics and partly because Ruth Berlau's photographic record of the production was never published. Although both Günther Reus and Gudrun Klatt have published brief accounts of the production, they do not attempt any textual analysis.[4] Furthermore, their failure to consult even such basic sources as the programme leads them to overlook important aspects of the staging. Thus, whereas Reus claims that Brecht's production attempted to resume the agitational theatre of the Weimar Republic, it actually distanced the play from the proletarian-revolutionary tradition. Reus also alleges that none of the play's agitation or topical relevance was lost, whereas the production actually downplayed most agitational elements while intensifying the anti-war argument. Even though Klatt locates the production more firmly in its historical context, she—like Reus—fails to note the intensified anti-war agitation and the extent to which Brecht's new approach reflected his awareness of the widespread antipathy to Communism in the GDR.

The extent to which Brecht made tactical concessions in the GDR has attracted more scholarly interest. Matthew Philpotts has recently criticized scholars such as Theo Buck for overprivileging tactical explanations of Brecht's actions in the GDR.[5] Rightly stressing Brecht's fundamental support for the regime, Philpotts argues that his productions at the BE generated 'non-intentional dissent', primarily due to Brecht's aesthetic distance from Socialist Realism.[6] He thus agrees with James Lyon, who characterizes the GDR Brecht as 'a dissident conformist, with emphasis

---

[4] Günther Reus, 'Die historisierende Neuinszenierung von Brechts *Mutter* 1951', in *Oktoberrevolution und Sowjetrußland auf dem deutschen Theater: Zur Verwendung eines geschichtlichen Motivs im deutschen Schauspiel von 1918 bis zur Gegenwart*, 2 vols (Bonn: Bouvier, 1978), ii. 254–8; Gudrun Klatt, 'Brechts *Mutter*: Zur Geschichte eines Theatermodells', *Connaissance de la RDA*, 9 (1979), 187–200.

[5] Matthew Philpotts, *The Margins of Dictatorship: Assent and Dissent in the Work of Günter Eich and Bertolt Brecht*, British and Irish Studies in German Language and Literature, 34 (Bern: Peter Lang, 2003), 283–4.

[6] Ibid. 294.

on the "conformist" '.[7] I argue here that Brecht was wholly committed to the Socialist goals and the creation of an anti-fascist society, and that he was willing to make short-term concessions precisely because he shared the regime's long-term political objectives. These concessions were not just for the benefit of the authorities, but also for that of the audience—a crucial dimension which Lyon and Philpotts do not consider.

1.3 Source Material

In order to assess how Brecht and his set designer Caspar Neher created a new *Gesamtgestus* (overall *Gestus*)[8] for the 1951 production, I have consulted a wide range of evidence, including Berlau's photographic record, Hans Jürgen Syberberg's ten-minute silent film (1953), Manfred Wekwerth's film documentation (1958), and Neher's set designs and models.[9] I also use the BE's unpublished records, published memoirs by company members, and evidence from my own interviews with Brecht's former pupil Wera Küchenmeister (née Skupin) and assistant Manfred Wekwerth. When discussing the production's reception, I use newspaper reviews, internal SED documents, and the BE's own records of audience response.

The sheer difficulty of identifying which script was used in 1951 may explain why neither Reus nor Klatt attempted any textual analysis. In fact, the Brecht Archive contains three texts which relate to this production: 'Brechts Regiebuch' ('Brecht's director's script'), 'Soufflierbuch Fassung Berliner Ensemble' ('prompt book, Berliner Ensemble version'), and 'Bühnenmanuskript 1951' ('stage manuscript 1951').[10] 'Brechts Regiebuch' is a typescript of the 1933 edition, with handwritten amendments that incorporate both the changes made by

[7] James K. Lyon, 'Brecht in Postwar Germany: Dissident Conformist, Cultural Icon, Literary Dictator', in *Brecht Unbound*, ed. Lyon and Hans-Peter Breuer (London: Associated University Presses, 1995), 76–88 (76).

[8] The director Manfred Wekwerth explains: 'Ein ganzes Stück kann einen bestimmten Gestus haben, zum Beispiel den der Provokation. Oder des Appells. Oder der Verunsicherung. Ja, ein und dasselbe Stück kann durch den Wechsel des Gestus seinen Inhalt verändern.' ('An entire play can have a specific *Gestus*, for example that of provocation. Or of an appeal. Or of undermining certainties. Indeed, one and the same play can change its content if the *Gestus* is altered.') Wekwerth, 'Was spricht eigentlich gegen Brecht?', *Das Argument*, 226 (1998), 531–42 (539).

[9] 'Das Mutter-Modellbuch', BEA; *Syberberg filmt bei Brecht*, dir. Hans Jürgen Syberberg, 1953, ISBN 3-923854-80-3; cf. Introduction, n. 35.

[10] 'Brechts Regiebuch', BBA 195; 'Soufflierbuch Fassung Berliner Ensemble', BBA 1572; 'Bühnenmanuskript 1951', BBA 637.

Brecht for the 1938 edition and some additional changes made for the 1951 production, mostly by Brecht but also by Ruth Berlau and the assistants Käthe Rülicke and Peter Palitzsch. The cast list in the 'Regiebuch' is incomplete, and the revolutionaries' names—which were actually changed for the 1951 production—remain the same as in the 1933 and 1938 editions. So, although Fuegi assumes that the 'Regiebuch' was 'Brecht's own directing text', Brecht probably used it only in the early phase of the production's preparation.[11] Comparison of the 'Regiebuch' with the 'Soufflierbuch' reveals that the 'Soufflierbuch' was produced later, for this typescript incorporates the 1938 changes, the revolutionaries' new names, and some handwritten alterations present in the 'Regiebuch'. Nevertheless, some handwritten amendments in the 'Soufflierbuch' correspond to alterations in the 'Regiebuch', thus indicating that the texts were probably used simultaneously for some time. The 'Bühnenmanuskript' is essentially a fresh typescript of the 'Soufflierbuch' and its alterations, but it also contains subsequent, additional handwritten amendments. My analysis relies primarily on the 'Bühnenmanuskript' because it contains both the typescript that was almost certainly performed at the première and changes that were made later in the run.

2. THE PROCESS OF PRODUCTION

The BE's unpublished logbooks, rehearsal notes, and nightly reports of performances (*Abendberichte*) enable us to form a detailed picture of Brecht's theatrical practice in the GDR. This evidence reveals continuities between his staging methods in 1932 and 1951, despite the aesthetic and political differences between his two Berlin productions of *Die Mutter*. Analysis of the *Fabel* again provided the initial basis for rehearsals, and Brecht continued to encourage his co-workers to collaborate on every aspect of the staging. In 1951, however, this collaboration had a strong pedagogical dimension. Now that Brecht had his own subsidized theatre company, he was able to train young assistants in his methods. This aspect of Brecht's work was important, for after his death on 14 August 1956 his assistants continued to develop his methods in new productions at the BE.

---

[11] Fuegi, *Essential Brecht*, 227 n. 13.

In January 1950 *Die Mutter* was staged for the first time in the GDR, by Ruth Berlau at the Kammerspiele in Leipzig. Although Klatt assumes that this was a dry run for Brecht's 1951 production, her account may well be misleading. The BE's logbook reveals that *Die Mutter* was actually a last-minute replacement for *Leben des Galilei*, which Brecht had been forced to postpone when the lead actor, Leonhard Steckel, declared that he would not be available until the 1951–2 season.[12] None the less, the experiences gained from Berlau's staging proved valuable, and the BE did subsequently test out several plays on audiences outside Berlin in preparation for its own productions. Benno Besson, for example, directed *Don Juan* in Rostock in 1952 before attempting to stage it in Berlin in 1954.[13]

Despite the changed political situation, Berlau attempted to revive her audience's interest in the German revolutionary tradition by adhering closely to Brecht's 1932 model. As she had done in Copenhagen in 1935, Berlau used photographs to reconstruct the original set and blocking, and Brecht assisted her by rehearsing with the lead actress, Charlotte Küter, and attending the final rehearsals.[14] Significantly, the production was premièred on 15 January, the anniversary of Rosa Luxemburg's death, and the programme contained Brecht's poems to her and Karl Liebknecht, plus an essay by Hans Mayer entitled 'Karl und Rosa'.[15]

It soon became clear that Berlau had paid insufficient attention to the gulf between the expectations of spectators in 1932 and 1950. Thus, although reviewers praised the quality of her production, some expressed reservations about its effect on the audience and even its political content. One critic commented that the audience lost interest after the interval, while another declared that Brecht's Marxist advocacy of self-reliance filled spectators with dread.[16] Moreover, the functionary Georg Kaufmann privately informed Brecht of the SED's reservations about the play's 'avant-garde' form and 'sectarian' content.[17] According to Kaufmann's son, he asked: 'War es nicht politisch schädlich, wenn Brecht eine Position "links von der Partei" einnahm, wenn er

---

[12] 'Inszenierung *Das Leben des Galilei*', in 'Logbücher BE '50–'52', BEA.

[13] *BFA*, ix (1992), 417.

[14] Berlau's notebook, Ruth-Berlau-Archiv (henceforth RBA) N152, AdK RKP.

[15] Stadtgeschichtliches Museum Leipzig.

[16] A. M. U., 'Bertolt Brecht: *Die Mutter* nach Maxim Gorkijs Roman', *Leipziger Volkszeitung*, 17 Jan. 1950; anon., 'Marxistisches Theater in Leipzig', *Die Union* (Dresden), 21 Jan. 1950.

[17] Hans Kaufmann, 'Wie er nicht im Buche steht: Erinnerungen an Brecht', *Juni-Magazin für Literatur und Politik*, 24 (1996), 77–90 (88).

Teile der Bevölkerung verprellte, die als Ganzes für die antifaschistisch-demokratische Ordnung gewonnen werden sollte?'[18] As Kaufmann's question indicates, the SED's main concern at this early stage was not to re-activate the Party faithful, but to win over hostile sections of the population. Four months later, when Berlau supervised a production in Schwerin based on her Leipzig staging, Brecht acknowledged the difficulties of injecting humour and grace into the model: 'Das Modell wirkt noch als Zwangsjacke, in der die Werbung ums Publikum natürlich stark behindert ist.'[19] Berlau's experiences in Leipzig and Schwerin suggested that a new approach was needed to win over the audience.

Brecht's readiness to make substantial textual changes for his productions shows how he instinctively combined the roles of writer and director, an approach that quickly became central to the BE's practice. Even before rehearsals began, the provisional script for the 1951 production differed substantially from the 1933 edition. First, it contained the changes that Brecht had made for the 1935 Theatre Union production and the 1938 edition. Thus, the scene 'Die Partei ist in Gefahr' ('The Party is in Danger') was now performed before, not after, the scene at the street corner, so that Wlassowa's illness appeared to result from her grief over Pawel's death, not from political resignation following the failure of her anti-war agitation. Second, Brecht, Berlau, Palitzsch, and Rülicke made additional changes for the BE production: for instance, by redistributing sections of the dialogue they created a new character, Semjon Lapkin, as the revolutionaries' leader. This provided a prominent role for Ernst Busch who, now aged 51, could no longer play Pawel as he had done in 1932. Brecht and his co-workers also renamed several other characters, probably to distinguish the new script from the published editions. Thus, Anton, Karpow, and Sostakowitsch became Archip, Smychow, and Sigorski, respectively. Andrej Maximowitsch Nachodka was renamed Stepan Iwanowitsch Pregonski, and the teacher, Nikolai Iwanowitsch Wessowtschikow, became Fjodor Trofimowitsch Lapkin. According to Elisabeth Hauptmann, Brecht mischievously refused to explain these changes in subsequent editions: '[er] verwies lachend darauf, daß die Germanisten und Philologen doch

---

[18] 'Wasn't it politically damaging if Brecht positioned himself "to the left of the Party", if he alienated sections of the population which needed to be won over as a whole for the anti-fascist, democratic order?' Ibid. 89.

[19] 'The model still acts as a straightjacket, which of course makes it much harder to court the audience.' *BFA*, xxvii (1995), 310.

auch später mal etwas zu tun haben müßten. Natürlich drückte er sich nicht so fein aus.'[20]

Like Brecht's script, Eisler's score contained changes made for the Theatre Union production and some new additions. Thus, it included 'Das Lied vom Flicken und vom Rock' ('The Song of the Patch and the Coat'), which Brecht and Eisler had inserted into Scene 3 in 1935.[21] This song took the workers' arguments against reformism to their logical conclusion: the demand for revolution. The BE's resources allowed Eisler to re-orchestrate the score for a slightly larger ensemble: flute, clarinet, trumpet, horn, trombone, percussion, banjo, and double bass. Finally, he wrote a new musical accompaniment for the first demonstration scene, which comprised a montage of quotations from the play's other songs and Communist classics such as the 'Internationale'.[22]

Although German theatres commonly employed a dramaturge to find and adapt plays for performance, the BE's pre-rehearsal work on the script departed qualitatively and quantitatively from the norm. As in 1932, Brecht and his assistants focused on the *Fabel*, identifying the key points in each scene and relating them to the overall arc of the play's development, a method which reflected three of Brecht's priorities.[23] First, he strove to present his characters as changeable and changing by showing how they developed in response to their experiences. In 1952, he explained: 'Wir bauen nicht Figuren auf, die dann in eine Fabel hineingeworfen werden, sondern wir bauen die Fabel auf.'[24] Second, analysis of the *Fabel* provided the basis for blocking and helped Brecht to devise clear, focused stagings as an antidote to the prevailing superficiality and false pathos of post-Nazi theatre.[25] Third, Brecht's focus on the

---

[20] 'He pointed out, laughing, that the Germanists and philologists would also need something to do later. Of course, he didn't put it so politely.' Letter from Elisabeth Hauptmann to Käthe [Rülicke], 6 Aug. 1958, EHA 693. Brecht probably borrowed 'Semjon Lapkin' from Iwan Iwanowitsch Lapkin and Anna Semjonowna Samblizkaja, the hero and heroine of Chekhov's *Der böse Junge* (*A Naughty Boy*); 'Fjodor Trofimowitsch' from Stepan Trofimowitsch, the teacher in Dostoevsky's *Böse Geister* (*The Devils*), and Dostoevsky's first name, Fjodor. 'Smychow' is the name of a suburb of Prague; 'Sigorski' may have been inspired by the Russian-born aeronautical engineer and inventor of the helicopter, Igor Sikorsky, and/or Poland's wartime leader in exile, General Wladyslaw Sikorski.

[21] BBA 637/18.   [22] HEA 1660.

[23] Wera Küchenmeister, personal interview, 6 Dec. 2000. Unless otherwise indicated, subsequent statements attributed to Küchenmeister are also taken from this interview.

[24] 'We do not build up characters which then get thrown into a *Fabel*, but we build up the *Fabel*.' 'Über unsere Inszenierungen', *BFA*, xxiii. 192.

[25] 'Einige Bemerkungen über mein Fach', ibid. 150–2.

Fabel re-asserted the importance of story-telling in his productions. He explained, probably in 1951, that when a director stages a play, 'er bringt eine Geschichte vor das Publikum'.[26] By emphasizing this aspect of epic theatre, Brecht challenged the common prejudice that it constituted an abstract, theoretical stage form. Indeed, his writings between 1951 and 1956 both emphasize his plays' power to provoke 'naïve' reactions, like joy, curiosity, and anger, and document his growing dissatisfaction with the controversial term 'epic theatre'.[27]

After two weeks of textual preparations, rehearsals with the cast began on 28 October 1950.[28] Although generous state funding allowed Brecht the luxury of long rehearsal periods, rehearsals for *Die Mutter* took two and a half months, a relatively short period compared to the eleven months devoted to *Der kaukasische Kreidekreis*. This was probably because Brecht, Berlau, and Neher already had considerable experience of producing the play, while three of the actors, Weigel, Busch, and Bienert, had acted in the 1932 première, and Ernst Kahler had played Pawel in 1950. After the actors had read the play together, the production was blocked in three rehearsals. Detailed work on the scenes and music followed in the sixty-five play rehearsals, fifty-two music rehearsals, and sixteen orchestra rehearsals before the production was rehearsed in full in the final run-throughs and dress rehearsals. As in 1932, Brecht tested the production's effect on spectators in closed performances before the première, which took place on 12 January 1951.[29]

Professional training and political education played a far greater role in the preparations for this production than they had for the 1932 première. Brecht expected his assistants to learn on the job, and Wera Küchenmeister remembers that Gert Beinemann, Peter Palitzsch, and Wolfgang Struck attended most rehearsals and were required to make detailed notes. Besides rehearsals, the actors attended classes in gymnastics, music theory, and elocution three times each week, and Weigel arranged showings of classic Soviet silent films, including Vsevolod Pudovkin's *The Mother* (1926), which directly influenced Brecht's presentation of the prison scene.[30] The ideological education inherent in the play was also supplemented by weekly discussions of

---

[26] 'He puts a story before the audience.' '[Fragen über die Arbeit des Spielleiters]', ibid. 177–8 (177).

[27] e.g. ibid. 299, 300–2, 386.   [28] 'Logbücher BE '50–'52', BEA.

[29] BBA 1969/84.

[30] 'Logbücher '50–'52', BEA; Hans Lauter (ed.), *Der Kampf gegen den Formalismus in Kunst und Literatur, für eine fortschrittliche deutsche Kultur* (East Berlin: Dietz, 1951),

Marxism, and from 7 October these took the form of two-hour lectures on the Russian Revolution by Jacob Walcher, a former founding member of both the KPD and the KPD-Opposition.[31] Walcher's co-operation with the BE can only have confirmed the SED's suspicions regarding Brecht's ideological 'reliability', since Walcher was denounced as a member of criminal factions in January 1951 and was not rehabilitated until 1956, during the political thaw that followed Stalin's death.[32]

As in 1932, Brecht's approach to the production was instinctively collaborative. During each phase he welcomed constructive comments from his co-workers, irrespective of their area of responsibility. For example, on 25 January 1951 Brecht thanked his costume designer, Kurt Palm, for his many and varied contributions: 'Ich muß Ihnen auch wieder sagen, daß Ihr behutsames und produktives Eingreifen in eigentlich alle Aspekte einer solch komplizierten Aufführung mir große Freude bereitet hat.'[33] Caspar Neher's set designs and models helped to shape the entire production concept, and while John Heartfield and Wieland Herzfelde worked on the photo-projections, Slatan Dudow helped to produce the closing film.[34] Thus, Brecht's team consisted of trusted colleagues with whom he had worked in the Weimar Republic and young practitioners who were new to professional theatre—a combination that reflected his deep mistrust of those theatre practitioners who had collaborated with the Nazi regime.

3. BRECHT'S NEW APPROACH: COURTING THE AUDIENCE

3.1 Revolution as Family History

Since Brecht's aim in 1951 was to conciliate, he combated his spectators' anti-Communist prejudices by courting their sympathy for the harmless story of Wlassowa and her son. Wekwerth explained to me:

67; Maxim Gorky, *Mother*, dir. Vsevolod Pudovkin, 1926, re-released by Tartan Video, 1997, TVT 1275.

[31] 'Logbücher '50–'52', BEA.
[32] Dieter Hoffmann, Helmut Müller-Enbergs, and Jan Wielgohs (eds), *Wer war wer in der DDR? Ein biographisches Lexikon*, 2nd rev. edn (Berlin: Ch. Links, 2001), 885.
[33] 'I must tell you again that I am very pleased with your tactful and productive interventions in really every aspect of such a complicated production.' Petra Stuber, 'Helene Weigel und ihre Rolle als Intendantin zwischen 1949 und 1954', *Brecht Yearbook*, 25 (2000), 252–75 (269).
[34] 'Logbücher '50–'52', BEA.

Nachdem die Revolution von den Nazis in der barbarischsten Weise [geschildert worden war], mit dem Messer im Mund, Kinder mordend, Frauen vergewaltigend, da wollte er dieses Bild einfach beseitigen und sprach davon, daß er das Liebenswerte hervorkehren wollte.... Eine Revolution als etwas Liebenswertes dargestellt, sei gefährlicher für die Konterrevolution als die geballte Faust.[35]

Brecht exploited the potential for identification with Wlassowa that already existed in the text, in the hope that the spectators would then follow her political adventure with interest. Thus, he instructed Weigel to emphasize Wlassowa's initial scepticism towards Communism so that spectators could see that she represented their concerns. At the rehearsal of Scene 3 on 23 November Wera Küchenmeister noted: 'Verkümmert und unlustig kommt sie.... Denn sie tut es gegen ihr Gewissen, die Sache gefällt ihr ja auch nicht...'[36] According to the novelist Anna Seghers, this approach was highly effective: 'Als Wlassowa steht [Helene Weigel] zuerst unwissend und verzagt da, und viele Frauen hören ihr zu und begreifen ganz gut, wovor sie Angst hat. Es wäre ihnen genau so zuwider, wenn Fremde sich bei ihnen breitmachen würden. Zuerst versagen sie mit der Wlassowa, verlieren dann mit ihr Bedenken und Sorgen.'[37]

In 1951, Brecht also encouraged spectators to identify with Pawel and Semjon Lapkin. To enable the SED's new, young converts to identify with Pawel, Brecht presented him in the early scenes as a novice who is uncertain how to behave. Instead of explaining revolutionary theory to Wlassowa—as in 1932—Pawel listened with her to Semjon's explanations and interjected 'so ist es' ('that's how it is') to show his eagerness and assent.[38] Ernst Kahler, who played Pawel in 1951,

---

[35] 'After the Revolution [had been described] by the Nazis in the most barbaric terms—revolutionaries with knives in their mouths, murdering children, raping women—he simply wanted to remove this image and spoke of wanting to bring out its endearing side.... A revolution depicted as endearing was, Brecht said, more dangerous for the counter-revolution than a clenched fist.' Wekwerth, personal interview, 13 Dec. 2000. Unless otherwise indicated, subsequent statements attributed to Wekwerth are also taken from this interview.

[36] 'She approaches, lethargically and reluctantly.... For she is acting against her conscience; she doesn't approve of this business either...' Ditte Buchmann (ed.), *'Eine Begabung muß man entmutigen ...': Wera und Claus Küchenmeister erinnern sich an Brecht* (East Berlin: Henschel, 1986), 92–3.

[37] 'As Wlassowa [Helene Weigel] stands there, ignorant and despondent at first, and many women listen to her and quite understand her fears. They would find it equally abhorrent if strangers were to take over their home. At first they fail with Wlassowa, then they lose their doubts and worries as she loses hers.' Anna Seghers, 'Die Sprache der Weigel', BBA 683/36–8.

[38] BBA 637/24. The fact that Brecht re-assigned many of Pawel's lines to Semjon explains why the 1960 tour gave Roland Barthes the impression that Pawel awakens his

explains how his gestures supported this presentation: 'Ein Kopfnicken als Bestätigung der eben gehörten Meinung, ein fragender Blick zu Lapkin bei einer schwierigen Stelle, ein Senken des Kopfes, gefolgt von einem überraschten Aufblicken, als hätte sich ein bisher dunkler Zusammenhang aufgehellt.'[39] By presenting Semjon as an older, trusted authority on political matters, Brecht showed that Pawel had gained a father-figure through the movement. Young people in the GDR were desperately short of male role models, since even those fathers who had survived the War were often implicated in the crimes of National Socialism. Ernst Busch, who played Semjon, was an ideal Socialist role model, since he had participated in the sailors' mutiny at Kiel in 1918, fought in the Spanish Civil War, and been imprisoned under Hitler.

In order to win the audience's sympathy for the revolutionaries, Brecht's changes portrayed them as disciplined, kind, and considerate. For example, after the police inspector had destroyed Wlassowa's few possessions during the house search, the revolutionaries replaced the broken mirror and lard-pot and provided a new cover for the torn sofa, a *Gestus* of solidarity.[40] Where, in the 1933 and 1938 editions, the May demonstration had included some 'Verzweifelte ...', die durch die Arbeitslosigkeit zum Äußersten getrieben waren', in 1951 Brecht cut this line so that only 'ordentliche Leute' ('decent people') participated.[41] This change was particularly significant because it portrayed the Communists as respectable and showed that the police had no justification for firing on them. Brecht's new version also emphasized that the revolutionaries needed to learn from the arguments of the initially sceptical Wlassowa and, by extension, of the audience. So instead of presenting the discussion of Marxist economics in Scene 4 as a lesson for the audience, Brecht ensured that Wlassowa's questions kept tripping up the revolutionaries.[42] This emphasis on Wlassowa's scepticism increased the significance of her subsequent conversion by showing that the revolutionaries had won an important victory.

mother to social consciousness through praxis rather than speech: 'Pavel est essentielle-ment *silencieux*' ('Pawel is essentially *silent*'). Roland Barthes, 'Sur *La Mère* de Brecht', in *Essais Critiques*, rev. edn (Paris: Editions du Seuil, 1981), 143–6 (145).

[39] 'A nod of the head to confirm the opinion he has just heard, a questioning glance to Lapkin at a difficult point; a bow of the head, followed by a surprised look up, as if light had been shed on a previously obscure link.' *Theaterarbeit*, 150.

[40] BBA 637/22.

[41] 'Desperate people driven to extremes by unemployment.' *BFA*, iii. 282 and 348; BBA 637/28.

[42] Wekwerth, 13 Dec. 2000.

Further textual changes toned down potentially controversial elements that might have alienated spectators. For example, the major part of Wlassowa's anti-religion speech was cut, even though Brecht had called the speech the ideological core of the entire scene when the Theatre Union had cut it in 1935.[43] In 1951, he may well have made the cut in response to the SED's criticism of the 1950 production. Berlau's unpublished notes show that after the Leipzig première, she changed the pithy line 'besser die Bibel zerrissen als das Essen verschüttet' to the considerably more convoluted 'schade um das schöne Buch! Aber wenigstens ist das Essen nicht verschüttet worden. Ich habe nichts dagegen, daß ihr glaubt, was ihr glaubt, wenn ihr nur wißt, was ihr wissen mußt.'[44] In 1951, Brecht simply cut the line, together with the caption 'Religion ist Opium fürs Volk' ('Religion is opium for the people') and the stage direction 'die Bibel geht in Fetzen' ('the Bible falls to pieces').[45] Even so, his changes failed to satisfy the East German CDU newspaper *Neue Zeit*, which called for the Bible scene to be cut because many people had found it repugnant.[46]

In his attempt to win the audience's interest, Brecht also exploited the play's potential for humour, particularly through gesture. The 1953 and 1958 films show that the humour was sometimes slapstick. In Scene 2, for instance, the revolutionaries lifted the sofa while Wlassowa was still sitting on it, forcing her to clamber down in a hurry, and in Scene 3 she spun round in the factory turnstile. Brecht also used humour to expose the hypocrisy of the bigoted landlady, and *Theaterarbeit* describes how pantomime subverted the strikebreakers' patriotic rhetoric in Scene 8b: 'Sie aßen aus einer Schüssel mit großen Löffeln, und wenn sie sich gegen die versteckten Angriffe des Gutsmetzgers verteidigten, ging gleichzeitig ein stiller, aber heftiger Kampf um die Schüssel zwischen ihnen vor sich. Sprach der eine, so zog der andere die Schüssel an sich, und der Sprecher mußte sie sich zurückerobern.'[47] These humorous elements countered the widespread prejudice that didactic theatre was incompatible with

---

[43] *BFA*, xxiv. 140.

[44] 'Better a torn Bible than spilled food'; 'shame about the fine book! But at least the food has not been spilled. I have nothing against you believing what you believe, so long as you know what you need to know'. BBA 1911/04.

[45] BBA 637/60–7.

[46] Ypsi, 'Bertolt Brecht: *Die Mutter*', *Neue Zeit* (East Berlin), 14 Jan. 1951.

[47] 'They ate from a bowl with large spoons, and when they defended themselves against the estate butcher's covert attacks, they simultaneously fought silently, but vehemently, over the bowl. If one spoke, then the other would pull the bowl to himself, and the speaker would have to win it back.' *Theaterarbeit*, 146.

entertainment, a view which had been implicit in several reviews of the 1932 première and 1935 American production.[48]

3.2 The Historical Frame

In 1951, Brecht used Wlassowa's biography to offer a personal perspective on Russian history. Whilst the Leipzig programme had attempted to revive the memory of the Spartacists, the Berlin programme focused on the history of the Russian Revolution. It contained 'Der große Oktober' ('The Great October'), Brecht's enthusiastic hymnic poem in praise of the Russian Revolution, plus a chronology of the events leading up to the overthrow of the Tsarist regime. Changes in the script also located the action firmly in its historical context. For example, in Scene 4 Brecht added the question: 'Und wie war es vor drei Monaten in Petersburg am "Blutigen Sonntag", wo die Polizei des Zaren tausend Arbeiter abschlachtete, weil sie ihm eine Bittschrift überreichen wollten?'[49] Following this comment, the murder of Smychow—formerly Smilgin—in the following scene became an example of the universal police oppression that was sanctioned by the regime. Moreover, Brecht included a reference to uprisings in Moscow in Scene 9, where one of the workers revealed that 'der Moskauer Sowjet der Arbeiterdeputierten hat vorgestern zum Generalstreik aufgerufen'.[50] By presenting Wlassowa's revolutionary activities as just one small part of the broader historical development, these additions prepared the audience for the final, triumphant demonstration.

Brecht's emphasis on the historical context of the stage action must not be confused with his own use of the term *Historisierung* (historicization). In a postscript to the *Messingkauf* Brecht explained that *Historisierung* destroys the illusion that familiar phenomena are eternal: 'was ist, war nicht immer und wird nicht immer sein'.[51] Thus interpreted as a form of *Verfremdung*, *Historisierung* actually describes Brecht's approach to

---

[48] e.g. Dr. Richard Biedrzynski, 'Marxistische Theaterschule', *Deutsche Zeitung* (Berlin), 18 Jan. 1932; Howard Barnes, 'The Theaters', *Herald Tribune* (New York), 20 Nov. 1935.

[49] 'And what happened three months ago in Petersburg on "Bloody Sunday", when the Tsar's police slaughtered a thousand workers because they wanted to hand him a petition?' BBA 637/26.

[50] 'The Moscow Soviet of workers' representatives proclaimed a general strike the day before yesterday.' BBA 637/57.

[51] 'What is, was not always so, and will not remain so forever.' 'A9 Nachtrag zur Theorie des *Messingkaufs*', *BFA*, xxii.2. 701–2 (701).

staging the play in 1932, before he began to use the term in his theoretical writings, not in 1951. So where Brecht's 1932 production used the analogy with Tsarist Russia to argue that the Weimar Republic could also be overthrown by revolution, the historical frame of the 1951 production simply familiarized the spectators with Russian history and invited them to accept this as the revolutionary heritage of their own new state. After all, as far as the SED was concerned, the German 'Revolution' had been successfully completed when the GDR was founded in 1949.

3.3 'The Lovely Mother'

Brecht's desire to win his audience's sympathy for Wlassowa led him to abandon some of his previous views on how *Die Mutter* should be staged, so that Wekwerth summed up his impression of the 1951 production as 'the lovely Mother'. Although Neher retained the basic structure of the 1932 set for the homes of Wlassowa and the teacher, he used different materials to create a predominantly realistic environment. In Wlassowa's room, for example, the white sheets of 1932 were replaced by wooden panelling, whilst the teacher's home was decorated with wallpaper and ornate lamps, and at the copper collection point the white sheets were replaced by a solid wooden fence and building, decked with patriotic flags and an elaborate sign.[52]

This new emphasis on milieu was reinforced by the Russian costumes, which represented another major U-turn from Brecht's earlier pronouncements on how *Die Mutter* should be staged. When the Theatre Union had used Russian costumes for its production, Brecht had called this 'a politically dubious measure, since it produces a picture-book impression and makes the activity of the revolutionary workers seem exotic and localised'.[53] But in 1951 a 'picture-book impression'—an equally apt description of Hainer Hill's painted projections—promised to arouse the audience's interest in the 'innocuous' events on stage. Significantly, although Brecht printed his poem 'Brief an das Arbeitertheater "Theatre Union"' ('Letter to the Workers' "Theatre Union"') in the programme, he omitted the stanza that criticized the American staging—a sign that the realistic aspects of the BE's aesthetic had more in common with the Theatre Union's original design than with the 1932 première.[54]

---

[52] *Theaterarbeit*, 122–9, 137–8, 147.   [53] BBA 341/14–18.
[54] For a detailed discussion of this dramaturgical poem, see White, 144–58.

Even so, these substantial aesthetic changes were by no means a capitulation to Naturalism, for Brecht aimed to achieve 'ein Realismus, der das sozial Wichtige herausarbeitet'.[55] This approach can be characterized as Gestic Realism: whilst a Naturalist presentation uses a multitude of objects, often selected apparently at random, to create an impression of authenticity, Gestic Realism requires that all the elements on stage contribute to the company's interpretation of the play. According to the critic Hugo Fetting, the production satisfied this requirement: 'Alle Stücke zeigten Spuren des Gebrauchs, dienten der Charakterisierung der Menschen, die mit ihnen lebten und umgingen.'[56] For example, Wlassowa's iron stove was balanced precariously on a pile of tiles, thus indicating that she was losing her battle to keep her home in order, as the song 'Wie die Krähe' argues.[57] Brecht's successors strove to adhere to the principles of Gestic Realism throughout the staging's long run.[58]

The production's aesthetic distance from Socialist Realism, as well as Naturalism, was immediately apparent from Neher's use and division of the stage space. As his set designs, models, and the two films show, the new realistic interior occupied only one section of the stage, as if reality were being depicted in quotation marks.[59] The chorus stood outside this realistic area when singing 'Wie die Krähe', the 'Grabrede', and 'Steh auf', so that it was clear that the songs commented independently on the action. In the background, Hill's painted projections portrayed the broader social context of Wlassowa's family history.[60] During Scenes 1, 2, and 4, for instance, the factory towered threateningly over Wlassowa's room, and the Tsarist eagle on the factory gate highlighted the alliance

[55] 'A realism that brings out what is socially significant.' Letter from Brecht to Kurt Palm, 25 Jan. 1951, in Stuber, 'Helene Weigel', 269.

[56] 'All the props showed signs of use, helped to characterize the humans who lived with them and used them.' Hugo Fetting, 'Caspar Neher: *Die Mutter*, Berliner Ensemble, 1951', *Theater der Zeit*, Nov. 1979, 1.

[57] Rülicke-Weiler, 212; BBA 637/03.

[58] e.g. letter from Wekwerth to Meier, 13 Feb. 1958: 'vielleicht können wir für die nächste *Mutter*-Vorstellung das alte Muttersofa alt und speckig machen, da es jetzt neu aussieht' ('perhaps we could make the Mother's old sofa old and greasy for the next performance of *The Mother*, as it looks new now'); Wolf Biermann, 'Abendbericht MUTTER', 17 June 1959: 'Herr Hardtloff trägt in der Szene "Landagitation" hellgewaschene Edel-Fußlappen—die versilberte Säge, mit der nie gesägt wurde...' ('Mr Hardtloff is wearing fine, cleanly washed rags on his feet in the "countryside agitation" scene—the silver-plated saw which never sawed anything...'). Both in 'Die Mutter 1951', 5a, 2.11–2.12, BEA.

[59] Neher's set models are displayed in the Keller-Restaurant at the Brecht-Haus, Chausseestraße 125, Berlin.

[60] *Theaterarbeit*, 161–2.

2. Caspar Neher's sketch of Scene 1, 1951.

between autocracy and capitalism even before Wlassowa asked in Scene 4: 'Was hat die Polizei mit diesem Suchlinow zu tun?'[61] When the chorus sang 'Wie die Krähe', projected photographs of three female peasants showed that women across the world shared Wlassowa's predicament, and in Scene 11 projected photographs depicted her adversaries: Tsar Nicholas II, Kaiser Wilhelm II, and British Foreign Secretary Sir Edward Grey. Whilst the painted projections recalled the nineteenth-century painted backcloth, these photo-projections and the chorus gestured towards the more radical aesthetic techniques associated with Piscator and agitprop. So even though Brecht and Neher had made substantial aesthetic concessions, their continued reliance on epic techniques was guaranteed to offend the SED's cultural politicians.

Although Küchenmeister and Wekwerth both claim that the new emphasis on milieu only coincidentally distanced the production from the proletarian-revolutionary tradition, the 1951 programme was clearly designed to pre-empt accusations of Formalism. It emphasized the play's relationship to Gorky's novel, whose Socialist Realist credentials were impeccable, and included Brecht's poem 'Grabinschrift für Gorki' ('Epitaph for Gorky') and quotations from Gorky's writings. Furthermore, the programme reminded the audience that *Die Mutter* was based on real-life events since it contained an interview with Anna Kriliowna Salomowa, who, according to Gorky, was the prototype for Pelagea Wlassowa. This move suggested that *Die Mutter* satisfied both the SED's call for 'volksverbundene Kunst'[62] and Friedrich Engels's demand for 'die getreue Wiedergabe typischer Charaktere unter typischen Umständen'.[63]

The programme also attempted to protect Eisler from charges of Formalism. Georg Knepler, who had accompanied Weigel at concerts in 1932, wrote an essay that foregrounded the score's relationship with the classical tradition. He contrasted Eisler with the Formalist New Music movement, arguing that the latter sought to renew music using form, technique, and tone, without seeing that form could not make uninteresting content interesting. Instead, Knepler asserted that

---

[61] 'What have the police got to do with this man Suchlinow?' BBA 637/26.

[62] 'Popular art' (literally: 'art tied to the people'). '[Entschließung der Ersten Zentralen Kulturtagung der SED]', in *Dokumente zur Kunst-, Literatur- und Kulturpolitik der SED*, ed. Elimar Schubbe (Stuttgart: Seewald, 1972), 91.

[63] 'The faithful representation of typical characters in typical circumstances.' Letter from Friedrich Engels to Margaret Harkness, Apr. 1888, in Karl Marx and Friedrich Engels, *Über Kunst und Literatur*, ed. Manfred Kliem, 2 vols (East Berlin: Dietz, 1967), i. 157–9 (157).

Eisler's originality lay in the fact that he had found an important form for important content. Thus, although Küchenmeister and Wekwerth question the suggestion that the 1951 production was intended to allay the SED's concerns, the programme implies that this consideration was very much at the forefront of Brecht's mind.

Yet, far from transforming *Die Mutter* into a Socialist Realist drama, Brecht's new approach actually created fresh tensions. Although the historical detail and milieu fostered the illusion of reality and encouraged the audience to identify with Wlassowa, Semjon, and Pawel, the epic elements disrupted this illusion and openly articulated the play's political lessons.[64] According to Wekwerth, Palitzsch considered that the style of acting directly opposed the function of the epic devices; he allegedly commented that the acting was far too psychological for the audience to distance themselves from the actors.[65] Furthermore, Brecht insisted that the songs should, as in 1932, be separated clearly from the action. As Küchenmeister explained to me: 'Sie setzen absichtlich erstmal einen Ruhepunkt.... Denken wir mal gemeinsam nach, ... überlegt euch, was wir euch hier sagen, und dann fahren wir in der Geschichte weiter.'[66] Besides demonstrating that the text resisted Brecht's new aesthetic approach, these tensions also highlight the conflict between two of his aims in 1951: to present a clear production that focused on the play's political purpose and to draw the spectators into the story so that they would learn unconsciously.

3.4 The Cunning to spread the Truth

At the time, several of Brecht's co-workers saw his new approach as an unacceptable betrayal of the play.[67] According to Wekwerth, Palitzsch argued: 'Die Aufführung sei gegenüber der von 1930 [*sic*]

---

[64] Carl Weber, who joined the BE in 1952, overlooks these tensions when he claims that the BE's production of *Die Mutter* 'was in many respects the most faithful rendering of the epic theatre concept as he [Brecht] had defined it before and during his exile years'. Weber, 'Brecht and the Berliner Ensemble: The Making of a Model', in *The Cambridge Companion to Brecht*, ed. Peter Thomson and Glendyr Sacks (Cambridge: Cambridge University Press, 1994), 167–84 (172).

[65] Manfred Wekwerth, *Erinnern ist Leben: Eine dramatische Autobiographie* (Leipzig: Faber & Faber, 2000), 90.

[66] 'They are designed to provide a pause for reflection.... Let us reflect together, ... think about what we are telling you here, and then we will continue with the story.'

[67] The subheading ('Die List, die Wahrheit zu verbreiten') is taken from 'Fünf Schwierigkeiten beim Schreiben der Wahrheit', *BFA*, xxii.1. 74–89 (81).

verwässert, das Bühnenbild mit seinen Fabrik- und Häuserprojektionen unerträglich illustrativ…. Es fehle Kargheit, somit Provokation.'⁶⁸ As Berlau pointed out ten days before the première, the elegant, crafted aesthetic also risked presenting a sanitized version of working-class life: 'Die Kostüme großartig, doch könnten … noch *verlumpter* sein, speziell *Fußbekleidung*…. Arbeiter im Streik und auch in Arbeit haben keine Stiefel—und wenn, dann umgewickelt, damit die Reste von Sohlen festgehalten werden.'⁶⁹ Brecht's refusal to address controversial topical issues in the production particularly frustrated Berlau, who argued that the play was burningly topical, whether Brecht saw it or not. She urged him to add topical references to Scene 8a in order to agitate against anti-social farmers and the fact that 'die Bauern lieber alles verrotten lassen oder in Erde runtergraben, als billig verkaufen—daß die Bauern, selbst die Kleinbauern, den Arbeitern nicht helfen, sondern ausplündern'.⁷⁰

Despite these criticisms, Brecht offset his tactical concessions by intensifying the play's agitation against war, his most urgent concern during this period.⁷¹ Following the outbreak of the Korean War in June 1950 and the proposed creation of a European Defence Community, remilitarization in West Germany and an East–West conflict appeared increasingly likely. In the programme, three photographs related the play's arguments specifically to the Korean War: the first bore the caption 'Amerika 1950: Weinende Mütter sehen die Abreise ihrer Söhne an die Front';⁷² the second, headed 'Korea 1950', depicted a mother grieving over her dead infant; and the third showed a peasant woman carrying her child. Just to drive the point home, the final verse of Brecht's poem 'An Meine [*sic*] Landsleute' ('To My Compatriots') was superimposed on the third picture with the closing plea: 'Ihr Mütter, lasset eure Kinder leben' ('You Mothers, let your children live'). Moreover, Weigel

---

⁶⁸ 'The production is watered down compared to the one in 1930 [*sic*], the set with its projected factory and houses is unbearably illustrative…. What it lacks is frugality and hence provocation.' Wekwerth, *Erinnern*, 90.

⁶⁹ 'The costumes are great, but they need … to be more *ragged*, especially the *footwear*…. Workers on strike or even at work do not have any boots—and if they do, then they are tied on so that the remains of the soles are held on.' Ruth Berlau, 'Notate über *Die Mutter*', 3 Jan. 1951, BBA 971/86–7. Where possible, Berlau's erratic orthography has been standardized.

⁷⁰ 'The farmers prefer to let everything rot or to bury it underground, rather than sell it cheaply—that the farmers, even the smallholders, do not help the workers, but rob them of all that they have.' Ibid.

⁷¹ e.g. '[In die Welt ist ein neuer Schrecken gekommen]', *BFA*, xxiii. 158.

⁷² 'America 1950: tearful mothers watch their sons depart for the front.'

delivered Wlassowa's indictment of those mothers who supported the war and sent their sons to die for the wrong cause with a new ferocity. Berlau commented on the change in Weigel's delivery as follows:

[Als] die Mutter [1932] Antikriegspropaganda [trieb], führte sie diese Arbeit heiter und freundlich aus, damals stand Berlin noch, jetzt in den Ruinen zeigt die Weigel Ungeduld und Härte, wenn sie gegen den Krieg spricht—so wie sie deutlich zeigt, daß nur die Mütter der Söhne, die gegen Hitler kämpften, Mitleid erwarten können, nicht die, die selber ihrem Sohn das braune Hemd nähten und nicht wissen wollten, daß es sein Todeshemd war.[73]

Quite apart from the intrinsic importance of Brecht's changes, the audience's own experiences of the Second World War further heightened the impact of his anti-war argument. In 1951, the memory of war was more immediate than it had been in 1932, and its effects on civilian life had been far greater, due to aerial bombardment, invasion, and occupation. In 'Einige Irrtümer über die Spielweise des Berliner Ensemble' Brecht noted how his argument struck home:

In der Aufführung der *Mutter* sah ich beim Publikum Tränen, als Arbeiter am Vorabend des ersten Weltkriegs der alten Wlassowa die Flugblätter gegen den Krieg nicht mehr abnehmen. Das sind … politische Tränen, vergossen über die verstopften Ohren, die Feigheit, die Läßlichkeit. Mancher, der hier entsetzt zusah, war immer noch gegen die Bolschewiki, … er mochte … klassenmäßig fast außerstande sein, sich mit der Wlassowa zu identifizieren, aber er … vereinigte sich mit den neben ihm Sitzenden in einem Entsetzen über solche, die nicht wissen, was sie tun und nicht tun.[74]

Thus, far from betraying the play's political function, Brecht's tactical concessions actually allowed him to promote his anti-war argument

---

[73] 'When the Mother agitated against the war [in 1932], she carried out her task in a cheerful and friendly manner; back then, Berlin was still standing; now, in the ruins, Weigel is impatient and harsh when she speaks against the war—just as she shows clearly that only mothers whose sons fought against Hitler can expect sympathy, not those who sewed their son's brown shirt with their own hands, refusing to realize that it was his shroud.' Ruth Berlau, '*Die Mutter* Modell', BBA 1969/134–8.

[74] 'Some misconceptions about the Berliner Ensemble's performance methods': 'In the production of *The Mother* I saw tears in the audience's eyes when workers no longer accept anti-war leaflets from the ageing Wlassowa on the eve of the First World War. These are … political tears, shed over their deaf ears, cowardice, negligence. Many a person watching here, horrified, was still against the Bolsheviks, … may have been almost incapable of identifying with Wlassowa in class terms, but united with his neighbours in horror at people who do not realize what they are doing and failing to do.' *BFA*, xxiii. 323–38 (326). Brecht styled this essay as a fictive conversation and attributed this comment to 'R.' [Käthe Rülicke].

successfully. Consequently, Wekwerth now appreciates the skill of Brecht and Neher in tailoring the production to their audience: 'Sie haben jedenfalls versucht, einzugehen auf das Publikum, das man hatte. Und das finde ich sehr wichtig.... Brecht meinte, man muß auf das Publikum eingehen, das da ist, wobei er immer sagte, daß er das nicht besonders liebt.'[75]

4. THE PRODUCTION'S RECEPTION

4.1 Attracting Working-Class Audiences

The BE's attempt to attract working-class spectators was a logical development of Brecht's efforts in 1932, now with state support. Brecht sent Wera Küchenmeister to factories where she arranged for records of the songs from *Die Mutter* to be broadcast over the tannoy and then spoke to workers about the production. This policy was not motivated primarily by economic considerations but by a desire to broaden access to the theatre. As Küchenmeister explains: 'Das wichtigste war, sie vertraut zu machen ... mit einer neuen Sache.'[76] If workers agreed to see the production, then the BE arranged transport and provided cut-price tickets, an approach that it developed even further in 1953 when it staged Erwin Strittmatter's *Katzgraben*. Then the company discussed its plans with villagers in Klein-Kölzig and Eichwege, where it subsequently performed the finished production on tour.[77] Küchenmeister recalls 'daß natürlich der Wissensstand des Publikums damals Brecht besonders interessierte: was wissen sie denn insgesamt über die Arbeiterbewegung, was haben sie noch nicht begriffen, was wissen sie schon, aber was sehe ich anders?'[78]

Significantly, the BE's first tour took *Die Mutter* directly to a working-class audience. In May 1951 the company staged performances in Weimar, Chemnitz, and Gera during a week-long trade union theatre festival. Concerned that workers, many of whom had never

---

[75] 'At any rate they tried to engage with the audience that was there. And I think that is very important.... Brecht said you have to engage with the audience that is there, although he did always say that he didn't particularly enjoy it.'

[76] 'The most important thing was to familiarize them ... with something new.'

[77] *BFA*, xxiii. 383, 597.

[78] 'That of course the level of the audience's knowledge at that time particularly interested Brecht: what do they know overall about the workers' movement, what have they not yet understood, what do they already know, but what do I see differently?'

visited a theatre before, might lose interest during a three-hour performance, the BE served pea soup to them at the start of the show.
Although this fare may have seemed particularly appropriate given
Wlassowa's opening monologue, several workers in Weimar were offended by the BE's well-intentioned but patronizing gesture. One worker
objected: 'Erbsensuppe gehört nicht für [*sic*] Theaterbesuch', while
another explained: 'Die Verabreichung der Erbsensuppe vor Beginn der
Vorstellung war nicht angebracht. Erforderlich wären zwei Brötchen
und eine Tasse Kaffee.'[79] This incident suggests that the BE's ideal-
istic experiments were sometimes hindered by a lack of familiarity
with the—rather bourgeois—expectations of workers from the factory
floor.

4.2 The Responses of Different Sections of the Audience

Although the production divided theatre critics into pro- and anti-Brecht
camps, even the anti-Brecht camp reacted enthusiastically to the quality
of the acting, partly because it was predominantly realistic. Nevertheless,
cultural politicians and critics close to the SED were suspicious of the
songs, captions, and photo-projections because of their association with
the agitprop tradition.[80] For example, in the SED newspaper *Neues
Deutschland*, Johanna Rudolph argued that the captions had become
superfluous now that the spectators were committed to the people's
interests.[81]

Despite Brecht's textual changes, the production was also criticized on political grounds. For example, in *Die Tägliche Rundschau*,
the official newspaper of the occupying Soviet authorities, Walther
Pollatschek complained about Brecht's inadequate treatment of the
farmers' question.[82] Shortly afterwards, the production was discussed
by the *Politbüro*, which decided that further changes were necessary:
'Es soll mit Bert Brecht gesprochen werden, daß einige Korrekturen an

---

[79] 'Pea soup isn't appropriate for a theatre visit'; 'handing out pea soup before the
start of the performance was not appropriate. We needed two bread rolls and a cup of
coffee.' 'Die Mutter 1951', file 5, MK12, BEA.

[80] e.g. Johanna Rudolph, 'Wertvolle Bereicherung des Berliner Theaterlebens', *Neues
Deutschland* (henceforth *ND*, East Berlin), 14 Jan. 1951; Max Schroeder, 'Neunzehn
Jahre nach der Uraufführung', in *Von hier und heute aus* (East Berlin: Aufbau, 1957),
111–14; Lauter, 51, 131.

[81] Rudolph, 'Wertvolle Bereicherung', *ND*, 14 Jan. 1951.

[82] Walther Pollatschek, 'Die Bühne als Anleitung zum Handeln', *Tägliche Rundschau*
(East Berlin), 16 Jan. 1951.

der Aufführung vorgenommen werden.'[83] Following these criticisms, Brecht changed the dialogue in Scene 8a so that it emphasized the alliance, rather than the hostility, between workers and agricultural labourers.[84] As in 1932, he responded quickly to the Party's criticism of his political line.

The forty-three sets of workers' comments from the 1951 tour provide a useful comparison with the opinions of these professional reviewers.[85] Like the theatre critics, the workers enthused about the quality of the acting and set. Many workers, particularly women, identified directly with Wlassowa's experiences. Charlotte Pennewitz felt that the play was taken straight out of the lives of the people, while Karl Weinhold, a metal worker from Langefeld, called the production excellent and true to life. Nevertheless, Brecht's theatre was very much a novelty to the workers, many of whom regarded the songs and captions with uncertainty but not outright hostility. One argued that the production was unusual but good, and another commented that it took a while to get used to the songs. Some workers even suggested how the production might be improved: one thought that the songs should be placed between the scenes to entertain the audience during the long scene changes, and another suggested replacing the captions with a narrator. Then again, one anonymous worker objected to the half-curtain, complaining that spectators in the circle could see the scene changes, a view endorsed by Hans Jahn and Frau Beyer. Such criticisms were not just a failure to understand Brechtian *Verfremdung* on the part of an audience accustomed to traditional conventions, they also highlighted a tension in the staging. Whereas the half-curtain was designed to reveal the mechanics of the production (the scene changes), the detailed, historicized set seemed to encourage an illusion of reality.

Hostility towards Brecht's experimentation increased in March 1951, when the Fifth Conference of the Central Committee launched a campaign against Formalism. The published records of this conference show that several functionaries strongly criticized the production of *Die Mutter*. For example, Fred Oelßner, the Secretary of the *Politbüro* argued that it was not theatre but some kind of cross between Meyerhold and *Proletkult*. Acknowledging Brecht's literary

---

[83] 'Someone should speak to Bert Brecht about making several corrections to the performance.' Stiftung Archiv der Parteien und Massenorganisationen der DDR (henceforth SAPMO) im Bundesarchiv (henceforth BArch) DY 30 IV 2/2/129 (minutes of the meeting on 23 Jan. 1951).

[84] *Theaterarbeit*, 134–5.   [85] 'Die Mutter 1951', file 5, MK12, BEA.

talent, Oelßner called on him to write a well-constructed play that really hung together.[86] These comments were seconded by the manager of the Theater der Freundschaft, Hans Rodenberg, who accused *Die Mutter* of Formalism,[87] and the head of the Culture Department, Hans Lauter, even argued that *Die Mutter* disorientated people in the class struggle. Pointing out that the two demonstrations were narrated, not enacted, Lauter argued that Brecht had deliberately taken the drama and excitement out of revolutionary events in order to weaken their impact.[88] Yet Wekwerth recalled that these scenes had precisely the opposite effect on spectators: 'wenn im Stück am Anfang nicht geklatscht wurde, weil die Leute erst einmal sich einfinden mußten, wenn der 1. Mai lief …, dann brach ein großer Beifall aus'.[89] Nevertheless, Lauter concluded: 'das Ganze ist fehlerhaft und ein Beispiel für Formalismus', suggesting that a dogmatic aesthetic conservatism had already distanced cultural politicians from the tastes of ordinary East Germans.[90]

Brecht and Weigel worked hard to defend the production against these criticisms. At the 1951 conference, as at the 1953 Stanislavsky conference, Weigel spoke on Brecht's behalf and assured the delegates that their concerns were misplaced.[91] In October 1952, Brecht fought successfully for permission to include *Die Mutter* in the repertoire for the BE's forthcoming tour of Poland, telling Helmut Holtzhauer, a member of the *Staatliche Kommission für Kunstangelegenheiten* (State Commission for Artistic Affairs):

Es ist … eine der schönsten Aufführungen des Ensembles, das Gegenstück zu *Mutter Courage*, positiv und sozialistisch. Einige Einwände, Einzelheiten betreffend, sind berücksichtigt worden: es wurden Änderungen vorgenommen. Gorki selbst hat … das Stück gelesen und autorisiert. Auf den ersten Blick scheint das Stück vielleicht beeinflußt vom Agitprop-Theater, seiner Musikelemente wegen, aber in Wirklichkeit folgt es der klassischen deutschen Bauweise (vom *Götz* bis zum *Wozzeck* [*sic*]).[92]

---

[86] Lauter, 51.   [87] Ibid. 131.   [88] Wekwerth, *Erinnern*, 88.

[89] 'Whenever there was no applause at the start of the play because people needed to find their way into it, then the 1 May scene … would unleash massive applause.'

[90] 'The whole thing is defective and an example of Formalism.' Wekwerth, *Erinnern*, 88.

[91] Lauter, 64–8.

[92] 'It is … one of the Ensemble's finest productions, the counterpart to *Mother Courage*, positive and Socialist. Several objections concerning details have been heeded: changes were made. Gorky himself read and authorized the play…. At first glance the play may seem influenced by agitprop theatre, because of its musical elements, but in

Furthermore, the BE's 1952 publication *Theaterarbeit* emphasized the production's popularity with actual spectators. In addition to quoting enthusiastic comments by workers who had seen the 1951 tour, Brecht reprinted a letter demonstrating the play's positive political influence: 'Ich bin ein Genosse aus Westberlin und es kam so, daß ich in letzter Zeit etwas müde wurde, gegen die Bösheit der Klassenfeinde und die Dummheit der Klassengenossen zu kämpfen. Und gestern habe ich Deine *Mutter* gesehen und da habe ich wieder einen großen Mut bekommen.'[93] Brecht even secured the endorsement of the *Held der nationalen Arbeit* (National Labour Hero), 49-year-old Hans Garbe, and his wife Erika, both of whom—conveniently—praised the controversial epic devices. After explaining that he understood things much more quickly if he read them first, Garbe described how the production had struck a chord with his own experiences: 'Das war alles so, als ob ich meine Vergangenheit auf dem Theater gesehen hätte. Ich habe immer wieder meine Frau angestoßen und gesagt, das ist doch ganz so, wie ich es erlebt habe.'[94] Brecht's strategy was clever, for the SED's cultural rhetoric prized *Volksverbundenheit* and *Volksnähe* (closeness to the people). Accordingly, the authorities allowed *Die Mutter* to remain in the BE's repertoire.

5. THE 1967 REVIVAL: CHANGE AND DEVELOPMENT

By the end of the 1958–9 season, *Die Mutter* had been performed 163 times at the BE.[95] This long run had taken its toll on the production, not least because many of the actors were bored with the staging and even with the play's ideology. Indeed, at a meeting of the whole company in 1956, Käthe Rülicke had considered it necessary to remind the actors that it was important to perform plays like *Katzgraben*, *Die Mutter*, and *Die Gewehre der Frau Carrar*, even if they did not

reality it follows the classic German method of construction (from *Götz* to *Wozzeck* [*sic*]).' Brecht to Holtzhauer, 4 Oct. 1952, *BFA*, xxx (1998), 142.

[93] 'I am a comrade from West Berlin and it so happened that I became rather tired recently of fighting against the malice of our class enemies and the stupidity of our class comrades. And yesterday I saw your *Mother* and took heart again.' *Theaterarbeit*, 338.

[94] 'It was all as if I was watching my past in the theatre. I kept nudging my wife and telling her: that's exactly how I experienced it.' Ibid. 168–70 (169).

[95] 'Repertoire-Aufstellung', in 'Statistik des BE bis 1959', BEA.

find them much fun.[96] By June 1959 it had become clear that the long-running stagings had deteriorated significantly, and so the BE formed a committee to monitor their quality.[97] But even though its members watched performances and reported their findings in person, this measure tackled only the symptoms, not the causes of stagnation.

After Brecht's death, the BE's long runs contributed significantly to its public image as a Brecht museum, even though performances of classic productions like *Die Mutter, Leben des Galilei*, and *Mutter Courage* occupied only a small proportion of the programme. *Die Mutter* was particularly vulnerable to accusations of anachronism because of its detailed, realistic aesthetic. Compared with the BE's more recent productions, such as O'Casey's *Purpurstaub (Purple Dust)*, and with Besson's experiments at the Deutsches Theater, the production increasingly seemed like a relic from a bygone era. This problem was compounded by the production's failure to take account of any of the major political events in the Eastern bloc since 1951, such as the East German uprising in 1953 and the Hungarian one in 1956. Although the BE addressed the reasons for the construction of the Berlin Wall in its staging of *Die Tage der Commune (The Days of the Commune,* 1962), long-running productions could not tackle such an issue because they had been designed for an earlier set of circumstances. As the hopes invested in the early GDR faded, the popularity of *Die Mutter* diminished further, because it was treated as a *Staatsfeststück* (play used for state celebrations) and performed, above all, on major anniversaries of the October Revolution.

The simplest means of increasing the production's topicality was to update the closing film, which continued the action from 1917 to the present. Indeed, the different versions of the film show how the BE repeatedly rewrote the history of Socialism between 1951 and 1971. Although the 1951 version showed the storming of the Winter Palace and speeches by Lenin, Stalin, and Mao Tse-tung, Stalin's picture was cut in 1956, after Khrushchev had denounced his cult of personality, and Mao's image met the same fate after he had criticized Khrushchev.[98] The 1967 film also suggests that Brecht's anti-war argument had receded, for it included pictures of the annual military parade on Red Square.

---

[96] 'Protokoll der Betriebsvollversammlung am 4. Januar 1956', in 'Protokolle 50er', BEA.

[97] 'Aus einem Protokoll einer Parteiversammlung im Juni 1959', in '1949–1962 Ensembleaufstellung, Probenstatistik', BEA.

[98] *Theaterarbeit*, 167.

After thus demonstrating the USSR's victory in the arms race, the film turned to the space race and showed images of Soviet cosmonauts. These images replicated the rhetoric of the Cold War by demonstrating the alleged superiority of the Socialist system.[99]

Despite these topical changes, the production's main asset remained Helene Weigel, whose performance as Wlassowa had already entered theatre history. Indeed, although the revival was billed as a commemoration of the fiftieth anniversary of the October Revolution, its co-director Alexander Stillmark told me that its chief purpose was to provide a showcase for Weigel: 'Damals wurde eine große Rolle für die Weigel gesucht .... Die *Courage* [wurde] noch einmal aufgebaut, aber es waren die körperlichen Anstrengungen der Rolle, die es verhinderten.... Es waren ganz praktische Gründe, daß sie das nicht mehr durchhielt.'[100] Weigel's advancing age and physical frailty added to the production's pathos, most famously in her final performance in Nanterre on 3 April 1971, less than five weeks before she died of lung cancer.[101] Advertisements for the 1967 revival capitalized both on this pathos and Weigel's personal renown, and Stillmark suggested to me that Weigel's performance even verged on sentimentality: 'daß sie nicht doktrinär war, daß sie sehr das Mütterliche, immer wieder das Persönliche betonte, gegen eine scheinbar objektive Härte des Textes.... So geriet sie manchmal in die Nähe der Sentimentalität, aber sie fand auch enorm große Momente.'[102] So although Brecht had insisted in 1951 that Weigel should resist sentimentality, by 1967 both her performance and the production's publicity had shifted in this very direction.[103]

This increase in pathos was offset by a new emphasis on generational conflict which exploited the potential already present in the text. For

[99] Anon., 'Publikum in Bann gezogen', *Der Demokrat* (Schwerin), 5 Oct. 1967.

[100] 'At the time we were looking for a major role for Weigel.... The stage was set up for *Courage* again, but the physical demands of the role made it impossible.... It was for the entirely practical reason that she could no longer cope with it.' Alexander Stillmark, personal interview, 7 Dec. 2000.

[101] Hecht, *Helene Weigel*, 124–31. Even though Weigel broke two ribs when she was embraced by Pawel in Scene 9, she still struggled through the rest of the performance.

[102] 'That she was not dogmatic, that she emphasized the maternal aspects a great deal, kept on emphasizing the personal element, against the apparently objective harshness of the text.... She sometimes verged on sentimentality, but she also found tremendously great moments.' Stillmark, 7 Dec. 2000. For the poster advertising the 1967 revival, see Friedrich Dieckmann and Karl-Heinz Drescher (eds), *Die Plakate des Berliner Ensembles 1949–1989* (Hamburg: Europäische Verlagsanstalt, 1992), 123.

[103] Joachim Lang and Jürgen Hillesheim (eds), *'Denken heißt verändern...': Erinnerungen an Brecht* (Augsburg: Maro, 1998), 88.

example, in Scene 2 Pawel tells the revolutionaries that his mother 'ist nicht mehr jung genug und könnte uns doch nicht helfen'.[104] In *Neues Deutschland*, Rainer Kerndl praised the topical relevance of Hilmar Thate's portrayal of Pawel: 'Pawel rettet sich ... in jungenhafte Bockigkeit, will den Überlegenen (über die "zurückgebliebene" Mutter) markieren. Durch diesen kleinen Akzent ist uns die Figur mit einem Male sehr nahe, hat etwas Heutiges, assoziiert gar nicht so unaktuelle Verhaltensweisen, ohne auch im mindesten ihre historische Konkretheit aufzugeben.'[105] Even so, both this new emphasis on generational conflict and the obvious effects of Weigel's advancing age entirely escaped Margot Piens, who discussed the production in a brief dissertation of 1968.[106]

Recasting produced further changes, particularly in the characterization of the landlady. Although Angelika Hurwicz and Charlotte Brummerhoff had both played the role as a caricature, Wekwerth—who supervised the final rehearsals in 1967 in his capacity as the BE's chief director—advised Gisela May against following their example:

Darum legte ich auch so großen Wert auf den sehr mitleidvoll schiefen Kopf zu Anfang, der anzeigt, sie ist gekommen, einen alten Streit zu begraben, nicht einen anzufangen.... Wir hatten immer Schwierigkeiten, gerade diesen Punkt der Bibel-Szene darzustellen.... Ich kenne die Versuchung, die von dieser Szene ausgeht; schließlich erlag ihr auch Angelika Hurwicz und auch die Brummerhoff, die es vor Dir spielten.[107]

Despite Wekwerth's instructions, the new interpretation was achieved only on 7 May 1968, when Felicitas Ritsch stood in for May, who was

---

[104] 'Is no longer young enough and could not help us anyway'. BBA 637/04.

[105] 'Pawel takes refuge ... in boyish stubbornness, wants to show that he is superior (compared to his "backward" mother). This little touch suddenly brings the character very close to us, makes him seem contemporary, reminds us of modes of behaviour which are actually quite topical, without relinquishing his historical concreteness in the slightest.' Rainer Kerndl, 'Mit der heiteren Vernunft der Sieger', *ND*, 5 Oct. 1967.

[106] Margot Piens, 'Über Gesetzmäßigkeiten bei der Anwendung von Modellen am Beispiel der Inszenierungen von Bertolt Brechts Stück *Die Mutter* am Berliner Ensemble unter Berücksichtigung des besonderen Charakters des Lehrstücks' (unpublished *Diplomarbeit*, Theaterwissenschaftliche Abteilung der Theaterhochschule 'Hanns Otto' in Leipzig, 1968).

[107] 'That is why I attached so much importance to her very sympathetically bowed head at the start, which signals that she has come to bury an old quarrel, not to start one.... We always had difficulty in conveying precisely this point in the Bible scene.... I know the temptation that arises from this scene; after all, both Angelika Hurwicz and Brummerhoff, who played it before you, succumbed to it.' Letter from Wekwerth to Gisela May, 3 Oct. 1967, in 'Die Mutter 1951', file 5a, 2.11, BEA.

ill. Stillmark's report indicates that her new characterization transformed the scene:

Sie zeigte eine sehr interessante Figur. Keine Karikatur einer bösen Frömmlerin, sondern eine tief gläubige, reiche Frau, die während der ganzen Szene nicht versteht, wieso Häuser etwas mit Gott zu tun haben sollten…. Es erscheint also nicht eine geschwächte, in den letzten Zuckungen lächerliche Kirche, sondern es erscheint eine Institution, die im zaristischen Rußland durchaus staatserhaltende und restaurierende Funktion hatte. Also stand in dieser Szene die Mutter einer sehr ernst zu nehmenden Gegnerin gegenüber.[108]

Although the press reception of the 1967 revival was surprisingly positive in both parts of Germany, several West German reviewers highlighted the old-fashioned elements in the staging. Writing for the *Süddeutsche Zeitung*, Jürgen Beckelmann told his readers: 'Tatsächlich wirkt das Stück, 1951 noch aktuell, heute historisch, sogar eine Spur antiquiert. Die scharfen Agitprop-Töne, die nun einmal dazugehören, klingen jetzt gleichsam romantisch, wie Echolaute auf Stimmen aus der Vergangenheit.'[109] Yet just months later, in May 1968, political events lent the production a fresh, topical edge when it was performed on tour in Cologne.

The West German première of *Die Mutter* was guaranteed to cause controversy, particularly in an East German production. As it transpired, the tour could not have been better timed, for the backdrop of industrial unrest and anti-Vietnam protests made *Die Mutter* relevant and topical. Thus, Hauptmann—who continued to advise the BE in an unofficial capacity—wrote to Stillmark's co-director Isot Kilian on 24 April: 'das Stück, wenn Ihr es in Köln zeigt, [ist] dort von einer ungeheuren Aktualität…. Deshalb bin ich so für Ernst, Frische, Einmaligkeit.'[110] Even more fortuitously, the first performance on 9 May coincided with a national demonstration against the new emergency laws. Stillmark remembered seeing protesters leaving the main station in Cologne for

[108] 'She portrayed a very interesting character. Not a caricature of a malicious bigot, but a deeply religious rich woman, who does not understand during the entire scene why houses should have anything to do with God…. So the Church does not appear as weakened, ridiculous in its death-throes, but as an institution which did indeed help to bolster and revive the state in Tsarist Russia. So in this scene the mother confronted a formidable opponent.' Stillmark, 7 Mar. 1968, in 'Die Mutter 1951', file 5a, 2.12, BEA.

[109] 'Indeed the play, still topical in 1951, now comes across as historical, even a touch antiquated. The sharp agitprop sounds, which are an integral part of it, now seem romantic as it were, like echoes of voices from the past.' Jürgen Beckelmann, 'Im Zeichen des Roten Oktobers', *Süddeutsche Zeitung* (Munich), 14 Oct. 1967.

[110] 'When you perform the play in Cologne, it will be enormously topical…. That's why I am so concerned that it should be serious, fresh, unique.' Letter from Hauptmann to Kilian, 24 Apr. 1968, EHA 430.

Bonn: 'Die Züge waren rot, über und über bedeckt mit roten Fahnen, und die Demonstranten wie Fußballfans … überall war Polizei … eine ziemlich brisante Stimmung.'[111]

The Cologne tour shows how a new audience and performance context can transform the reception of a production, even when only minimal changes are made to the staging. With the agreement of its host, the trade union IG Metall, the BE simply exchanged the 1967 film images for new pictures of the Vietnam War, Martin Luther King, and recent demonstrations in West Germany.[112] Although this film was not shown until the end of the production, the text's subversive force was immediately apparent to the BE's left-wing audience, consisting mainly of delegates to IG Metall's Eighth Youth Conference. The police brutality depicted in Scenes 2, 3, and 5 was particularly topical; the delegate Peter Kroytowski noted that only a few of those present had escaped the police batons during the recent demonstrations.[113] Thus, from the discussion of wage cuts in Scene 2 onwards, every scene was interrupted by applause as the spectators heard the characters on stage articulate grievances that were only too familiar.[114] In the conference pack, a quotation from Scene 8b summed up the delegates' mood: 'Zorn und Unzufriedenheit genügen nicht. So etwas muß praktische Folgen haben.'[115] As the reviewer Hannes Schmidt commented, this was 'politisches Theater von gestern in politischer Wirklichkeit von heute'.[116]

6. THE MODEL AND THE MUSEUM EXHIBIT

By 1968, Brecht's model had been replicated in at least a further seventeen East German stagings of *Die Mutter*, not to mention productions as far afield as Cuba and Japan. This had been possible only because

[111] 'The trains were red, covered with red flags everywhere, and the demonstrators were like football fans … Police were everywhere … It was a pretty charged atmosphere.' Stillmark, 7 Dec. 2000.

[112] Letter [from Weigel?] to Wekwerth, Tenschert, Kilian, and Hosalla, 1 Mar. 1968, in 'Tourneen' (Cologne 1968), BEA.

[113] Elvira Mollenschott, 'Wer seine Lage erkannt hat …', *ND*, 25 May 1968.

[114] H. C., 'Ovationen für das Berliner Ensemble', *tatsachen* (Duisburg), 25 May 1968.

[115] 'Anger and discontent are not enough. Something like this must have practical consequences.' 'Die Mutter 1951', file 5, BEA.

[116] 'Political theatre from yesterday in the political reality of today.' Dr. Hannes Schmidt, 'Helene Weigel spielte die Mutter der russischen Revolution', *Neue Ruhr-Zeitung* (Essen), [1968], Schloß Wahn Theatersammlung, Cologne (henceforth SW).

Ruth Berlau had documented the production in a *Modellbuch* (model book), containing several hundred photographs. Her invention of the *Modellbuch* was inspired by her own approach to staging *Die Mutter* in 1935, and her main task at the BE was to supervise the compilation of similar records of the company's productions.[117] Brecht regarded this work as vital to the dissemination of his staging methods, as he told Berlau in a letter of 1956.[118]

Berlau argued that this form of documentation was particularly suitable for 'epische Stücke, epische Regie und epische Darstellungskunst' ('epic plays, epic directing, and epic acting').[119] This was because Brecht used blocking to convey the social relationships between characters in a series of visual tableaux, stripped of superfluous movement and gesture. On 8 April 1951, Brecht explained his approach to Käthe Rülicke, whose unpublished notes state: 'Alles auf Nachahmbarkeit gestellt, Zufälliges und Einmaliges scharf getrennt vom Richtigen und Grundsätzlichen.... Nur diese Aufführungen sind "fotografierbar", ergeben Bilder in jedem Moment des Spiels.'[120] Nevertheless, as Werner Hecht and Brecht's co-workers have argued, the concept of the model was also tailored to the historical context in which Brecht worked: he was concerned about the poor quality of post-Nazi productions and hoped to influence the theatre by providing examples of good practice. As he noted in his journal on 30 June 1951: 'Diese Modelle und die Neueinstudierungen, die sie erweitern und säubern, sind so nötig, weil die Künste ... zumindest zeitweise von schnellem Verfall bedroht scheinen.'[121] Furthermore, Brecht hoped that the *Modellbücher* would encourage a scientific approach to theatre whereby directors would exchange their findings, just as he himself had borrowed freely from Pudovkin's film.[122] Finally, the *Modellbücher* enabled Brecht to control other stagings of his plays. Whilst his desire to do so was not new, it had become particularly acute in the early GDR because he was so vulnerable to accusations of Formalism.

---

[117] Hans Bunge (ed.), *Brechts Lai-Tu: Erinnerungen und Notate von Ruth Berlau*, 2nd edn (Darmstadt: Hermann Luchterhand, 1985), 54–5.

[118] *BFA*, xxx. 417.   [119] Bunge (ed.), *Brechts Lai-Tu*, 280–4 (281).

[120] 'All the emphasis is on making it imitable; what is coincidental and unique must be strictly separated from what is correct and principled.... Only these productions are "photographable", provide pictures in every moment of the performance.' BBA 1340/53.

[121] 'These models and the new productions which extend and clean them are so necessary because the arts ... seem, at least at times, under threat of rapid decay.' *BFA*, xxvii. 321.

[122] e.g. 'Hemmt die Benutzung des Modells die künstlerische Bewegungsfreiheit?', *BFA*, xxv (1994), 386–91 (389).

Although Brecht's theoretical statements about the model mention only the first two of the above considerations, his actions suggest that the third was no less important. As he admitted: 'Die Talente unter den Regisseuren hätte ich am meisten zu fürchten, sie wären am originellsten.'[123] Consequently, Brecht insisted that directors should use the *Modellbücher* and accept his assistants' advice, and on occasions he even intervened personally.[124] For example, in a letter to Karl Köther, the manager of the Eisenacher Landestheater, Brecht listed the additional changes that he required in the theatre's production of *Die Mutter* even though this was already based on the model.[125] Whilst Brecht's theoretical statements asserted that directors were free to reject the suggestions in the *Modellbücher*, in practice he only accepted alternative productions by directors like Harry Buckwitz whose work he knew and trusted. Thus, although Brecht consistently condemned slavish imitation of the models, the tension between his desire to inspire and his determination to control meant that the danger of such imitation was always present.[126]

Photographs of nine GDR productions of *Die Mutter* between 1957 and 1967 clearly show that faithful reconstructions of Brecht's model were the norm.[127] As Gerhard Pröhl, the director of the Quedlinburg production (1967) wrote to his cast: 'Es braucht wohl nicht besonders betont zu werden, daß das Modellbuch der *Mutter*-Inszenierung des BE Grundlage für unsere Arbeit sein wird.'[128] Each director reconstructed the 1951 set, costumes, and blocking, simply adapting the set to fit the stage and sometimes making changes to cut costs: the Quedlinburg production, for example, dispensed with the side walls for the interior scenes. Most other differences were negligible: in 1957, for instance, a different pattern was used for the teacher's wallpaper in a production

---

[123] 'The talented directors that I should fear the most would be the most original ones.' '[Originale Auffassungen zu Brechtstücken]', *BFA*, xxiii. 127.

[124] e.g. *BFA*, xxv. 386.

[125] *BFA*, xxx. 116–17.

[126] e.g. *Theaterarbeit*, 306, 346.

[127] AdK RKP Fotosammlung zum deutschsprachigen Theater, 1694 (Theater der Stadt Brandenburg, 1960), 1695 (Landesbühnen Sachsen, Dresden-Radebeul, 1957), 1697 (Bühnen der Stadt Gera, 1961), 1698 (Theater in der Universitätsstadt Greifswald, 1957), 1699 (Landestheater Sachsen-Anhalt, Halle, 1958), 1700 (Arbeitertheater Karl-Marx-Stadt, 1960), 1701 (Friedrich-Wolf-Theater, Neustrelitz, 1957); AdK RKP Theaterdokumentation, TM 41 (Städtische Bühnen Quedlinburg, 1967) and 53 (Altenburg Landestheater, 1967).

[128] 'It is probably unnecessary to stress that the model book of the BE's production of *The Mother* will form the basis of our work.' AdK RKP Theaterdokumentation, TM 41.

in Greifswald. Although such faithful reconstructions can be valid and interesting in their own right, stagnation sets in quickly if they become the norm. Moreover, the demand for reconstructions was minimal while the original production was still being performed at the BE.

The perpetuation of Neher's detailed, realistic aesthetic allowed *Die Mutter* to be appropriated as a *Staatsfeststück* in the GDR. Even though the songs and projections had so offended cultural politicians in 1951, they were gradually rendered innocuous by overfamiliarity. In 1967, at least six theatres staged productions of the model in honour of the fiftieth anniversary of the October Revolution. Indeed, Eberhard Richter, the director of a production at the Landestheater in Altenburg (1967), complained that he was able to borrow the *Modellbuch* only for a short period because of the high demand.[129] As a result of its old-fashioned performance aesthetic and new status as a *Staatsfeststück*, *Die Mutter* was increasingly perceived as a dull history lesson, and performances in 1967 at the BE and the Landestheater in Anklam were attended mostly by party functionaries and schoolchildren.[130] However hard actors tried to convey the text's humour and relevance, by 1967, on the eve of seismic disturbances in the Eastern bloc, these elements had been occluded by the performance context and aesthetic.

7. CONCLUSION

In 1951 Brecht transformed the *Gesamtgestus* of *Die Mutter* by changing the text, aesthetic, acting, and programme. The audience's predominantly positive response testified to both the production's artistic quality and Brecht's tactical compromises. Indeed, Brecht's willingness to compromise indicates that he had become significantly more sensitive to political and cultural realities since the American *débâcle* of 1935. At the same time, it is important not to view Brecht's concessions as a capitulation to his audience and the SED, for they actually enabled him to communicate his anti-war argument and present Communism in a positive light. These concessions do indicate, however, that the production should not be regarded as the definitive way of staging *Die Mutter*.

---

[129] AdK RKP Theaterdokumentation, TM 53.
[130] 'Protokoll zum Dreitheatergespräch am 7.1.1968', AdK RKP In. 34.

The 1951 production also suggests that Brecht's aesthetic practice had shifted away from the austere epic theatre of 1929–32. Brecht's approach was closely related to his new audience: whereas in 1932 *Die Mutter* had been staged primarily for workers, far left-wing intellectuals, and avant-garde theatre-goers, in 1951 it was performed for a socially more inclusive public. Thus, Brecht and Neher replaced the earlier stark aesthetic with a design that foregrounded craftsmanship, elegance, and beauty—qualities that distinguished it both from the improvisation of 1932 and the opulence of (post-) Nazi theatre. Whilst some of Brecht's earlier stagings had contained traces of this approach, it dominated his work only at the BE, where he had far greater resources at his disposal.

At the BE Brecht created an apparatus that would develop and disseminate his staging principles. He was highly effective in identifying and nurturing new talent, and three of his assistants—Besson, Palitzsch, and Wekwerth—eventually ranked among the great postwar European directors. Brecht's foresight proved crucial since, by his death, his assistants had acquired the experience and expertise needed to take over the BE's artistic management and continue his context-specific approach in productions of new plays. Nevertheless, although the *Modellbücher* provided an invaluable record of Brecht's productions, they were simply no substitute for Brecht's personal training, because they encouraged directors to imitate his stagings instead of exploring their underlying principles. This problem was aggravated by the fact that Brecht and his heirs used the *Modellbücher* to control stagings of his plays, even though his context-specific productions were, by definition, unsuitable as long-term models. For these reasons, it was not until the 1970s, after Weigel's death, the Prague Spring, and the 1968 protests, that directors in East and West Germany began to challenge Brecht's model by pursuing their own context-specific interpretations of *Die Mutter*.

3

The Politics of Performance: *Die Mutter* in West and East Berlin, 1970 and 1974

1. INTRODUCTION

In the early 1970s, *Die Mutter* was staged by two of the divided Germany's most prominent theatres: the Schaubühne am Halleschen Ufer in West Berlin (1970) and the BE in East Berlin (1974). These productions differed profoundly in almost every respect: their textual interpretations, their aesthetic approaches, and the responses of the audience and critics. These differences were rooted in the divergent politico-cultural contexts and the contrasting priorities of the principal directors, Peter Stein and Ruth Berghaus, who selectively developed Brecht's methods in accordance with their own distinctive political and artistic programmes.

These two productions stand out because of the talent of Stein and Berghaus, their innovative interpretations of *Die Mutter*, and their theatrical approaches. This was the first time that theatres in both German states had entered into a productive new dialogue with the text: previous GDR stagings had simply copied Brecht's model, while the FRG had boycotted the play entirely until it was staged by the Westfälisches Landestheater in Castrop-Rauxel (1969). Even though Stein and Berghaus still envisaged a relatively broad audience, they adopted the risky strategy of moving ahead of their spectators' expectations: Stein politically, Berghaus aesthetically. Their approach thus raises the question of how far, without the kinds of concessions that Brecht had made in 1951, *Die Mutter* could appeal to a wide audience. Furthermore, since the productions occurred at pivotal points in each company's history, they also illuminate their institutional development. This is particularly important with regard to the BE, because only brief accounts of Berghaus's tenure have hitherto been published.[1]

---

[1] Friedrich Dieckmann, 'Meine Schleef-Mappe: Einar Schleefs Berliner Bühnenbildner-Jahre', in *Einar Schleef*, ed. Gabriele Gerecke, Harald Müller, and

2. CULTURAL AND POLITICAL CONTEXT

By 1970, political theatre was undergoing a process of redefinition in East and West Germany, albeit for different reasons. In the West, theatre had been re-politicized in the 1960s, when documentary dramatists had breached taboos concerning the Nazi past and young directors had staged agitational productions against the Vietnam War.[2] The demand for such theatre was closely related to the rise of the APO (*Außerparlamentarische Opposition*/Extra-Parliamentary Opposition) which promoted direct civic involvement as the answer to the perceived lack of effective opposition in parliament. Even so, the inefficacy of public protest became clear in May 1968, when the *Bundestag* finally ratified the controversial emergency laws. Ideological divisions within the APO were then exacerbated in August, when Communist factions refused to condemn the Warsaw Pact's invasion of Prague. So when Willy Brandt's left-liberal coalition replaced Kurt Kiesinger's unpopular Grand Coalition in October 1969, many moderates transferred their hopes for social reform to the new government. As the APO splintered along ideological lines, alternative politics and political theatre both entered a phase of re-assessment. This context helps to explain the historical focus and muted tenor of the Schaubühne's production of *Die Mutter*, premièred on 8 October 1970: instead of agitating for revolution in the present, it explored how solidarity, now so elusive, had been generated in the past.[3]

During the late 1960s, Walter Ulbricht's increasingly repressive politics and the suppression of the Prague Spring destroyed the last vestiges of enthusiasm for affirmative political theatre in East Germany.

Hans-Ulrich Müller-Schwefe, Theater der Zeit Arbeitsbuch, 11 (Berlin: Podewil, 2002), 20–7; Dieter Kranz, 'Die Zeichen-Künstlerin: Zum Tode von Ruth Berghaus', *Theater heute*, 37 (Mar. 1996), 70; Karl Mickel, 'Das Berliner Ensemble der Ruth Berghaus', *Theater der Zeit*, Mar./Apr. 1996, 50–1; Sigrid Neef, *Das Theater der Ruth Berghaus* (East Berlin: Henschel, 1989), 74–93.

[2] e.g. Rolf Hochhuth, *Der Stellvertreter* (*The Deputy*, 1963); Peter Weiss, *Die Ermittlung* (*The Investigation*, 1965); Peter Stein's production of Weiss's *VietNam Diskurs* (*Discourse on Vietnam*) in Munich (1968).

[3] Cf. e.g. Rob Burns and Wilfried van der Will, *Protest and Democracy in West Germany: Extra-Parliamentary Opposition and the Democratic Agenda* (London: Macmillan, 1988); Hermann Glaser, *Kleine Kulturgeschichte der Bundesrepublik Deutschland 1945–1989* (Munich: Hanser, 1991); Martin Hubert, *Politisierung der Literatur—Ästhetisierung der Politik: Eine Studie zur literaturgeschichtlichen Bedeutung der 68er Bewegung in der Bundesrepublik Deutschland* (Frankfurt/Main: Peter Lang, 1992).

Yet in 1971 Ulbricht's replacement as First Party Secretary by Erich Honecker signalled an important shift towards greater tolerance of aesthetic experimentation. Indeed, at the Fourth Conference of the Central Committee in December 1971, Honecker's reference to 'keine Tabus' ('no taboos') effectively promised an end to accusations of Formalism.[4] Nevertheless, this new freedom was strictly limited, for Honecker stipulated that artists must still proceed ideologically from 'der festen Position des Sozialismus' ('the firm position of Socialism').[5] Even so, by using previously proscribed aesthetic techniques and asserting individual needs and aspirations, artists could challenge the orthodox model of affirmative theatre and literature. This approach underpinned Berghaus's innovative and provocative production of *Die Mutter*, which was premièred on 18 October 1974.

Despite the major cultural and political differences between East and West Germany, their theatres faced similar changes in the late 1960s and early 1970s as the first postwar generation of *Intendanten* (theatre managers) retired. In East Berlin, the BE changed hands in 1971, the Deutsches Theater in 1969 and 1972, and the Volksbühne in 1974, and Walter Felsenstein was keen to retire from the Komische Oper.[6] In March 1970, the West German periodical *Theater heute* announced that the management or artistic direction would probably change at eight theatres, including Stuttgart, Hamburg, and Munich.[7] These changes were highly significant, for a manager commanded immense power, controlling appointments, determining the theatre's overall artistic line, and even influencing the details of individual productions. So although the changes caused instability and uncertainty, they were also seen as an opportunity to revitalize theatre. Moreover, in West Germany the anti-authoritarian impetus of the APO was encouraging demands for 'die überholte feudale Struktur' ('the outmoded feudal

---

[4] Cf. e.g. Axel Goodbody, Dennis Tate, and Ian Wallace, 'The Failed Socialist Experiment: Culture in the GDR', in *German Cultural Studies: An Introduction*, ed. Rob Burns (Oxford: Oxford University Press, 1995), 147–207; Günter Erbe, *Die verfemte Moderne: Die Auseinandersetzung mit dem 'Modernismus' in Kulturpolitik, Literaturwissenschaft und Literatur der DDR* (Opladen: Westdeutscher Verlag, 1993), 111–16; Jäger, 119–86.

[5] '[Schlußwort Erich Honeckers auf der 4. Tagung des ZK der SED Dezember 1971, Auszug]', in *Dokumente zur Kunst-, Literatur- und Kulturpolitik der SED 1971–1974*, ed. Gisela Rüß (Stuttgart: Seewald, 1976), 287–8 (287).

[6] *Politbüro*, Anlage Nr. 8 zum Protokoll Nr. 8/74 vom 5.3.1974, SAPMO-BArch DY 30 J IV 2/2/1493.

[7] H[enning] R[ischbieter], 'Ein Modell?', *Theater heute*, 11 (Mar. 1970), 8.

structure') of *Intendantentheater* to be replaced by a democratic form of organization.[8]

3. THE SCHAUBÜHNE AM HALLESCHEN UFER AND THE BERLINER ENSEMBLE

In the early 1970s the Schaubühne and the BE each entered a crucial new phase in their development. The Schaubühne, hitherto a left-wing student theatre, was re-founded in 1970 along collective, democratic lines, with a new ensemble and new in-house directors, Peter Stein and Claus Peymann, and *Die Mutter* was its inaugural production.[9] The company's new ethos was reflected in the fact that three directors shared responsibility for the staging: Stein was joined by Wolfgang Schwiedrzik, with whom he had co-directed Peter Weiss's *VietNam Diskurs* (*Discourse on Vietnam*) in Munich, and Frank-Patrick Steckel, who had worked in student theatre with Peymann in Hamburg. Nevertheless, the rehearsal minutes indicate that Stein's experience and talent lent him a natural authority within the group, so that he became the leading force.[10] In 1971, there were also changes in the East of the city, when Helene Weigel's twenty-two-year reign at the BE ended and her successor, Ruth Berghaus, embarked on a major programme of artistic innovation. Berghaus's production of *Die Mutter* formed the centrepiece of this programme in the BE's Silver Jubilee year, 1974, by epitomizing her refusal to be restricted by the BE's artistic heritage.

In 1970 the re-opening of the Schaubühne was the most eagerly awaited event in the West German theatrical calendar.[11] This was partly because of the proven talent of those involved, the directors Stein and Peymann and actors like Bruno Ganz, Edith Clever, and Jutta Lampe. But it was also because the Schaubühne was attempting to create a new

---

[8] Wolfgang Schwiedrzik and Peter Stein, 'Demokratie ist auch Aktion', *Theater heute*, 9 (Sept. 1968), 2–3 (3).

[9] Cf. Peter Iden, *Die Schaubühne am Halleschen Ufer 1970–1979* (Munich: Hanser, 1979), 30–4; Michael Patterson, *Peter Stein: Germany's Leading Theatre Director* (Cambridge: Cambridge University Press, 1981), 37–45.

[10] e.g. 'Protokoll der 3. Probenkritik der Inszenierung DIE MUTTER (10.9.70)', in 'Protokolle', Schaubühne am Lehniner Platz Archive (henceforth SA).

[11] e.g. anon., 'Berlin geht neue Wege: Es sollen wieder Experimente stattfinden', *Oldenburgische Volkszeitung* (Vechta), 1 Apr. 1970; Ingeborg Keller, 'Theaterleute geben Auskunft: Die Schaubühne—ein Kollektiv und seine Pläne', *Der Telegraf* (West Berlin), 12 May 1970; R[ischbieter], *Theater heute*, 11 (1970), 8.

kind of theatre in which all the members had an equal say in decision making. Thus, the actors, technicians, and directors enjoyed equal representation on committees, received copies of the minutes of each meeting, and debated their concerns in regular assemblies of the whole company.[12] Consequently, the Schaubühne was significantly more open and transparent than any other German theatre, including the BE, where the management was obliged to consult members' representatives but reached most decisions in closed meetings.[13]

Although the Schaubühne was broadly anti-capitalist, it rejected left-wing dogmatism in favour of a more sensitive exploration of sociopolitical reality.[14] Correspondingly, the members' political allegiances ranged from the left wing of the SPD, through the SEW (Sozialistische Einheitspartei Westberlins/Socialist Unity Party of West Berlin), to the KPD and anarcho-syndicalist splinter groups. Furthermore, although its publicity also targeted workers, the ensemble accepted that its audience would consist primarily of middle-class intellectuals and students.[15] Nevertheless, by opening with *Die Mutter*, which West German theatres had boycotted until so recently, the Schaubühne fostered the misleading impression that it intended to campaign aggressively for radical social change.

From the mid-1960s onwards, the struggle for a post-Brechtian theatre dominated the BE. Whereas reformers like Wekwerth sought to combine Brecht's methods with new theatrical influences in productions such as O'Casey's *Purpurstaub* (*Purple Dust*), conservatives like Weigel essentially wanted to preserve Brecht's methods and models. Consequently, Weigel regarded Wekwerth's approach as a betrayal and argued: 'Es ist mir seit einigen Jahren ... immer klarer geworden, daß er den Weg Brechts verläßt.'[16] By May 1969 their differences had become so irreconcilable that Weigel accepted Wekwerth's resignation.[17] When several other directors, actors, and dramaturges followed him, it became so difficult to plan new stagings that the only 'premières' in the 1968–70 seasons were revivals of the models and performances of songs and

[12] 'Bei dem vorerst für zwei Spielzeiten geplanten Versuch...', in '1970 1971 MUTTER TASSO', SA.
[13] Cf. 'Berghaus Protokolle (Verwaltungs-Mat. 1971–3)', 'Protokolle, Leitungssitzungen 1973–76', BEA.
[14] e.g. '[Besprechung in Großgoltern vom 26. bis 30.3]', 10–11, in 'Protokolle', SA.
[15] Ibid. 11.
[16] 'Over the past few years it has become ... increasingly clear to me that he is departing from Brecht's path.' Weigel to Fredrik Martner, 7 Feb. 1970, in 'HW Allg. Briefw. 1970', BEA.
[17] Cf. Wekwerth, *Erinnern*, 236–7.

sketches.[18] In public Weigel denied rumours of the crisis, but in private she admitted: 'Man kann sicher von einer Krise des BE sprechen.'[19]

The government's response to this crisis indicates how much its concern about the GDR's international image had increased since the early 1950s, when it had no compunction about censoring Brecht's production of *Lukullus* and publicly criticizing his staging of *Die Mutter*. Having exploited the BE as a national status symbol since it was awarded first prize at the *Théâtre des Nations* festival in Paris (1960), the Culture Ministry and the Culture Department of the Central Committee were desperate to avoid a damaging scandal. For instance, Culture Minister Klaus Gysi warned his over-zealous colleagues against forcing Weigel's resignation, explaining: 'Folge wäre Skandal, dessen Folgen nicht abzusehen sind'; while Alexander Abusch had 'starke Bedenken, den 70. Geburtstag von H. Weigel mit politischem Krach zu verbinden'. The *Politbüro* member Kurt Hager summed up the worst-case scenario: 'Auf keinen Fall lassen wir das BE durch Brechts Witwe liquidieren.'[20]

Much to the authorities' relief, Weigel eventually agreed to restructure the BE, improve its long-term planning, and appoint a deputy manager, Ruth Berghaus, to lighten her administrative burden. In 1969–70 it was not yet apparent that Berghaus was even more committed to artistic innovation than Wekwerth, as she had directed only one production—*VietNam Diskurs*—at the BE. Moreover, in her role as the theatre's Party Secretary, she had steered a neutral course during Weigel's dispute with Wekwerth and thus seemed ideally suited to unite the different factions. As a result, the number of premières rose under the effective leadership of Berghaus and the *Rat der Intendanz*, a new advisory committee.[21] But as the dramaturge and critic Werner

[18] Uta Birnbaum, Werner Heinitz, Helmut Rabe, Georg Simmgen, Hilmar Thate, and Wekwerth left in 1968–9; Norbert Christian, Gisela May, Günter Naumann, and Renate Richter resigned in 1969–70. 'Vermerk über ein Gespräch mit den Mitgliedern des Berliner Ensembles … am 27. Oktober 1969', SAPMO-BArch DY 30 IV A 2/9.06/113; anon., 'Le Répertoire du Berliner Ensemble de 1949 à 1986', *Théâtre en Europe*, 12 (Oct. 1986), 70–1.

[19] 'One can certainly speak of a crisis at the BE.' Weigel to Martner, 7 Feb. 1970, in 'HW Allg. Briefw. 1970', BEA.

[20] 'It would lead to a scandal with unforeseeable repercussions'; 'strong reservations about linking the 70th birthday of H. Weigel with a political row'; 'under no circumstances will we let the BE be disbanded by Brecht's widow'. 'Ergänzendes Protokoll zur Beratung über die Berliner Theatersituation am 23.10.1969 beim Genossen Kurt Hager', SAPMO-BArch DY 30 IV A 2/2.024/30.

[21] Cf. Werner Hecht, 'Farewell to her Audience: Helene Weigel's Triumph and Final Exit', *Brecht Yearbook*, 25 (2000), 317–27 (320).

Hecht pointed out, the BE still lacked a long-term programme: 'Die seit 1968 herausgekommenen Inszenierungen sind in vieler Beziehung uneinheitlich, da die Regisseure nicht von einem gemeinsam erarbeiteten methodischen Prinzip ausgingen.'[22] His conclusion was endorsed by outsiders like the philosopher Wolfgang Harich, who argued: 'Die tiefste Ursache dieser Krise war und ist das Fehlen einer klaren Konzeption über die zentralen Aufgaben in der Zukunft, zunächst in den siebziger und achtziger Jahren.'[23] These comments suggest that the causes of the dispute between Weigel and Wekwerth had yet to be addressed.

The BE's decisive shift towards post-Brechtian theatre occurred only after Weigel's death in 1971, when Berghaus succeeded her as theatre manager. The most fundamental change involved her treatment of Brecht, whom she regarded as just one writer among many: 'Wir leben ja mit Brecht genau wie mit Schiller oder Lenz oder Büchner.'[24] By staging more contemporary plays, Berghaus hoped to gain fresh perspectives on Brecht's works and methods and thus to resist being intimidated by his status as a classic.[25] She argued that this was precisely the treatment that Brecht would have wanted and told her critics: 'Wir ehren ja nicht Brecht, indem wir ihm Denkmale setzen, sondern indem wir seine Wirkung in der sozialistischen Theaterkunst fördern', a view more famously espoused by Heiner Müller, the GDR's leading proponent of post-Brechtian theatre.[26] Yet Berghaus's professed commitment to Brecht was chiefly rhetorical: because the BE was still regarded as Brecht's theatre, she had to camouflage her experimentation in the conservative language of *Brechtpflege* (caring for Brecht). Furthermore, Brecht's methods were not even the major formative influence on her practice. Whereas Wekwerth had trained under Brecht, Berghaus

---

[22] 'The productions premièred since 1968 lack unity in many respects, since the directors did not forge and proceed from any common methodological principle.' 'Zur Analyse der letzten Spielzeiten', in 'BE (internes Mat.) 70er Jahre HAUS - GESCHICHTE', BEA.

[23] 'The most deep-seated cause of this crisis was and remains the lack of a clear concept about the central tasks for the future, starting with the seventies and eighties.' Wolfgang Harich to Kurt Hager, 14 May 1971, SAPMO-BArch DY 30 IV A 2/2.023/74.

[24] 'After all, we live with Brecht just as we live with Schiller or Lenz or Büchner.' 'Interview mit Ruth Berghaus und Felizitas [*sic*] Ritsch am 21.10.1976 im Kulturmagazin', in 'BE (internes Mat.)', BEA.

[25] Cf. 'Einschüchterung durch die Klassizität', *BFA*, xxiii. 316–18.

[26] 'We do not honour Brecht by erecting monuments to him, but by promoting his influence in Socialist theatre.' Berghaus, interview with Radio DDR, 4 Apr. 1973, in 'Berghaus Protokolle (Verwaltungs-Mat. 1971–3)', BEA; Heiner Müller, 'Brecht gebrauchen, ohne ihn zu kritisieren, ist Verrat', *Theater 1980*, Jahrbuch der Zeitschrift *Theater heute*, 134–6.

had studied choreography under Gret Palucca from 1947 to 1950 before directing operas at houses like the Deutsche Staatsoper. She was introduced to the BE only in 1964—by her husband, the composer Paul Dessau—when she first began to assist with theatrical productions.

The similarity between Berghaus's and Müller's views on Brecht was crucial, for Müller was a key member of Berghaus's team at the BE, which included some of the GDR's most innovative writers, dramaturges, designers, and directors. Besides Müller, there were the dramaturges Friedrich Dieckmann and Hans-Jochen Irmer; the poet, dramatist, and essayist Karl Mickel; the set designers Andreas Reinhardt and Einar Schleef; and Schleef's co-director B. K. Tragelehn—none of whom would have been content to work within a narrowly defined 'Brechtian' tradition. But the more conservative attitude towards *Brechtpflege* still had forceful advocates in Brecht's heirs, Barbara Brecht-Schall and her husband Ekkehard, and to a lesser degree in the director Peter Kupke and the dramaturge Wolfgang Pintzka. Differences within the company were aggravated when Müller and Schleef grew impatient at the slow pace of reform, so that by 1975 Berghaus faced criticism from both the conservatives and radicals in her team.[27]

4. REPERTOIRE

As its decision to stage *Die Mutter* suggests, the Schaubühne shared some of the BE's interests: indeed, Stein looked to the BE as a model of a politically committed theatre with a reputation for excellence. Furthermore, instead of simply imitating Brecht's models, as so many directors had done in the 1950s and 1960s, the Schaubühne—like the BE—applied his staging methods to different texts. For instance, they re-examined the classics from a historical-materialist perspective, locating works in their original contexts, and discovering points of contact with the present. In this respect, Stein's productions of *Peer Gynt* (1971) and *Prinz Friedrich von Homburg* (*Prince Frederick of Homburg*, 1972) stood in the same tradition as Brecht's staging of *Der Hofmeister* (*The Tutor*, 1950).[28] Both companies were also committed to contemporary

[27] Hans-Jochen Irmer, 'Ein Frühlings Erwachen im Berliner Ensemble: Über Einar Schleefs Anfänge als Regisseur', *Theater der Zeit*, Jan. 2002, 57–9 (57).

[28] e.g. Brecht *et al.*, *Theaterarbeit*, 68–120; Iden, 116–36, 150–8; Schaubühne am Halleschen Ufer, '*Peer Gynt*: Protokolle', in *Kreativität und Dialog: Theaterversuche der 70er Jahre in Westeuropa*, ed. Joachim Fiebach and Helmar Schramm (East Berlin: Henschel, 1983), 153–77.

drama: the Schaubühne premièred Handke's *Ritt über den Bodensee* (*Ride Across Lake Constance*, 1971), and the BE premièred Müller's *Zement* (*Cement*, 1973). Finally, the Schaubühne's practice of adapting texts for performance was partly inspired by the BE's dramaturgical work.

From 1970 to 1973, the Schaubühne's repertoire reflected the company's twin objectives: to explore its bourgeois identity and history and to investigate proletarian forces for change.[29] Thus, Stein's *Peer Gynt* examined the personal cost of the petit-bourgeois drive for social advancement, portraying Gynt as a 'kleinbürgerlicher Faust' ('petit-bourgeois Faust'), whereas productions of Enzensberger's *Verhör von Habana* (*Havana Inquiry*, 1971) and Schwiedrzik's *Märzstürme 1921* (*March Offensives*, 1972) depicted workers positively as historical agents.[30] But because these related interests were not communicated to the public at the outset, many observers mistakenly assumed that the Schaubühne would focus exclusively on proletarian drama. As a result, the company's repertoire doubly disappointed the far Left for, after 1973, it no longer included plays about workers.[31] In fact, this was precisely because the first three seasons had cast doubt on the demand for radical theatre in West Berlin and the strength of proletarian forces for change.

Although there was a clear rationale behind the Schaubühne's programme, Joachim Fiebach rightly argues that a certain eclecticism was apparent from the start.[32] This was only to be expected, given the contrasting interests and approaches of its directors and the fact that any member of the company could nominate plays. Indeed, at a planning meeting in April 1970, it was only after all the proposed plays had been listed that Stein and the dramaturge Dieter Sturm reiterated the need for a programmatic discussion, asking 'was, wozu und für wen würden wir in den kommenden zwei Spielzeiten arbeiten und vor allen Dingen warum?'.[33] Compromises had to be made, and Peymann's threatened

---

[29] '[Besprechung]', 10, in 'Protokolle', SA.   [30] Ibid. 4.

[31] e.g. Peter Rühmkorf criticized Stein 'der einmal aufbrach, die Gesellschaft zu bewegen, und dem unter der Hand ein Schlemmerlokal erwuchs' ('who once set out to change society and found himself presiding over a gourmet restaurant'). 'Gedanken aus der Dunkelkammer: Über das Entwickeln von Wirklichkeit auf dem Theater', *Literaturmagazin*, 1 (1973), 69–87 (70).

[32] Joachim Fiebach, ' "Das entscheidende [*sic*] für uns ... ist das Theater in Paradoxis": Zur Schaubühne am Halleschen Ufer von 1970 bis 1980', in *Theater seit den 60er Jahren: Grenzgänge der Neo-Avantgarde*, ed. Erika Fischer-Lichte, Friedemann Kreuder, and Isabel Pflug (Tübingen: Franke, 1998), 235–315.

[33] 'On what, for what purpose, and for whom will we work in the next two seasons, and above all why?' 'Protokoll Nr. 1 zur hausinternen Information über die Sitzung am 10. und 11. März 1970', in 'Protokolle', SA.

resignation prompted the company to agree, reluctantly, to stage *Ritt über den Bodensee*.[34] After the clarity of *Die Mutter*, Handke's depiction of the problems of apprehending reality and communicating at even the most basic level surprised those who, like the author and critic Peter Rühmkorf, had expected the Schaubühne to continue with far left-wing drama.

In East Berlin, the basic structure of the BE's repertoire had not changed since the 1950s, when Brecht had developed the company's distinct and popular profile.[35] First, and most importantly, there were his own plays, and by 1970 the Ensemble was focusing on such early and late works as *Im Dickicht der Städte* (*In the Jungle of the Cities*, 1971) and *Turandot* (1973), and inventing new stagings for such model productions as *Die Gewehre der Frau Carrar* (*Senora Carrar's Rifles*, 1971). Second, there were the classics, like Wedekind's *Frühlings Erwachen* (*Spring Awakening*, 1974); and third, there were contemporary Socialist dramas, such as Mickel's adaptation of Bek's *Wolokolamsker Chaussee* (*The Road to Volokolamsk*, 1972). A fourth component consisted of classic comedies with progressive politics, like Shaw's *Frau Warrens Beruf* (*Mrs Warren's Profession*, 1973), and further continuity was provided by the most popular long-running productions from Wekwerth's day, such as *Purpurstaub* (1966), and revivals of Brecht's models, like *Leben des Galilei* (1971). These revivals served as an important counterweight to Berghaus's experimentation by indulging those conservatives—and Western tourists—who expected the BE to preserve Brecht's legacy intact.

Within this overall structure, however, Berghaus initiated major shifts of focus, interpretation, and approach. Most importantly, she staged more experimental dramas and focused on contemporary problems facing individuals in the GDR. Thus, Mickel's version of Ferdinand de Roja's *Celestina* (1974) used the sixteenth-century text to explore how, in order to stabilize an oppressive regime, the Inquisition allows young people 'mit Spuren neuen Bewußtseins' ('with traces of a new consciousness') to go to their deaths.[36] This interpretation invited comparisons with the Stasi and the troops guarding the Berlin Wall, particularly since the play's young lover dies crossing the wall that

[34] Roland Koberg, *Claus Peymann: Aller Tage Abenteuer* (Berlin: Henschel, 1999), 123–5.
[35] This analysis is based on the table 'Le Répertoire du Berliner Ensemble', cf. n. 18.
[36] Ursula and Rudolf Heukenkamp, *Karl Mickel* (East Berlin: Volk & Wissen, 1985), 161.

separates him from his beloved. In *Zement*, Müller, Berghaus, and Reinhardt depicted the harsh struggle and personal cost of revolution, while in Strindberg's *Fräulein Julie* (*Miss Julie*, 1975) Tragelehn and Schleef abandoned the historical milieu and incorporated contemporary references to beat dance and lager.[37] In each case the directors abstracted the conflict from its historical context so that it might apply to the present. Because of their iconoclasm, *Zement*, *Die Mutter*, and *Fräulein Julie* caused the greatest controversies, amongst both theatre critics and the BE's own staff, not all of whom supported Berghaus's experimentation.

In the context of this artistic programme, *Die Mutter* offered Berghaus an opportunity to invent a new staging for one of Brecht's best-known models and provide an alternative to the standard GDR treatment of revolution. Her productions presented revolution 'nicht als Idylle, sondern als ständigen Kampf' ('not as an idyll, but as constant struggle'), an approach which would have been unthinkable in the Stalinist 1950s.[38] Back then, the Trotskyite doctrine of permanent revolution defied the official line that the GDR's revolution had been completed in 1949, but in the less doctrinaire 1970s *Die Mutter* could be used to press for the continuation of the revolutionary process. Thus, Berghaus reminded her colleagues: 'Man darf nicht vergessen, daß wir noch in Bewegung sind, wir haben doch das Ziel noch nicht erreicht. Es ist noch viel zu leisten.'[39] Yet restaging *Die Mutter* for this purpose was a provocative choice, not only because it was commonly regarded as a *Staatsfeststück* but also because Wlassowa had been Weigel's most famous role. Although Mickel and Müller backed Berghaus's project with alacrity, the conservative Pintzka feared that it would amount to sacrilege: 'Sollte man bei diesem Projekt nicht doch an die Nähe der Weigel denken und besser auf *Courage* gehen?'[40] This disagreement was an early indication that the finished production would exacerbate the BE's internal divisions concerning its relationship with Brecht's legacy.

[37] Neef, 83–7; Kreuzer and Schmidt, ii. 299–328.

[38] 'Protokoll zur Leitungssitzung am 14. Dezember 1973', 4, in 'Protokolle, Leitungssitzung 1973–76', BEA.

[39] 'People must not forget that we are still in progress, we have not yet reached our goal. A lot remains to be done.' 'Protokoll zur Leitungssitzung am 13. Juni 1974', 2, in 'Protokolle, Leitungssitzung 1973–76', BEA.

[40] 'Shouldn't we bear in mind how close this project is to Weigel and opt for *Courage* instead?' 'Protokoll der Regie- und Dramaturgiesitzung am 3.5.73', 4, in 'Protokolle 50er', BEA.

5. STAGING *DIE MUTTER*

5.1 The Production Concepts

Both production concepts illuminated new aspects of *Die Mutter*, show-ing the variety of interpretations and even genre definitions that are possible for the play. By approaching it as a *Lehrstück*, the Schaubühne hoped to explore the themes of solidarity, political organization, edu-cation, and agitation, and then to communicate its findings to the audience.[41] Such issues were not only relevant to its attempts to found a politically committed, democratic theatre but might also, it was hoped, provoke a re-assessment of the Left's fragmentation since 1968. In contrast, the BE presented *Die Mutter* as a tragedy, focusing on the themes of suffering and martyrdom. This was highly provocative, for it suggested disillusionment with the regime's rhetoric of success. By these means, both productions contributed towards a larger shift in political theatre, away from affirmation in the East and agitation in the West.

For the Schaubühne, the appeal of the *Lehrstück* lay in Brecht's emphasis on providing an educational experience for the practition-ers because the company's members all wanted to benefit personally from rehearsals. Thus, Stein explained to the press: 'Lehrstück heißt für diejenigen, die es machen, ein Lernprozess.'[42] Yet his approach ignored two significant aspects of Brecht's practice. First, where-as the Schaubühne's staging was a purely professional enterprise, some of Brecht's productions of the *Lehrstücke* had involved ama-teurs, including schoolchildren (*Der Jasager*) and workers' choirs (*Die Maßnahme*). Second, whilst the Schaubühne's spectators remained the passive consumers of a finished theatrical product, Brecht had expected the audiences of *Das Badener Lehrstück vom Einverständnis* and *Die Maßnahme* to adopt an active role, by singing or evaluating the pro-duction in questionnaires. Furthermore, the Schaubühne's lead actress and main authority on the *Lehrstück* was the leading German actress Therese Giehse, who had worked closely with Brecht only at the Berliner Ensemble in the late 1940s and early 1950s, by which time his practice had shifted substantially away from the *Lehrstück*. These differences

---

[41] 'Protokoll Nr. 6: Mitgliederversammlung in Zürich am 13., 14. und 15. Juni 1970', in 'Protokolle', 89–129 (123–4), SA.
[42] '*Lehrstück* means a learning process for those who stage it.' 'Protokoll Nr. 4 der Pressekonferenz vom 11. Mai 1970', in 'Protokolle', 61–79 (75), SA.

indicate how far Stein's approach was governed by his own, post-Brechtian priority of developing an alternative to *Intendantentheater*, rather than by any desire to imitate Brecht's practice faithfully.

The political context of 1970 prompted the Schaubühne to highlight the differences between the historical setting of *Die Mutter* and the present. After all, the anti-capitalist movement was far weaker in West Germany in 1970 than it had been in either Russia in 1917 or Germany in 1932, and the Schaubühne's predominantly bourgeois audience was unlikely to identify with Brecht's revolutionary workers. So instead of campaigning directly for revolution, the Schaubühne created a more neutral space in which to explore the play as a past Utopia. This approach reflected some of the actors' initial reactions to the text: Bruno Ganz had called it a fairy-tale, while Tilo Prückner had felt that some sections were simply too good to be true.[43] At the same time, by historicizing the action, the Schaubühne showed that workers once really had fought together for an alternative to the *status quo*. Thus, Stein's new approach actually corresponded to Brecht's theory of *Historisierung*, since it demonstrated that humans had behaved differently in the past and, by implication, could do so again in the future. But by focusing on the modest aim of reflecting on historical difference, the Schaubühne had already shifted significantly from the agitational theatre of 1968.

In contrast, at the BE Berghaus liberated *Die Mutter* entirely from the historical confines of Brecht's model. With Mickel's aid, she recast the play as a tragedy, focusing on the martyrdom of Smilgin and Pawel and treating the text almost as if it were a secular passion play for modern times. Indeed, Mickel's dramaturgical analysis drew attention to the biblical echoes in Wlassowa's stoning by the agricultural labourers and the butcher's denunciation of the strikebreakers, 'eine Fluch- und Schimpfrede biblischen Formats' ('a speech with curses and abuse in biblical proportions').[44] Similarly, in the sickbed scene, Berghaus reversed the image of Michelangelo's *Pietà* so that Wlassowa lay sick in the lap of a young worker, and in Scene 5 she created a tableau that has been compared with the Descent from the Cross.[45] Finally, she replaced the innocuous story and soft colours of the 1951 production

---

[43] 'Protokoll Nr. 6', in 'Protokolle', 125–6, SA.

[44] '1974 Konzeption', 7, 19, in 'Die Mutter', box file 67, BEA.

[45] Dieter Kranz, '*Die Mutter* im Berliner Ensemble', broadcast in 'Atelier und Bühne' on Berliner Rundfunk, 27 Oct. 1974, transcript in 'Die Mutter', box file 67, BEA; Christoph Müller, 'Die Mühen der Ebenen: Ein Report über die Theatersituation in der Hauptstadt der DDR', *Theater heute*, 15 (Dec. 1974), 16–28 (25).

with the harshness of the class struggle and the sacrifices made by its combatants.

The BE's new production was driven by a sense of urgency, which Berghaus conveyed by hinting at the terrible consequences of failure. She explained: 'Uns war bei der Vorarbeit wichtig der Satz: "Bedenkt, wenn ihr versagt." '[46] This crucial line occurs in the street corner scene, where workers ignore Wlassowa's warnings against the war:

> MUTTER   Jaa [*sic*], aber bedenkt, daß die ganze Welt (*schreiend, so daß die erschrockenen Arbeiter ihr den Mund zuhalten*) in einer ungeheuren Finsternis lebt, und ihr allein wart es bis jetzt, die noch für die Vernunft erreichbar waren. Bedenkt, wenn ihr versagt![47]

For Mickel, this was the lowest point in the play: even after the tragedy of Pawel's death, the 'Grabrede' had promised hope for the future via proletarian solidarity.[48] But Wlassowa's lines at the street corner show that without solidarity mankind is lost and can no longer be redeemed through reason. Berghaus considered this warning 'angesichts der Welt-lage für sehr wichtig und aktuell' ('very important and topical in view of the world situation'), almost certainly a reference to the Cold War arms race and risk of mutually assured destruction.[49]

5.2 Textual Changes

Even though Brecht's heirs had insisted that the company should remain faithful to the work and refrain from making any additions to the text, they raised no objections to the important new cuts and additions which the Schaubühne made to Brecht's text.[50] This may have been partly because some of the changes corresponded to those that Brecht had made in 1951, such as the new dates and the references to Bloody Sunday and the Moscow uprising.[51]

---

[46] 'The sentence "remember what will happen if you fail" was important in our preparations.' 'Interview mit Ruth Berghaus', in 'BE (internes Mat.)', BEA.

[47] 'Yes, but remember that the whole world (*screaming so that the startled workers cover up her mouth*) is living in monstrous darkness and that you were the only people up to now who could still be reached by reason. Remember what will happen if you fail!' *BFA*, iii. 317, 384.

[48] '1974 Konzeption', 24; *BFA*, iii. 310, 374–5.

[49] 'Interview mit Ruth Berghaus', in 'BE (internes Mat.)', BEA.

[50] Stefan Mahlke (ed.), *'Wir sind zu berühmt, um überall hinzugehen': Helene Weigel: Briefwechsel 1935–1971* (Berlin: Theater der Zeit, 2000), 232.

[51] Bertolt Brecht, 'Die Mutter', adapted by the Schaubühne am Halleschen Ufer, in *Die Mutter: Regiebuch der Schaubühnen-Inszenierung*, ed. Volker Canaris (Frankfurt/Main: Suhrkamp, 1971), 59, 66, 69, 73, 75–6, 81, 101.

The Schaubühne's most significant innovation was a narrative framework for the action. Since this consisted of five literary and historical texts, it was probably more immediately influenced by the documentary theatre of the 1960s than by Brecht, who had chiefly relied on songs, captions, and verse, or agitprop, which usually incorporated topical material. The texts included two extracts from Gorky's novel: a slightly abbreviated version of the opening chapter and the description of Wlassowa smuggling propaganda into the factory. The first extract described the play's social setting and showed how the oppressive factory dominated the lives of its workers whose personal relationships were poisoned by violence, hatred, and suspicion.[52] By emphasizing the monotony of this way of life and the ingrained resistance to change, this passage demonstrated the mental obstacles to social revolution. The second extract replaced Brecht's humorous episode between Wlassowa and the factory porter and transferred the emphasis from her comic wit and his laziness to the violence and unpleasantness of the guards, policemen, and spy, thus highlighting Wlassowa's achievement in outwitting several dangerous opponents. Furthermore, Gorky's use of interior monologue revealed Wlassowa's thoughts and feelings, thereby showing how the experience contributes to her conversion.[53]

The next two interpolated texts supplied factual material about historical developments in Russia. After Pawel's brief reunion with Wlassowa, a piece by Lenin on the 1905 Revolution described the strikes, workers' councils, peasant revolts, and Moscow uprising. Thanks to this historical overview, the subsequent report of Pawel's death in the Moscow uprising showed the intersection of the personal and the historical even more clearly than it had done in 1951.[54] The next extract, from the *Geschichte der kommunistischen Partei der Sowjetunion (Bolschewiki)— Kurzer Lehrgang (History of the Communist Party of the Soviet Union [Bolsheviks]—Short Course)*, described the years of repression after the 1905 defeat, the Mensheviks' expulsion from the Party in 1912, and the subsequent revival of the revolutionary movement.[55] Because this extract was delivered after the Bible scene, it bridged the historical gap between Pawel's death in the Moscow uprising and the outbreak of the First World War in the following scene, a gap that Brecht had created in 1951 by moving the date of Pawel's death from 1912 to 1905.

---

[52] Ibid. 9–12.   [53] Ibid. 25–6.   [54] Ibid. 79–80.   [55] Ibid. 87.

The fifth and final interpolated text was the second stanza of Brecht's 'Brief an das Arbeitertheater "Theatre Union" ', which Giehse delivered after the final scene, thus completing the narrative frame begun by the opening extract from Gorky's novel. This stanza presents Brecht's interpretation of the *Fabel*, giving the final word to the dramatist rather than his characters. In it Brecht reminds the audience that Wlassowa has both lost and won by the end of the play, suffering personal tragedy through her son's death, yet gaining a new family through the revolutionary movement:

Immer noch Mutter
Mehr noch Mutter jetzt, vieler Gefallenen Mutter
Kämpfender Mutter, Ungeborener Mutter.[56]

Brecht emphasizes Wlassowa's unceasing struggle by repeating 'Kampf' ('fight') ten times in various forms, moving from the initial familial conflict to the final struggle for state power. Then, towards the end of the stanza, a series of dialectical oppositions recalls the argumentative structure of the 'Lob der Dialektik', showing how Wlassowa lives by her own advice and refuses to admit defeat:

Verfolgte und Verfolgerin
Nichtgeduldete und Unduldsame. Geschlagene und Unerbittliche.[57]

By ending with Brecht's interpretation of the action instead of the triumph of the revolution, the Schaubühne re-opened the whole play for discussion.

The Schaubühne also made several changes to the sequence and thematic focus of Brecht's play. First, the presentation of Wlassowa's party card was postponed to the scene in the butcher's kitchen, where it replaced the 'Lob der Wlassowas'.[58] This change showed that Wlassowa had earned her party membership by saving the strike. Second, the Schaubühne shifted the thematic focus in the Bible scene from the fight against superstition to the struggle against rent increases, which it considered a more urgent priority. This was achieved partly by using a new announcement—'Pelagea agitiert gegen Mietwucher' ('Pelagea agitates against high rents')—and partly by cutting Wlassowa's anti-superstition

---

[56] 'Still Mother/Even more Mother now, Mother of many who have fallen/Mother of those fighting, Mother of those not yet born.' Ibid. 96.

[57] 'Persecuted and persecuting/Not tolerated and intolerant. Beaten and inexorable.' Ibid. 96.

[58] Ibid. 73.

speech and the niece so that the spectators would focus on the conflict between the landlady and her tenant.[59] Third, by reciting the 'Lob der Dialektik' after both the street corner scene and the final demonstration, the Schaubühne showed that the 1917 Revolution had been possible only because Communists like Wlassowa had refused to despair in the face of seemingly inevitable defeat.[60]

At the BE, the use of the characters' original names immediately distinguished Berghaus's staging from the 1951 model. Her script corresponded most closely to the 1938 edition, for it included the 'Lied vom Flicken und vom Rock' and observed the 1938 sequence, so that the street corner scene followed the sickbed scene.[61] It also contained fewer historical references than the model: Pawel, for example, did not die in the Moscow uprising but during his attempt to cross the Finnish border—probably an allusion to the contemporary consequences of trying to leave East Germany illegally.[62] In Berghaus's *Regiebuch*, one reference to Bloody Sunday survived in Scene 6d, but in the BE's live audio recording even this line was omitted.[63] Interestingly, the references in Scene 5 to the 'Internationale' and 'Brüder, zur Sonne, zur Freiheit' ('Brothers, to the sun, to freedom') are absent from the recording but not from Berghaus's *Regiebuch*, suggesting that they may have been cut at a late stage in rehearsals.[64] If this is so, then the cut may have been made because the songs had become part of the GDR's affirmative political culture and so had lost their revolutionary force.

Berghaus's most significant change was the introduction of an epic narrator who was positioned in one of the front boxes, away from the acting space. Dressed in a grey business suit, Ekkehard Schall symbolized 'das Gesetz der Revolution' ('the law of the Revolution') in contrast to 'das praktische Beispiel' ('the practical example') on stage. He also represented the modern revolutionary, showing that class struggle was still topical, only under different conditions.[65] Schall performed the songs as solos, except for the agitational 'Die Partei' and the closing 'Lob der Dialektik', and he also delivered the pieces that Brecht had intended Wlassowa to sing or recite, such as the 'Lob des Kommunismus', the 'Lob der dritten Sache', and the five lines of verse beginning 'Sehr aber erschrak er über das Elend' ('But he was greatly horrified at the

---

[59] Ibid. 82–6.   [60] Ibid. 92–5.
[61] 1974 Regiebuch, 13, 56, in 'Die Mutter', box file 67, BEA.
[62] Ibid. 48.   [63] Ibid. 32.   [64] Ibid. 20.
[65] 'Stichwort-Protokoll von der Diskussion über die Inszenierung *Mutter* am 29.10.74', in 'Die Mutter', file 67, BEA.

misery').⁶⁶ By almost completely severing the epic commentary from the action, these changes granted the audience a series of brief respites in which to reflect on the desperate struggles being played out on stage. They also created a prominent role for Schall, perhaps reflecting Berghaus's view that it was time that he played a major role again.⁶⁷ But far from establishing a meaningful link with the time and place of the performance, the narrator's presence and costume actually baffled spectators, from an anonymous pupil to the respected critics Günther Cwojdrak and Rainer Kerndl.⁶⁸ Similarly, after a post-show discussion on 29 October 1974, Thomas Günther reported that spectators were unclear only about the status and significance of the revolutionary.⁶⁹

Perhaps surprisingly, the BE's script retained subversive passages such as the 'Lied im Gefängnis' and 'Lob der Dialektik', both of which attack state oppression. For example, the 'Lied im Gefängnis' warns that persecution cannot permanently shore up a regime against the popular will:

PAWEL   Eines Tages, und das wird bald sein
               Werden sie sehen, daß ihnen alles nichts nützt.
               Und da können sie noch so laut 'Halt!' schrein
               Weil sie weder Tank noch Kanone mehr schützt!⁷⁰

The 'Lob der Dialektik' is equally subversive:

ALLE (*singen*) Das Sichere ist nicht sicher.
               So, wie es ist, bleibt es nicht.
               Wenn die Herrschenden gesprochen haben
               Werden die Beherrschten sprechen.⁷¹

An anecdote from Heiner Müller sheds some light on how these lines were perceived in the GDR. Once, when travelling by bus from Friedrichstraße to Alexanderplatz, he met one of the BE's technicians who was taking some heavy equipment to the theatre workshop. Since

⁶⁶ Audio recording.
⁶⁷ 'Protokoll zur Leitungssitzung am 14. Dezember 1973', 3, in 'Protokolle, Leitungssitzung 1973–76', BEA.
⁶⁸ 'Stichwort-Protokoll', box file 67, BEA; Günther Cwojdrak, 'Brecht, Baierl, Vallejo, Schatrow', *Die Weltbühne*, 29 (1974), 1386–7; Rainer Kerndl, 'Versuch einer anderen Sicht', *ND*, 23 Oct. 1974.
⁶⁹ '*Die Mutter* am 29.10.74', in 'Die Mutter', box file 67, BEA.
⁷⁰ 'PAWEL One day, and it will come soon/They will see that all this can no longer save them/And they can shout "Stop!" as loud as they want/Because neither tank nor canon will protect them any more!' 1974 Regiebuch, 36.
⁷¹ 'ALL (*sing*) What is certain is not certain/Things will not remain as they are/When the rulers have spoken/The ruled will speak out.' Ibid., final [unnumbered] page.

an FDJ (Free German Youth) congress was being held in the Palast der Republik (Palace of the Republic), the bus had to make a detour, and so the technician had further to walk:

Er war sauer und sagte: 'Scheiß FDJ. Heiner, kennste det? "Und eines Tages, und es wird bald sein, werden sie merken, daß ihnen das alles nichts mehr nützt." ' Ein Zitat aus der *Mutter* von Brecht. Da fiel mir auf, daß nie jemand in der DDR in der *Mutter*-Aufführung diesen Text verstanden hatte, wahrscheinlich wegen der schönen Musik von Eisler. Also die Rolle der Kunst als Verschleierung und Beruhigung, als Schlafpille.[72]

This anecdote indicates the latent and largely unexploited power of the material. Both Eisler's music and the play's reputation as a *Staatsfeststück* allowed potentially controversial lines to escape censorship—which meant that while observant spectators like the technician could perceive their contemporary relevance, less alert spectators would have been blinded to their subversive force.

Both the Schaubühne and the BE cut the copper collection scene. At the BE, the omission of this scene and the closing demonstration was vital to Berghaus's interpretation: if *Die Mutter* was to work as a tragedy, it needed to end with Wlassowa's failure to convince the workers at the street corner, rather than her success at the copper collection point and during the closing demonstration. Thus, in the new version, Wlassowa's final line was the powerful and desperate 'bedenkt, wenn ihr versagt!' ('remember what will happen if you fail!'), so that the 'Lob der Dialektik' became a challenge to resist even apparently inevitable defeat. In contrast, pragmatic concerns about the production's length probably explain why the Schaubühne omitted the copper collection scene since the new narrative framework had significantly increased the running time. It is also possible that the anti-war agitation in this scene, based on Brecht's experience of the First World War, simply seemed inadequate in a nuclear age, so that Stein and Berghaus preferred to let their audiences consider how to respond to Wlassowa's warning.

The importance of Berghaus's cuts became abundantly clear after the première, when she re-incorporated the final two scenes, following

---

[72] 'He was annoyed and said: "Sodding FDJ. Heiner, d'you remember? 'And one day, and it will come soon, they will notice that all this can no longer save them.' " A quotation from *The Mother* by Brecht. Then it struck me that no one in the GDR had ever understood this text in the production of *The Mother*, probably because of Eisler's beautiful music. It goes to show how art covers things up and placates people, how it acts as a sleeping pill.' Heiner Müller, *Krieg ohne Schlacht: Leben in zwei Diktaturen* (Cologne: Kiepenheuer & Witsch, 1992), 208.

criticisms from Brecht's heirs.[73] Several of her colleagues argued that this destroyed the logic of the production. For example, Peter Konwitschny wrote: 'Schlecht: der inkonsequente Schluß. Die Zuschauer sind schlauer als vermutet, sie merken den Bruch nach dem 12. Bild, das ursprünglich das letzte war. Der offene Schluß wird als historisch heute [*sic*] richtiger angesehen, auch setze er mehr bei *unseren* Zuschauern in Bewegung. Die Bilder 13 und 14: ein Grabgesang auf die Konzeption.'[74] Siegfried Meves endorsed these claims: 'Die Aufnahme der "Kupfersammelstelle" beschädigt meiner Ansicht nach die Konzeption der Inszenierung erheblich. Der neue Blick auf die Figur der Mutter wird damit in der Schlußphase zurückgenommen und die vorher angelegten Intentionen werden unverständlich. Gespräche mit Zuschauern nach der Vorstellung bestätigten mir das deutlich.'[75] These enforced changes demonstrate the very real constraints that, even in a Socialist state, private property rights imposed on Berghaus's artistic practice: even though she was the BE's manager, Brecht's heirs still had a say in stagings of his plays.

5.3 The Performance Aesthetic

Both productions reacted against the crafted aesthetic of Brecht's 1951 staging, but with contrasting results.[76] By 1970, Neher's 'picture-book' set and Hill's painted projections seemed to support the charge that the model had become a museum piece. For instance, Canaris argues: 'Nehers Bauten und Prospekte, in einer nuancierten Skala von Braun- und Grautönen gehalten, zeichneten liebevoll eine vergangene Welt, in der sich ein Geschehen von großer Bedeutung abspielt.'[77] Instead of this

[73] Ursula Ragwitz to Hager, 1 July 1975, SAPMO-BArch DY 30 IV B 2/9.06/69.

[74] 'Bad: the inconsistent ending. The spectators are cleverer than we thought, they notice the break after Scene 12, which was originally the last one. The open ending is seen as historically more correct today; it also has a greater impact on *our* spectators. Scenes 13 and 14: a death-knell to the production concept.' *Abendbericht*, 21 May 1975, in 'Abendberichte 1975', BEA.

[75] 'In my view, the addition of the "copper collection point" damages the production concept considerably. It removes the new perspective on the Mother's character in the final phase, making the intentions set out earlier incomprehensible. Conversations with spectators after the performance confirmed this to me clearly.' *Abendbericht*, 14 May 1975, in 'Abendberichte 1975', BEA.

[76] Sections 5.3 and 5.4 are based on the video of the Schaubühne production, AdK RKP, and photographs of the BE production, BEA and Stadtmuseum Berlin (henceforth SB).

[77] 'Neher's buildings and backdrops, kept in a nuanced scale of shades of brown and grey, lovingly showed a past world in which events of great importance are taking place.'

reverential approach, the Schaubühne opted for an austere, functional set that provided a neutral space for the action, whilst the BE created a visually shocking environment that symbolized the characters' desperate plight.[78]

In the West, Klaus Weiffenbach's set reflected the dual function of the Schaubühne's performance: a parable for the audience and a collective achievement by and for the practitioners. In order to emphasize the political import of the action, Weiffenbach framed it with two projections showing Lenin addressing the masses and writing at a desk. The ensemble also wanted to bring the spectators as close to the action as possible, in order to focus their concentration.[79] In addition to achieving this aim, Weiffenbach's arena stage also softened the emphasis on propaganda by opening the action on three sides so that the actors did not confront all the spectators directly.[80] To stress their solidarity and show that the performance was also being staged for their benefit, the rest of the actors watched the performance from the back wall.

In some respects this austere aesthetic marked a return to Brecht's 1932 approach. Props were kept to a minimum: for example, the tables and benches used for the strikers' blockade were subsequently re-arranged to form the butcher's kitchen. As in 1932, the costumes indicated characters' social standing rather than any historical or cultural difference from the time and place of the performance. Thus, Wlassowa's coat was too small, showing her poverty, whereas the police inspector's long coat and fur collar indicated that he was well paid for his efforts on the regime's behalf. Nevertheless, the Schaubühne's approach was actually even further removed from Naturalism than the 1932 aesthetic had been. This was partly because no walls were used for the interior scenes and partly because the Schaubühne departed from Brecht's realistic use of stage space, enlarging the distances in Wlassowa's home to make it easier for the audience to appreciate the significance of the blocking.

Volker Canaris, 'Bertolt Brechts *Mutter* an der Schaubühne—ein Lehrstück', in *Die Mutter: Regiebuch*, 103–18 (103).

[78] For photographs of the productions, see *Die Mutter: Regiebuch*; Neef, 88–93; Wolfgang Storch (ed.), *Material Brecht—Kontradiktionen 1968–1976: Erfahrungen bei der Arbeit mit den Stücken von Bertolt Brecht*, Ausstellung und Broschüre aus Anlaß des 4. Kongresses der Internationalen Brecht Gesellschaft (West Berlin: Albert Hentrich, 1976), 42–5, 49–51; Verband der Theaterschaffenden der DDR (ed.), *Regisseure der DDR inszenieren Brecht: Materialien und Fotos zu zwölf Inszenierungen* (East Berlin: Verband der Theaterschaffenden, 1977), 2.

[79] 'Protokoll Nr. 6', in 'Protokolle', 129, SA.   [80] Iden, 100.

The Schaubühne's clear, functional set contrasted sharply with the BE's provocative landscape. Andreas Reinhardt, who had designed the controversial sets for *Purpurstaub* and *Im Dickicht der Städte*, created 'ein Trümmerfeld als Spielfläche' ('an expanse of rubble as the performance space').[81] He set the stage at an angle and covered it with scrap metal, car parts, and rubble, with a plain white cyclorama at the back. This approach was clearly post-Brechtian, for Reinhardt had rejected Gestic Realism in favour of symbolism and substituted crude, industrial materials for Neher's handcrafted aesthetic. Indeed, his design was so anti-realistic that it forced a dissociation from Russia and its history and pointed instead to a bleak, fully industrial, perhaps even post-nuclear age. Before each performance the company highlighted the play's international relevance by scattering the stage with handwritten signs bearing the words 'Die Mutter' in at least six different languages. When the spectators filed in, the curtain was already open so that they could examine the startling set.[82] Reinhardt's design thus exercised a powerful *Verfremdungseffekt* by forcing the audience to see Brecht's familiar story from an entirely fresh perspective.

Aside from its deliberate shock value, Reinhardt's set also reinforced Berghaus's view that *Die Mutter* depicted extreme, desperate situations. As she explained: 'Wir wollen zeigen, unter welchen existentiellen Bedingungen der Klassenkampf zwischen Bourgeoisie und Proletariat stattfindet. Für die Proleten ist diese ihre alltägliche Umgebung die schlechteste aller Welten, und hier beginnt das Ringen um ein neues Weltsystem.'[83] Berghaus made some ingenious points through the set: for example, in the factory scene, some of the workers looked out from their hiding places in upturned crates, as if they were caged by the system. She also argued that the sheer physical and acoustic difficulty of negotiating the set would help the actors to achieve the kinds of *Gestus* appropriate to illegal activity: 'Eine Schräge aus Metall, das beim Betreten einen Ton von sich gibt, dadurch werden die Haltungen gefördert bei allen illegalen Sitzungen und bei den Lohnkämpfen, ohne daß man

---

[81] 'Während der Proben notiert', 1974 programme, BEA.

[82] Heinz Klunker, 'Ein Endspiel von Brecht', *Deutsches Allgemeines Sonntagsblatt* (Hamburg), 27 Oct. 1974.

[83] 'We want to show the existential conditions under which the class struggle between bourgeoisie and proletariat takes place. For the proletariat these, their daily surroundings, are the worst of all possible worlds and are where the struggle for a new world order begins.' 'Während der Proben notiert', 1974 programme, BEA.

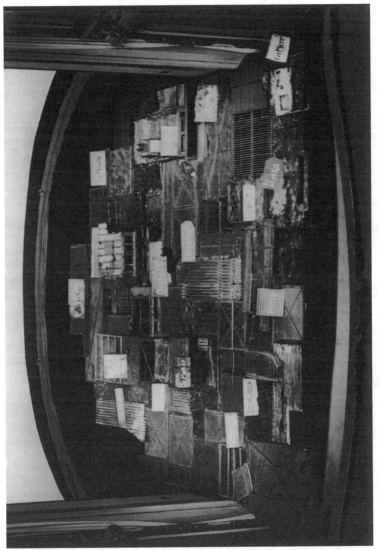

3. The Wlassowas of all countries at the BE, 1974 © Maria Steinfeldt.

Milieu geben muss.'[84] Even though the lead actress, Felicitas Ritsch, found the set highly provocative, she acknowledged that it helped her to do her job.[85] These points demonstrate that the set made an important, independent contribution to Berghaus's staging, like the designs used for Brecht's productions. Yet this fact alone does not qualify Reinhardt's design as 'Brechtian': after all, the same principle had governed the practice of directors like Leopold Jessner, even before Brecht's first stagings.

The Schaubühne and the BE devised different ways of representing the social distance between Wlassowa's working-class surroundings and the teacher's petit-bourgeois home. Like Brecht, the Schaubühne used different props and furnishings to depict the new social environment, and because the company's use of props had been minimal in the earlier scenes, their very presence also marked a shift in genre, supporting Stein's argument that the teacher's scenes were 'richtige Genre-Szenen ... (wie bei Hauptmann)' ('real genre scenes ... like in Hauptmann').[86] So here the furnishings included a screen, a portrait of the Tsar, carved wooden chairs with upholstered seats, a table with a lace cloth, and a rug. To illustrate the teacher's change in consciousness, the screen was removed at the same time as the portrait, restoring the openness and transparency of the earlier scenes.[87] In contrast, the BE draped the whole stage in transparent plastic sheeting so that the previous environment remained visible. This symbolic solution demonstrated two additional points: first, that the same problems and instability persisted beneath the trappings of petit-bourgeois society, and second, that Wlassowa's struggle had lost none of its desperate urgency—whereas the Schaubühne's production suggested that she had found a more comfortable environment. Reinhardt's technique, which may have been inspired by the experiments of visual and environmental artists like Christo, was criticized by aesthetically conservative reviewers: for example, Werner Pfelling argued in *Junge Welt* that the plastic sheeting was 'modernistisch-verspielt' ('modernistic and fanciful'), code in the GDR for negative criticism.[88]

---

[84] 'A metal slope which makes a sound when trodden on; this facilitates the actors' physical attitudes throughout the illegal meetings and wage struggles, without us having to add milieu.' 'Protokoll zur Leitungssitzung am 13. Juni 1974', 1, in 'Protokolle, Leitungssitzung 1973–76', BEA.

[85] Unedited transcript of interview with Berghaus and Ritsch, 1976, in 'Berghaus Protokolle 2', BEA.

[86] 'Protokoll der 3. Probenkritik', 5, in 'Protokolle', SA.   [87] Ibid. 6.

[88] Werner Pfelling, 'Ein Bühnenbild bestimmt den Spielverlauf', *Junge Welt* (East Berlin), 25 Oct. 1974; Rolf-Dieter Eichler, 'Die andere *Mutter*—die anderen Mütter', *National-Zeitung* (East Berlin), 22 Oct. 1974.

5.4 Acting Methods

In these productions, Stein and Berghaus moved beyond Brecht's practice by selectively incorporating and developing his techniques on their own terms. Even though Stein had declared his intention of adhering to Brecht's staging methods, he actually interpreted the *Lehrstück* from the perspective of 1970. And whilst Stein continued to prioritize Brecht's text, Berghaus used other performance elements to complement and challenge it far more, generating a wider range of meanings. Indeed, a major reason why her theatrical stagings encountered such controversy was that they were taken as a rejection of *Sprechtheater* (spoken theatre), which had been perceived as being under threat ever since the first decades of the twentieth century, when it was challenged by the historic avant-gardes.[89]

In order to show that the production was partly for the benefit of the practitioners, Stein, Schwiedrzik, and Steckel increased the prominence of the actor/character split. At the start of the performance, the actors filed in and sat down in a line at the back of the stage, thus closing off the fourth side of the acting space as if the play were being performed in the round. When they were needed on stage, they simply stepped forward so that the seam between the demonstration and the act of demonstrating was clearly visible. Similarly, when Wlassowa left the acting space, ostensibly to fetch some cloth to muffle the sound of the printing press, Giehse just sat down at the back of the stage, in full view of the audience. The actors also foregrounded the actor/character split by delivering the narrative elements out of character. For example, by putting on her glasses to read aloud from Gorky's novel, Giehse emphasized the difference between herself, the literate actress, and Wlassowa, the illiterate character. By reading such narrative sections aloud, instead of reciting them from memory, the actors also showed that they were presenting the opinions of their authors, Gorky, Lenin, and Brecht. Although these techniques followed on from Brecht's theories, they went far beyond his stage practice.

Like Brecht, Stein paid close attention to the *Fabel* and elucidated social relationships through the blocking. In the factory scene, for example, the blocking showed not only the workers' defection from Karpow to the revolutionaries, but also the contrast between Karpow's

---

[89] e.g. in his letter to Hager of 14 May 1971, Harich warned that *Sprechtheater* was under threat at the BE because its directors prioritized set design over dialogue.

hierarchichal relationship with the workforce and the revolutionaries' egalitarian one with their peers. Thus, although Karpow stood on a chair and spoke down to the workers, they soon drifted away and regrouped in a tight circle around Iwan, who was standing on their level. Like Brecht, Stein also stripped away details that were irrelevant to the plot—an approach which, according to the rehearsal minutes, conflicted with the actors' instinctive practice: 'Die Spieler der Zelle beschreiben noch zu sehr emotionale Zusammenhänge, dadurch entstehen nicht notwendige Füllsel. Besser ist, die Szene 2 anzugehen, indem man fragt, was sie grundsätzlich erzähle, wobei Füllsel wegfallen könnten.'[90] Nevertheless, Stein's efforts eventually paid off, and Elisabeth Hauptmann, who had seen a finished performance, reported to Helene Weigel: 'Die Aufführung ist interessant und erzählt die Fabel sehr deutlich und unterhaltsam, trotz Kürzungen und eingeschobenen Lenintexten.'[91] Indeed, Hauptmann's verdict may even explain why Weigel did not protest at the Schaubühne's textual changes.

Again like Brecht, the Schaubühne used concrete detail to convey information about characters' social circumstances. But whereas Brecht had vested such detail in both the acting and the props, the Schaubühne vested it solely in the acting. In the butcher's scene, for instance, Giehse showed how much Wlassowa's earlier, principled refusal to eat food cooked for strikebreakers had cost her. She held the plate close to her mouth, shortening the distance that the food had to travel, and savoured every hungry mouthful. After scraping her plate, Giehse tipped it vertically to catch the last drops in her spoon before licking both sides of the spoon clean. Indeed, Canaris argues that Giehse's entire performance was a montage of socially concrete detail: 'Die Giehse setzt die Wlassowa aus vielen Details zusammen, sie lädt zur emotionalen Identifikation ein, um zur Übernahme der politischen Praxis zu verlocken.'[92] Although his first claim holds true, the reliance on emotional identification actually corresponded more to Weigel's approach in 1951, when Brecht tried to entice spectators

[90] 'The actors playing the revolutionaries are still describing emotional links too much, producing unnecessary padding. It is better to approach Scene 2 by asking what basic story it tells and thus allowing the padding to fall away.' 'Protokoll der 1. Probenkritik zur Inszenierung von DIE MUTTER', in 'Protokolle', SA.

[91] 'The production is interesting and tells the *Fabel* in a very clear and entertaining manner, despite the abbreviations and forcible addition of texts by Lenin.' Hauptmann to Weigel, 9 Dec. 1970, in Mahlke, 242–3 (242).

[92] 'Giehse pieces Wlassowa together from many details; she invites emotional identification in order to entice spectators into adopting her political practice.' Canaris, 104.

into forgetting their political prejudices. In contrast, by combining identification with critical distance, the Schaubühne encouraged its audience to reflect on the political convictions of both the character and the actress.

At the BE, Berghaus developed Brecht's use of ideologically and socially coded *Gestus* in a controversial new direction. Influenced by her choreographic training and operatic work, Berghaus stylized each *Gestus* far more than Brecht had done in 1932 or 1951, so that it became clearly anti-naturalistic. The resulting series of tableaux expressed far stronger emotions than Brecht's stagings, showing the workers' desperate struggle for survival. Indeed, several reviewers, including Rainer Kerndl, Heinz Klunker, and Dieter Kranz, commented on the stylistic similarities between these tableaux and the art of Käthe Kollwitz, Ernst Barlach, and Fritz Cremer.[93] This was because Berghaus, like these three artists, depicted archetypal images of social misery. These images were startlingly effective on stage, partly because they fitted the stark, anti-naturalistic set and partly because they derived fresh power from the new theatrical context.

This heightened use of *Gestus* corresponded to Berghaus's increased emphasis on the non-textual aspects of theatre. Whether producing opera or drama, she consistently treated all the elements of performance as independent, including the blocking, gesture, lighting, and sound, so that her stagings were more polyphonic and contradictory than Brecht's own. Indeed, Mickel saw 'das konsequente Arbeiten an synchronen Vorgängen mit verschiedenen Aussagemitteln' as the defining principle of her work.[94] This practice was a logical extension not just of Brecht's theory of the separation of the elements, but also of Palucca's approach towards choreography. As Katja Erdmann-Rajski explains, Palucca brought out the difference and independence of music, movement, and gesture, exploiting the tension of the contrasts even between different parts of one dancer's body.[95] The parallels between Palucca's practice and Brecht's theories suggest that Berghaus was responding to

[93] Kerndl, 'Versuch einer anderen Sicht', *ND*, 23 Oct. 1974; Klunker, 'Ein Endspiel', *Deutsches Allgemeines Sonntagsblatt* (Hamburg), 27 Oct. 1974; Kranz, '*Die Mutter* im Berliner Ensemble', box file 67, BEA; Müller, 'Die Mühen der Ebenen', *Theater heute*, 15 (Dec. 1974), 25.

[94] 'Working systematically on synchronous processes with different means of expression.' Quoted in Neef, 91.

[95] Katja Erdmann-Rajski, *Gret Palucca: Tanz und Tanzerfahrung in Deutschland im 20. Jahrhundert: Weimarer Republik, Nationalsozialismus, Deutsche Demokratische Republik* (Hildesheim: Georg Olms, 2000), 184, 206, 323.

the broader cultural context in which epic theatre had evolved, and not exclusively or even primarily to Brecht's practice.

5.4.1 Scenes 5 and 7

Now that I have identified the main distinguishing features of Stein's and Berghaus's theatrical practice, I shall examine how their stagings of Scenes 5 and 7 helped to convey their different interpretations of *Die Mutter*. These scenes are just two examples of how their methods worked at the micro-level and how they departed from Brecht's model.

In the 1951 version of Scene 5, the revolutionaries stood in front of a painted projection of a street. Smilgin remained entirely still and silent during the past-tense report so that the section in which he delivered his lines in the present tense clearly functioned as a flashback. When the shot was fired, he fell to one knee before keeling over.[96] The Schaubühne's version differed from this in three key respects. First, the actors came on one by one during the scene, thus showing the process by which solidarity was achieved. Second, by the end there was a long line of twenty workers instead of just the party cell, Wlassowa, and Smilgin. Thus, the absence of any numerical difference between the two demonstrations implied that historical circumstances allowed the revolutionaries to succeed in 1917 where they had failed in 1905 and, by extension, in 1968. Third, the Schaubühne presented the entire scene as a re-enactment, not a flashback, in accordance with their treatment of the play as a *Lehrstück*. So instead of collapsing when he was shot, the actor playing Smilgin simply laid down the flag and stood aside, leaving the action like the pilot in Brecht's *Badener Lehrstück vom Einverständnis*.[97]

In contrast, Berghaus's presentation of Scene 5 focused on Smilgin's martyrdom and his comrades' grief, thus advancing her interpretation of the play as a tragedy. The scene opened with a gestic tableau in which the revolutionaries held Smilgin aloft, mourning his loss—an image reminiscent of both the Descent from the Cross and Cremer's memorial sculptures at Buchenwald and Ravensbrück.[98] Like Cremer, Berghaus presented the revolutionaries as a group but individualized their expressions of grief, in order to show that they retained their individuality within the collective. The revolutionaries set Smilgin down for the flashback, whereupon he walked off the stage, leaving a gap in

---

[96] *Die Mutter*, dir. Manfred Wekwerth, DEFA, 1958.   [97] *BFA*, iii. 45.

[98] Cf. Eichler, 'Die andere *Mutter*', *National-Zeitung* (East Berlin), 22 Oct. 1974.

their ranks that emphasized their loss and his sacrifice.[99] So whereas Stein presented the individual as replaceable, Berghaus highlighted the individual's importance for the group. Furthermore, the anguish of Berghaus's version contrasted sharply with the sobriety of Stein's staging and the gentle emotion of Brecht's model.

The two versions of Scene 7 show how the Schaubühne incorporated selected aspects of the model and how Berghaus's separation of the elements worked in practice. At the Schaubühne, Wlassowa and Pawel faced each other along the horizontal axis, across a free-standing barrier that indicated rather than represented the prison setting. Like Brecht, the Schaubühne presented the dual conversation realistically: questions like 'hilfst du im Haushalt, Mutter?' ('are you helping with the housework, Mother?') made the guard lose interest and wander off so that the secret information could be exchanged.

In contrast, Berghaus opted for an entirely anti-naturalistic solution that revealed far more than the earlier, realistic presentations. Her new approach was evident from the very beginning of the scene because the three characters were positioned along the vertical axis, with Pawel upstage facing the audience, the guard in the middle facing Pawel, and Wlassowa downstage with her back to the audience. Hans-Joachim Frank, who played Pawel, used his pronunciation and delivery to communicate their own independent message. Thus Dieter Kranz commented: 'Bei seinen ersten gequetschten Worten ahnt man sein verschwollenes Gesicht, seine eingeschlagenen Zähne. Er schluchzt fast und reißt sich wieder zusammen.'[100] Lighting changes marked the shifts between the two levels of dialogue, so that the inconsequential family conversation took place in full light, whereas the illegal information was exchanged under cover of darkness. Moreover, Frank's and Ritsch's delivery reversed the usual associations of light (positive) and darkness (negative), as Sigrid Neef explained: 'Im Dunkeln sprechen sie normal, können sich verständigen, wird es hell, müssen sie ihre politischen Geheimnisse verbergen, Sprache reißt, die Vokale werden langgezogen.'[101] The difference between the two modes of delivery showed that Wlassowa and Pawel could communicate naturally only through

---

[99] Kranz, '*Die Mutter* im Berliner Ensemble', box file 67, BEA.

[100] 'On hearing his first distorted words, you imagine his swollen face, his smashed teeth. He almost sobs and pulls himself together again.' Ibid.

[101] 'In the dark they speak normally, can make themselves understood; when it becomes light, they have to hide their political secrets: language tears, the vowels are stretched out.' Neef, 93.

4. Martyrdom and grief at the BE, 1974 © Maria Steinfeldt. Felicitas Ritsch as Wlassowa, far left.

5. Scene 7 at the Schaubühne, 1970 © Harry Croner. Therese Giehse as Wlassowa, far left.

6. Scene 7 at the BE, 1974 © Maria Steinfeldt. Hans-Joachim Frank as Pawel, left, and Felicitas Ritsch as Wlassowa, right.

their revolutionary work, as the 'Lob der dritten Sache' subsequently suggests.[102] Moreover, in combination with the contrast between light and darkness, the actors' delivery suggested that oppression had so deformed relationships in the public sphere that truth and justice survived only in illegal revolutionary activity. By these means, Berghaus's anti-naturalistic, multi-layered approach invoked disturbing parallels with the repressive practices of the modern police state.

5.5 Publicity and Audiences

The publicity for the Schaubühne and BE productions was closely geared towards their intended audiences. Most of the Schaubühne's publicity appealed to politically like-minded spectators: left-wing intellectuals and students. Since the company wanted to attract workers but knew that West Berlin was hardly a centre of heavy industry, it also targeted apprentices. In contrast, the BE aimed some of its publicity at young spectators because *Die Mutter* was on the GDR school syllabus. Both theatres could also rely on attracting a wider theatre-going audience, for Berghaus's innovations had revived interest in the BE and favourable reports of the Schaubühne's experiment in *Mitbestimmung*, the attempt to replace hierarchical management principles with collective decision making, had featured prominently in even the right-wing Springer press.[103]

The Schaubühne's commitment to *Mitbestimmung* and its decision to open with a Communist play generated the false expectation that it would campaign aggressively for revolution. Whilst the programme and the poster continued the documentary thrust of the script by including historical texts, the fact that they were by Lenin, Clara Zetkin, and Mao Tse-tung did little to dispel public expectations, particularly because the programme also included an essay in which the economist Elmar Altvater drew parallels between the situations in 1905, 1932, and 1970.[104] At the same time, the programme included so much of the Schaubühne's preparatory political and historical research that its sheer length—twenty-four pages of small print—and theoretical nature were overwhelming. For some spectators, this impression may have been strengthened by the monochrome, newspaper

[102] 1974 Regiebuch, 48.
[103] Arnim Borski, 'Die Praxis hat begonnen: Peter Steins Truppe bei der Arbeit', *BZ* (West Berlin), 18 Oct. 1970.
[104] 1970 programme, Landesarchiv Berlin, Rep. 129, Acc. 4465, Nr. 593.

format of both the programme and the poster. Consequently, the company's well-intentioned attempt to open up its internal learning process to the spectators seems to have met with little success. Indeed, Wessowtschikow's lines 'Könnt ihr eure Zeitungen nicht etwas unterhaltender schreiben? Das liest doch niemand' elicited the loudest laughs in the filmed performance.[105] Owing to the partial disparity between the Schaubühne's production and publicity, it was easy for middle-class reviewers to praise the performance while dismissing its contemporary ideological relevance.

This partial disparity testified to deeper internal differences regarding the Schaubühne's function and priorities. For example, although Stein and Peymann were sceptical about the efficacy of political theatre, the actor Michael König advocated a more agitational stance.[106] These differences were aggravated by the fact that the Schaubühne was attempting to serve two different audiences: workers and middle-class left-wingers. Thus, although a leaflet for apprentices made a strong case for the play's contemporary relevance, the actual production located agitation firmly in the past. Furthermore, it soon became clear that the apprentices were not particularly interested in the play, a problem that a faster pace, the omission of the interpolated texts, and the reduction of the play to the first five scenes all failed to solve.[107] This disappointing response prompted the Schaubühne to stage plays separately for each of its target audiences in future and to mount agitational productions in workers' clubs in the 1971–3 seasons.[108] But when even this approach failed to arouse significant interest, the company reluctantly concluded that there was insufficient demand for left-wing workers' theatre in West Berlin. Thus, the production of *Die Mutter* accelerated the Schaubühne's reassessment of political theatre after the failure of the 1968 protests which had, after all, been dominated by middle-class students.

Every aspect of the BE's publicity presented Berghaus's production as topical and fresh. On Karl-Heinz Drescher's poster, the red and blue type stood out against a white background, invoking the tricolour and hence the topos of revolution, while the larger font size drew attention to the word 'Neuinszenierung' ('new production'). A succinct quotation from

---

[105] 'Can't you make your newspapers a bit more entertaining? No one reads them.'
[106] 'Papier von Michael König, 14.9[.1970]', in 'Protokolle', SA.
[107] 'Protokoll Nr. 22 (abschließende Diskussion der *Mutter* Produktion am 14.10.1970)', in 'Protokolle', 297–304 (304), SA; Rolf Michaelis, 'Der Schaubühne anderes Gesicht', *Theater heute Sonderheft*, 14 (1973), 42–7 (43).
[108] Michaelis, 43.

Mickel's production concept indicated the play's parabolic function and the company's desire to provoke reflection: 'Das Verhalten der Mutter und ihrer Genossen ist Modellverhalten: Warum, unter welchen Umständen und wie müssen Menschen zu kämpfen beginnen?'[109] In the programme, another extract from Mickel's production concept explained the company's interpretation, and an insert depicted part of a frieze by the Greek sculptor Phidias, showing a mother holding her dying son. Whilst this image fitted the tragic thrust of the production and the archetypal tableaux on stage, it none the less risked implying that *Die Mutter* depicted the universal, timeless suffering that both Brecht and Berghaus opposed.

The publicity for this production also suggests that the focus of the BE's outreach work had shifted away from factory workers and towards school pupils. One dramaturge, Jörg Mihan, was specifically responsible for liaising with local schools and produced a pamphlet especially for pupils, containing photographs, the *Fabel* from Brecht's 'Brief an das Arbeitertheater "Theatre Union"', and a short reading list.[110] He invited pupils to attend rehearsals, canvassed their opinions, and adopted their suggestion that his leaflet should include an assessment of the play by a pupil by commissioning a brief report from Heike Bernau, a Year 12 pupil from the Bertolt-Brecht-Oberschule in Bad Freienwalde.[111] The leaflet also featured an interview with the BE's youngest actor, 22-year-old Hans-Joachim Frank, who highlighted the play's contemporary relevance to the situation in Chile after Pinochet's *coup* against the Allende Government in 1973.

The BE's publicity and outreach work attracted many young spectators, and the theatre's records show that at least thirteen of the nineteen performances were well attended, while four were even sold out.[112] On two occasions, rowdy teenagers disrupted the performance, but otherwise spectators followed it with interest and applauded enthusiastically at the end. Nevertheless, audiences often took time to adjust to Berghaus's aesthetic approach: for example, on 23 October 1974 Peter Konwitschny reported: 'Zunächst sprang das Publikum nicht an, aber zum Schluß hin gab es immer mehr Reaktionen und Applaus, der Schlußbeifall war

---

[109] 'The behaviour of the Mother and her comrades is model behaviour: why, under what conditions, and how must people begin to fight?' For the poster, see Dieckmann and Drescher, 133.

[110] In 'Die Mutter', box file 67, BEA.

[111] 'Einführungsblatt *Mutter* für Schulen', in grey folder, box file 67, BEA.

[112] 'Abendberichte 1975', BEA.

stärker als bei der Premiere.'[113] Indeed, his comments suggest that after the initial shock, ordinary theatre-goers responded more positively to the production than the first-night guests, who would have included press critics and cultural politicians. Even so, the relatively low total of performances indicates that the majority of the BE's spectators still preferred the entertainment of long-running comedies like *Purpurstaub* to Berghaus's aesthetically and politically challenging approach.

6. CULTURAL POLITICS IN EAST AND WEST

Although both productions deliberately courted controversy, their political reception actually deviated from the pattern of the 1950s and early 1960s, when Communist productions were usually boycotted in West Germany and aesthetically or politically challenging stagings were banned in the GDR. At the Schaubühne, the anticipated scandal was actually sparked off two months after the première, when tendentious extracts from the company's internal minutes were leaked to the CDU and the right-wing press. On 10 December the CDU cited this evidence before the West Berlin Senate, argued that the Schaubühne had contravened the Constitution by spreading Communist propaganda, and called for the company's generous subsidy to be blocked.[114] Besides its desire to prevent a left-wing theatre from receiving public funds, the CDU was also keen to score political points against the SPD, which had granted the subsidy, in the run-up to the Senate elections of March 1971. Even so, it was actually supported by sections of the local SPD, which viewed the campaign as an opportunity to register their opposition to Chancellor Brandt's *Ostpolitik*, the policy of opening negotiations with the Eastern bloc. The reactions of the national press confirm the impression that the campaign derived largely from local political machinations and West Berlin's unique geo-political position. For instance, in the left-liberal *Frankfurter Rundschau*, Werner Dolph commented: 'Die CDU-Fraktion, in Berlin, geht durch alle Parteien. Ihren Schwerpunkt hat sie in Berlins SPD.'[115]

---

[113] 'At first the audience did not react, but towards the end the reactions and applause mounted, the final applause was stronger than at the première.' *Abendbericht*, 23 Oct. 1974, in 'Abendberichte 1975', BEA.

[114] Cf. 'Thema der Vollversammlung', in 'Protokolle 2', SA.

[115] 'The CDU parliamentary party, in Berlin, cuts across all parties. Its centre of gravity lies in Berlin's SPD.' Werner Dolph, 'Die versuchte Ermordung der "Schaubühne"', *Frankfurter Rundschau*, 20 Jan. 1971.

The relative ease with which Stein averted this threat indicates how far, in the rest of the FRG, attitudes towards far left-wing theatre had changed since the popular Brecht boycott of the 1950s and early 1960s. On 14 December Stein skilfully won the support of the national media at a press conference when he attributed the CDU's charges to electioneering tactics and traditional prejudice against political theatre.[116] Jürgen Schitthelm, one of the Schaubühne's five managers, suggested that the CDU had acted in league with West Berlin's private theatres, which had a vested interest in seeing the Schaubühne lose its subsidy.[117] Stein then corrected the impression generated by the publicity for *Die Mutter* by explaining that the company's political views were heterogeneous, that none of the members had been forced to attend the political seminars, and that contacts with the SEW and FDJ were purely for marketing purposes. But he also raised the stakes by warning that unless public payments recommenced, two-thirds of the Schaubühne's staff would have to be dismissed and the entire theatre would close.[118] This tactic succeeded: after the press conference, sixteen of West Germany's leading theatre critics signed an open letter testifying to the Schaubühne's artistic significance. Meanwhile, the media rounded on West Berlin's CDU, accusing it of electoral opportunism and attempted censorship.[119] When the Senate's investigative committee eventually ruled in favour of the Schaubühne, the CDU quietly let the matter rest.[120]

The East German reception of Berghaus's staging also deviated partly from the pattern of the 1950s and 1960s, for although the production was politically and aesthetically subversive, it did not encounter any direct opposition from cultural politicians. Instead, the most forceful opposition came from Brecht's heirs, who never again permitted Berghaus to stage any of Brecht's plays. Just as Weigel had opposed Wekwerth's more experimental stagings, so Barbara

[116] 'Erklärung der Schaubühne zur Pressekonferenz vom 14. Dez. 1970', in 'Protokolle 2', SA.

[117] 'Protokoll No. 48 (Pressekonferenz vom 14.12.1970)', in 'Protokolle 2', 413–23 (413), SA.

[118] Ibid. 415–16, 418–19.

[119] Ivan Nagel, *Streitschriften: Politik Kulturpolitik Theaterpolitik 1957–2001* (Berlin: Siedler, 2001), 58–61. For more press reports see e.g. Peter Daniel, 'CDU-Schlag gegen die Demokratie: Theater im Würgegriff', *Die Tat* (Frankfurt/Main), 19 Dec. 1970; I[ngeborg] K[eller], 'Zensur auf Abwegen', *Telegraf* (West Berlin), 11 Dec. 1970; Rudolf Lorenzen, 'Theater in Spreewinkel: Die Berliner "Schaubühne am Halleschen Ufer" in Schwierigkeiten', *Die Weltwoche* (Zurich), 24 Dec. 1970.

[120] Nagel, 61.

Brecht-Schall believed that Berghaus had 'bei der *Mutter* politisch und künstlerisch versagt' ('failed politically and artistically with *The Mother*') and that '[man konnte ihr] Brecht nicht anvertrauen' ('[she could] not be trusted with Brecht').[121] Here, *anvertrauen* (trust) indicates how far the conservative concept of *Brechtpflege* still dominated the heirs' mentality. Given the centrality of Brecht's plays to the BE's repertoire, Brecht-Schall's decision undermined both Berghaus's position as manager and her innovative programme. As the conflict between Berghaus and Brecht's heirs split the theatre according to its members' artistic views and personal allegiances, both parties grew increasingly frustrated, and news of the BE's second crisis reached Western newspapers.[122]

Like the 1967–9 crisis, the conflict between Berghaus and Brecht's heirs posed problems for the regime because of the BE's role as a national status symbol. These difficulties were aggravated by the GDR's anniversary culture, which the SED had fostered as a means of enhancing the young state's historical legitimacy and cultural traditions. After the celebrations of Brecht's seventieth and seventy-fifth birthdays in February 1968 and 1973, it would have caused considerable embarrassment if the BE had failed to mark his eightieth birthday in similar fashion, with major new productions of his plays. Consequently, the Culture Ministry and Central Committee were anxious to resolve the crisis well before 1978,[123] and by December 1976 had decided to confront Brecht's heirs. Culture Minister Hoffmann explained: 'Wir setzen, wenn wir nicht handeln, Signale für heute lebende Autoren. Sollten wir den Weg nicht gehen, wird der Ärger mit einer nicht unbeträchtlichen Gruppe namhafter Theaterleute größer sein, als der mit Barbara Schall.'[124] This decisive shift from the earlier

---

[121] 'Gedächtnis-Protokoll eines Gespräches zwischen dem Minister für Kultur (Hoffmann) und Frau Barbara Schall am 29.9.1976', SAPMO-BArch DY 30 IV B 2/2.024/102.

[122] Cf. 'Berghaus Protokolle (Verwaltungs-Mat.)', 'Protokolle, Leitungssitzung 1973–76', 'Berghaus Protokolle 1973–76', BEA; SAPMO-BArch DY 30 IV B 2/2.024/102 and DY 30 IV B 2/9.06/69; Norbert Bauer, 'Neue DDR-Dramatik—hinter den Kulissen: Fraktionskämpfe im Berliner Ensemble', *Pfälzischer Merkur* (Saarbrücken), 29 Sept. 1975; Jürgen Beckelmann, 'Gerüchte um das Berliner Ensemble: Verläßt Ruth Berghaus das traditionelle Brecht-Theater?', *Stuttgarter Zeitung*, 7 June 1975; s. w., 'Er sieht keine Reformchancen: Andreas Reinhardt verläßt Ost-Berlin', *FAZ*, 30 July 1975.

[123] Hoffmann to Hager, 5 July 1976, SAPMO-BArch DY 30 IV B 2/9.06/69.

[124] 'If we do not act, we are sending out signals to authors alive today. If we do not take this approach, we will have more trouble with a not inconsiderable group of notable theatre practitioners than we already have with Barbara Schall.' Hoffmann to Hager, 2 Dec. 1976, SAPMO-BArch DY 30 IV B 2/2.024/102.

policy of containment and appeasement suggests that Brecht's heirs had overplayed their hand: despite their high public profile within the GDR, Brecht-Schall and her husband Ekkehard lacked Weigel's international renown and status. So, with Hager's agreement, Hoffmann instructed the publishing house Henschel to exercise its legal right to authorize Berlin productions of Brecht's plays in consultation with a committee headed by Brecht-Schall.[125] Although in theory this was a victory for Berghaus, in practice it did little to ease her position, because both Hoffmann and Hager had grown increasingly critical of her work.

Whereas Brecht's heirs had attacked Berghaus primarily on aesthetic grounds, cultural politicians focused on her dramaturgical and ideological approach. This marked another shift from the 1950s and 1960s, when aesthetics had been treated as intrinsically ideological. The thrust of the politicians' objections is clear from a Central Committee memorandum of January 1976: 'Genossin Berghaus sollte darauf hingewiesen werden, daß sie von der gegenwärtigen ideologisch-theoretischen Substanz ihrer Dramaturgie keinen ernsthaften Beitrag zur Brecht-Interpretation (konzeptioneller Art) wird erwarten können. Sie braucht einen politisch zuverlässigen Chefdramaturgen und muß sich auch von einigen Leuten trennen (Dieckmann, Mickel).'[126] After the productions of the 1970s Berghaus was no longer regarded as politically reliable, even though she had previously served as the BE's Party Secretary and was wholly committed to Socialism. As Dieckmann has recently testified, the withdrawal of state support made Berghaus's position untenable.[127] In April 1977, she resigned 'auf eigenen Wunsch aus gesundheitlichen Gründen' ('on her own request for health reasons') and returned to opera, staging twenty-one of her thirty-one productions during the 1980s in Western Europe.[128] At the BE, meanwhile, Wekwerth secured the position of manager in an uneasy alliance with Brecht's heirs, who had almost certainly come to regard his approach as the lesser of two evils.

[125] Ibid.; Hoffmann to Hager, 5 July 1976.

[126] 'Comrade Berghaus should be made aware that she will not be able to expect to make any serious contribution to the interpretation of Brecht (in terms of ideas), given the current ideological and theoretical substance of her dramaturgy. She needs a politically reliable head dramaturge and must also part from several people (Dieckmann, Mickel).' Ursula Ragwitz, 'Abt. Kultur, 19.1.1976: Einige Gedanken für das Gespräch mit Ruth Berghaus', SAPMO-BArch DY 30 IV B 2/2.024/102.

[127] Dieckmann, 'Meine Schleef-Mappe', 23–4.

[128] Klaus Bertisch, *Ruth Berghaus* (Frankfurt/Main: Fischer, 1989), 167–75.

When it became clear that Berghaus's days at the BE were numbered, most of her closest collaborators left the company. Müller and Dieckmann resigned in 1976, while Reinhardt and Schleef left the GDR entirely, frustrated by the constant political struggles. These developments were symptomatic of the situation in the GDR as a whole, since by 1976 the state was trying to re-assert its control in the cultural sphere—as Rainer Kunze's expulsion from the Writers' Union and Wolf Biermann's expatriation that November indicate. In 1978 Besson left the Volksbühne and went to live in the West, along with an increasing number of writers like Jurek Becker and Sarah Kirsch, and actors like Angelica Domröse and Hilmar Thate. Even so, now that a public space for experimentation had been created, those who remained were significantly more reluctant to comply with the cultural clamp-down. Consequently, a new generation of directors like Frank Castorf and Jo Fabian ensured that the process of theatrical modernization continued. Thus, although Honecker's more liberal cultural policy was short-lived, its effects continued to be felt long afterwards.

7. CONCLUSION

These two productions marked a shift towards a new phase of post-Brechtian theatre, during which the reception of Brecht became increasingly complex and his staging methods were adapted to serve new, contrasting purposes. Even though Stein consciously sought to learn from Brecht, his interpretation and staging methods still reflected his own commitment to a post-1968 model of anti-authoritarian theatre. At the BE, meanwhile, Berghaus's public references to Brecht mostly legitimated her own programme of experimentation instead of explaining specific artistic choices.[129] Her approach was significantly more selective and subversive than Stein's, because she developed Brecht's technique of ideologically coded gesture and movement in combination with a metaphorical treatment of set design, lighting, and sound. Moreover, the tensions that she created between the different elements of performance owed as much to Palucca as to Brecht, while some of her stage tableaux recalled the work of Kollwitz, Barlach, and Cremer. By combining

---

[129] e.g. 'Zehn Fragen an Ruth Berghaus'; 'Antwort auf den Gedanken von Minister Gysi', both in 'Berghaus Protokolle 2', BEA.

such different techniques and influences, Berghaus created a complex theatrical hybrid that cannot be described solely as post-Brechtian.

The two stagings also indicate that political theatre in East and West Germany was undergoing a process of redefinition in the early 1970s. In the West, the demand for agitation subsided after 1968, and left-wing theatre entered a more reflective phase. This transitional process accelerated as it became clear that the prerequisite for a successful proletarian theatre—a politically engaged working-class audience—was no longer present. In the East, meanwhile, aesthetic liberalization allowed innovative practitioners to challenge the affirmative model of political theatre and confront the failure of state Socialism, thus far, to deliver the promised Utopia. Yet the reception of Berghaus's production indicates the risks associated with aesthetically encoded criticism: because her approach was perceived as difficult and obscure, her staging attracted only a minority of the BE's regular audience. Indeed, she even commented ruefully: 'Qualität ist eine Sache und was das Publikum sehen möchte ist eine andere Sache.'[130] Despite the directors' conscious intentions, then, both productions marked a shift away from Brecht's socially inclusive approach of 1951, towards critical theatre for the middle classes at the Schaubühne and avant-garde experimentation for the artistic and intellectual élite at the BE.

Overall, the contrast between these productions and Brecht's model indicates how much had changed since the 1950s, and not just in the GDR. The political and cultural climate in both states was slowly becoming more liberal: even in West Berlin, just a few years after the end of the Brecht boycott, there were no calls for Brecht's Communist play to be banned, and the West German press strongly condemned the CDU's campaign against the Schaubühne. Furthermore, whereas the GDR authorities had condemned Brecht's aesthetically conservative approach as Formalist in 1951, they initially tolerated Berghaus's far more radical approach in 1974. Even so, the hopes vested in these productions were ultimately frustrated: in 1973, the lack of working-class demand for left-wing theatre forced the Schaubühne to abandon its commitment to staging such productions, while in 1977 combined pressure from Brecht's heirs and the GDR authorities brought an end to Berghaus's experimentation at the BE. The GDR authorities

---

[130] 'Quality is one thing and what the audience would like to see is another.' 'Protokoll zur Leitungssitzung am 19.8.1976', in 'Berghaus Protokolle 1973–76', BEA.

missed a crucial opportunity by failing to channel the creative potential and constructive criticism of artists like Berghaus and Reinhardt: by reverting to a more repressive approach, they forfeited the sympathy of large sections of the radical intelligentsia and accelerated the exodus of some of the state's most gifted artists to the West. In Chapter 5, I consider how this policy affected the BE's next staging of *Die Mutter* in 1988.

4

Translation and Transference since 1932

1. INTRODUCTION

1.1 Methodology

It was only after the Second World War that *Die Mutter* reached a truly worldwide audience, and only in the 1970s and 1980s that it became popular among politicized theatres in England and Scandinavia. For these two reasons, this chapter is an appropriate point at which to focus on the play's international reception and the problems of translation and transference. Although this approach interrupts my chronological discussion of German stagings, it actually continues my analysis of performance as a response to politico-cultural context by considering how, and how far, foreign-language productions have negotiated the differences between their audiences, Brecht's German text, and its Russian subject-matter.

Methodologically, my approach accords with the comparatively recent shift in emphasis in Translation Studies from linguistic transcoding to cultural transference. Following this 'cultural turn', most theorists now see the relationship between a text and its translations as culturally and historically conditioned.[1] Indeed, Susan Bassnett and André Lefevere have even argued that translators sometimes need to avoid 'faithful' renditions in order to reach their target audiences.[2] This theory corresponds to my analysis of Brecht's 1951 production—an example of intracultural transference—and suggests that more historical and cultural insights may be gained from exploring how and why

---

[1] Susan Bassnett and André Lefevere, 'Proust's Grandmother and the Thousand and One Nights: The "Cultural Turn" in Translation Studies', in *Translation, History and Culture*, ed. Bassnett and Lefevere (London: Cassell, 1995), 1–14.

[2] Susan Bassnett and André Lefevere, 'Where Are We in Translation Studies?', in *Constructing Cultures: Essays on Literary Translation*, ed. Bassnett and Lefevere, Topics in Translation, 11 (Clevedon: Multilingual Matters, 1998), 1–11 (4).

translations modify *Die Mutter* than from assessing their relative quality. Foreign-language productions also offer an opportunity to test two theories proposed by Rainer Kohlmayer and André Lefevere respectively: first, that directors are more likely to modify translated texts because they lack the protective aura of the original; and second, that relatively dominant cultures are more likely to adapt texts to domestic norms because they view their own practice as natural.[3]

In his historical study of translation theory, Laurence Venuti indicates the prolonged influence of Friedrich Schleiermacher's view of translation as a spectrum whose poles are domestication and foreignization.[4] Nevertheless, these terms have only limited critical value because they cannot do justice to the range of cultural practices which they imply. Domestication, for instance, can involve the assimilation of a text to domestic ideological and aesthetic norms, inclusion of local colour, and/or engagement with domestic issues. So my analysis focuses instead on three aspects of foreign-language productions: their theatrical approach, their treatment of politics and ideology, and their relationship with Brecht's foreign subject-matter and setting. Theatrically, a theatre may adapt *Die Mutter* to domestic norms, include some domestic techniques, or reject such techniques entirely. Politically and ideologically, it may engage critically with domestic issues, treat Brecht's politics simply as foreign colour, and/or alter the text's ideology. Finally, it may engage with Brecht's foreign subject-matter and setting, reduce the foreign to local colour, or even eliminate it entirely by rewriting the text.

1.2 Scope and Structure

My analysis begins in section 2 with an overview of international performances of *Die Mutter* in which I explore patterns of reception and consider the influence of the BE and politics. The rest of the chapter consists of three sets of contrasting case-studies. The first case-studies, in sections 3 and 4, exemplify opposing strategies of cultural relocation: whereas both the New York Theatre Union (1935) and

---

[3] Rainer Kohlmayer, *Oscar Wilde in Deutschland und Österreich: Untersuchungen zur Rezeption der Komödien und zur Theorie der Bühnenübersetzung* (Tübingen: Niemeyer, 1996), 89; André Lefevere, 'Chinese and Western Thinking on Translation', in *Constructing Cultures*, 12–24 (13).

[4] Laurence Venuti, *The Translator's Invisibility: A History of Translation* (London: Routledge, 1995); Friedrich Schleiermacher, 'Über die verschiedenen Methoden des Übersetzens', in *Das Problem des Übersetzens*, ed. Hans Joachim Störig, Wege der Forschung, 8 (Stuttgart: Henry Goverts, 1963), 38–70.

the Glasgow Citizens Theatre (1982) attempted to make *Die Mutter* conform theatrically and ideologically to their spectators' expectations, a production in Lille (1979) engaged more critically and creatively with the multiple theatrical, historical, political and cultural contexts associated with the text. Like the productions in Chapter 3, the Glasgow and Lille stagings also show different ways in which theatres have engaged with Brecht's theatrical methods and Marxist ideas since 1968. I pursue this theme further in my analysis of the second set of productions, by London's National Theatre (1986) and New York's Irondale Ensemble Project (1997). The stark political and theatrical contrasts between these stagings reflect broader differences between political theatre in Britain and the USA, where prejudice against Communism and didactic theatre were still endemic, over sixty years after the Theatre Union's unsuccessful staging. The third and final set of case-studies focuses on the agitational strand of post-1968 theatre and examines how English and Irish dramatists transferred *Die Mutter* to the sphere of contemporary domestic politics and culture by rewriting the play—the most far-reaching means of cultural relocation. Overall, the chapter illuminates not only translation and transference, but also the complexity and variety of post-Brechtian political theatre.

2. PRODUCTIONS OF *DIE MUTTER* WORLDWIDE

2.1 Chronological Overview

Die Mutter was rarely staged between 1932 and 1945, and then mostly by amateurs or independent collectives. In 1932 a left-wing group performed selected scenes in Dresden, and further productions were staged in the same year by workers in Budapest and an actors' collective in Sofia.[5] Brecht's personal connections helped him to secure two productions in exile in 1935: Ruth Berlau's amateur staging in Copenhagen[6] and the Theatre Union's production in New York, the only non-European production before 1960. During the Second World War, the only recorded staging was in neutral Switzerland, at the Volkshaus in Zurich (1941). The Nazi occupation of much of Europe precluded further productions.

---

[5] Anon., 'Maxim-Gorki-Feier des Linkskartells im Central-Theater', *Arbeiterstimme* (Dresden), 28 Dec. 1932.

[6] Bunge (ed.), *Brechts Lai-Tu*, 56.

In the late 1940s and the 1950s *Die Mutter* was staged almost exclusively in East Germany. It held little appeal for the West because of its Communist politics, for Eastern Europe because of its divergence from Socialist Realism, and for countries recently liberated from the Nazis because of its German origins. This situation began to change in the 1960s, partly thanks to the BE's performances in Poland (1952), Budapest and Bucharest (1959), and Paris (1960); and productions were staged in France (1961, 1966, 1968), Czechoslovakia (1961, 1972), Hungary (1965), Poland (1968), the USSR (1967/8), and Yugoslavia (1964, 1965, 1968, 1973, 1975).

After the 1968 protests, Western theatres outside France began to stage *Die Mutter*, and there were even clusters of productions in England and Scandinavia. Several non-European theatres also produced it during the 1970s: in Tokyo (1972), San Francisco (1973), and New Delhi (1978)—where one reviewer actually perceived the Brechtian half-curtain as a traditional Indian device.[7] In Latin America, where interest in Brecht had grown thanks to the Cuban government's dissemination of Spanish translations, *Die Mutter* was staged in Mexico City (1969), Uruguay (1971), and in the Chilean capital, Santiago (1971), shortly after Salvador Allende became the first democratically elected Marxist head of state.

Further amateur productions were staged from the 1940s onwards: for example, in Helsinki (1949), Karl-Marx-Stadt—now Chemnitz—(1960), Leipzig (1964), and Meißen (1966). After the Schaubühne's high-profile production, *Die Mutter* was also performed by amateur West German groups, including a student theatre in Hamburg-Billstedt (1973) and an amateur company in Marburg (1978).[8]

Some of these trends continued into the 1980s, when further productions took place in England, West Germany, and Scandinavia, and isolated non-European stagings occurred: for example, in Adelaide (1981), Wellington (1985), and Kabul (1985). In Latin America, however, censorship prevented theatres from performing *Die Mutter*: in Chile, for example, the Pinochet Government banned Brecht's works from 1973 to 1990. In Eastern Europe, there was just one production

[7] Meera Bhatia, 'Prayog's *Mother* Good', *Evening News* (India, city unknown), 19 Oct. 1978.

[8] Anon., 'Spaß am politischen Theater', *Spandauer Volksblatt* (West Berlin), 5 May 1973; Günter Giesenfeld, 'Wichtig ist, daß er aktiv wird', *Deutsche Volkszeitung* (Düsseldorf), 13 Apr. 1978.

outside the GDR in the 1980s, in the Ukrainian city of Donets'k (1980), and even in the GDR there was only a televised production (1981) and a new staging by the BE (1988). This decline suggests that interest in Brecht's pro-Communist play waned in the East as domestic resistance to the Soviet-backed regimes increased and free-market capitalism flourished in the West.

Before 1980, *Die Mutter* accounted for approximately 2 per cent of Brecht productions in Africa, Asia, Latin America, and the Socialist states.[9] There are no recorded productions in the Middle East, perhaps because such an independent, forceful heroine would challenge the patriarchal social order, or in China, where Brecht's works were banned during the Cultural Revolution and licensed for performance only in 1978.[10] The existence of only two recorded productions in the former USSR suggests that it may be harder for foreign adaptations to succeed in the original text's native country, where at least two directors, Nikolai Okhlopkov and Yuri Lyubimov, staged their own dramatizations of Gorky's novel (1933 and 1969).[11]

Even after the collapse of state Socialism in Eastern Europe, some theatres have staged *Die Mutter*. For instance, productions took place in Kassel and Paris (1991), Rio de Janeiro (1996), and Liège (1997), and Brecht's centenary was marked by further stagings in Berlin and Bochum (1998) and the revival of the Rio production. According to Alexander Stillmark, this Brazilian staging was 'furchtbar militant' ('terribly militant') and used the chorus 'wie eine Terroristengruppe' ('like a terrorist group') to confront the audience. Even so, Stillmark believed that the spectators found the production quite chic, suggesting that they were able to enjoy it without heeding its political implications.[12] In 2001 the English touring company Visiting Moon experienced similar

---

[9] Elifius Paffrath (ed.), *Brecht 80: Brecht in Afrika, Asien und Lateinamerika: Dokumentation*, Brecht-Zentrum der DDR, 2 (East Berlin: Henschel, 1980), 261–85; Karl-Claus Hahn (ed.), *Brecht 81: Brecht in sozialistischen Ländern*, Brecht-Zentrum der DDR, 3 (East Berlin: Henschel, 1981), 240–310.

[10] Cf. Wolfram Schlenker, 'Brecht hinter der Großen Mauer: Zu seiner Rezeption in der Volksrepublik China', *Brecht Yearbook*, 9 (1980), 43–137; Carl Weber, 'Brecht is at Home in Asia', *Brecht Yearbook*, 14 (1989), 30–43 (34).

[11] Nick Worrall, *Modernism to Realism on the Soviet Stage: Tairov—Vakhtangov—Okhlopkov* (Cambridge: Cambridge University Press, 1989), 154–7; Anatoly Smeliansky, *The Russian Theatre after Stalin*, trans. Patrick Miles (Cambridge: Cambridge University Press, 1999), 44–6.

[12] Stillmark, 7 Dec. 2000. For photographs of the production, see <http://www.ensaioaberto.com/a_mae_imagens.htm>; all websites referred to in this chapter were accessed on 21 Feb. 2005.

difficulties when it tried to provoke a debate about Labour's removal of Clause 4 from the Party's Constitution, which had previously committed it to nationalization. Although Visiting Moon had replaced Brecht's references to Communism with allusions to Socialism, spectators in Liverpool were far more interested in the topical relevance of Wlassowa's anti-superstition speech.[13] Here, the comment that farmers would do better to put their faith in insurance policies against 'Viehseuche', translated as 'foot and mouth disease', acquired an acute contemporary relevance when the performance run coincided with an epidemic of this very disease.[14] Unsurprisingly, spectators in rural Keswick received the speech in stony silence, since many of them were directly affected by the epidemic and lacked the necessary insurance cover.[15] Despite their different reactions, both audiences seem to have perceived only the play's coincidental contemporary relevance, not the larger issues that concerned Visiting Moon.

2.2 The Role of the BE

Ever since 1951 the BE has greatly influenced the international dissemination and reception of *Die Mutter*, just as Brecht intended. Several foreign productions were mounted by directors who had studied at the BE, like Néstor Raimondi in Cuba (1962) and Bernard Sobel in Paris (1991).[16] *Die Mutter* was also staged abroad by several of the BE's own directors, including Wekwerth in the Russian sector of Vienna (1953), Ulf Keyn in Cuba (1975), and Wolf Bunge in Soviet-occupied Kabul (1985), just after his departure from the BE. Other directors had seen the BE's model production: for instance, Jacques Rosner and Pierre-Etienne Heymann almost certainly saw the 1960 Parisian tour, and Koreya Senda saw a performance of the revival in 1968, eight years after directing his first, 'slightly over-enthusiastic staging' of *Die Mutter* in Tokyo.[17]

Even though the BE greatly facilitated the dissemination of Brecht's works and methods, its promotion of the model discouraged directors

[13] Visiting Moon, personal interviews, 1–2 Feb. 2001; post-performance discussion at the Liverpool Everyman Theatre, 27 Mar. 2001.

[14] *BFA*, iii. 313; Brecht, 'The Mother', trans. Steve Trafford, 49, Trafford's personal copy.

[15] Post-performance discussion.

[16] Havana 1962 programme, BBA; Colette Godard, *Le Théâtre depuis 1968* (Paris: J.-C. Lattès, 1980), 15.

[17] Koreya Senda, 'Instead of a Preface', in the Tokyo 1972 programme, 6, BBA. This translation by Kanae Aoyama and Laura Bradley.

from tailoring *Die Mutter* to their own politico-cultural contexts. Like East German directors in the 1950s and 1960s, many foreign directors simply imitated the model, even though it downplayed the text's agitation. For instance, after being 'completely shocked by the BE's staging, which moved me slowly, quietly but deeply', Senda attempted to set aside his initial reactions to the text and copy Brecht's model in 1972.[18] Nevertheless, cultural transference still left traces in the new stagings of the model. Wekwerth, for instance, recalls that the local acting conventions and dialect altered the 'feel' of the model when it was performed in Vienna in 1953: 'Wir haben dann die Rollen doch mehr im Sinne vom Volkstheater gespielt, und zwar im Wiener Dialekt.'[19] Similarly, when Raimondi staged the model in Havana immediately after Castro's Revolution, he armed all the characters in the final scene, including the women, with bayonets and ammunition belts. Even so, it was not until the 1970s that directors departed wholesale from the model, often by employing austere, functional styles that recalled the 1932 aesthetic. In New Zealand, for example, the Wellington Repertory Theatre (1985) used 'a clean, sparse set of white screens, black walls and grey furniture'.[20] As in the GDR, this delay indicates the difficulties that directors experienced in understanding, developing, and applying Brecht's methods, instead of simply imitating his achievements.

2.3 The Influence of Politics

Political factors have often influenced the timing of productions of *Die Mutter*, simply because it is so overtly political. It has often been staged at times of national crisis: for example, Senda's first production in Tokyo (1960) exploited public resistance to the renewal of the Japanese–American Security Pact, a production in Mexico City coincided with student unrest (1969), and a staging in Lisbon immediately followed a military *coup* (1976).[21] Theatres have also related *Die Mutter* to local political campaigns, often through the

---

[18] Ibid.

[19] 'We ended up playing the roles more along the lines of popular theatre after all; actually, in Viennese dialect.' Wekwerth, 13 Dec. 2000.

[20] Laurie Atkinson, 'Play Espouses Socialist Revolution', *Evening Post* (Wellington), 16 Oct. 1985.

[21] Tokyo 1960 programme, 24; Iwabuchi Tatsuji, 'Die Brecht-Rezeption in Japan aus dem Aspekt der Theaterpraxis', *Brecht Yearbook*, 14 (1989), 87–99 (92); Lisbon 1976 programme, BBA.

programme: for instance, the programme for Senda's second production in Tokyo (1972) featured an article about local working mothers' resistance to the government's plans to transfer a welfare research institute out of the city.[22] Meanwhile, the GDR authorities even used *Die Mutter* to improve relations with other states and advance Socialism abroad—which explains why they financed Raimondi's trip to Cuba and Bunge's visit to Kabul. As the official GDR press release shows, Raimondi's staging was designed to politicize local viewers: 'Das Nationale Dramatische Ensemble Kubas spielt ... Brechts *Mutter* vor Arbeitern, Bauern oder Angestellten in Betrieben. Die Schauspieler halten sich jeweils einen ganzen Tag bei ihren Zuschauern auf. Sie sprechen mit den Werktätigen über die Produktion und erläutern Stück und Inszenierung.'[23] But because *Die Mutter* had been designated an affirmative play only retrospectively, such bilateral projects sometimes had unexpected results. In Kabul, for instance, the actors actually used it to oppose Afghanistan's Soviet occupiers—which supports the argument that the play is subversive of established authority.[24] Yet this Afghan experience contrasted with productions of *Die Mutter* in the GDR itself, where—even after Berghaus's staging—it was still regarded as affirmative propaganda. In Chapter 5, I consider how four recent German stagings have dealt with this difficult legacy.

3. IDEOLOGICAL AND AESTHETIC APPROPRIATION: *MOTHER* IN NEW YORK, 1935

The safest method of negotiating cultural difference is to assimilate a text to the expectations of its new audience. This was the approach which New York's Theatre Union sought to adopt in 1935 by transforming the ideology, dramaturgy, and aesthetic of *Die Mutter* for its audience—much to Brecht's horror. Even though the events surrounding

[22] Kazuko Yamaie, 'Mothers and Female Workers Who Protect People's Lives', Tokyo 1972 programme, 19.
[23] 'The National Dramatic Ensemble of Cuba is performing ... Brecht's *Mother* to workers, peasants, or employees in factories. In each case the actors spend a whole day with their spectators. They talk to the workers about the factory's production and explain the play and the staging.' Anon., 'Brechts *Mutter* in Kuba', *Der Morgen* (East Berlin), 24 Mar. 1962; cf. anon., 'Brecht-Stück in Kabul aufgeführt', *Berliner Zeitung* (East Berlin), 3 Aug. 1985.
[24] Wolf Bunge, personal interview, 16 Sept. 2002.

this controversial production have been well-documented, the scripts prepared for it have never been examined in any detail.[25] What they reveal is a rare clash between two incompatible approaches towards cultural transference: whilst the Theatre Union sought to adapt *Die Mutter* to its usual repertoire, Brecht insisted on confronting the spectators with a near-literal translation.[26]

3.1 Political and Cultural Difference: Germany and the USA

Brecht's insistence on replicating the Berlin staging of 1932 stemmed from his failure to appreciate the major political and cultural differences between the German and American audiences and contexts. Unlike the KPD, the US Communist Party had neither a mass popular following nor any reason to believe that revolution might be imminent, even during the Great Depression. Furthermore, agitprop had never made the transition from amateur to professional theatre in the USA, whereas in Germany it had been the KPD's official aesthetic since 1922. On the rare occasions when professional American productions included agitprop techniques, they were poorly received: just months after the Theatre Union's production of *Die Mutter*, Piscator's epic staging of Theodore Dreiser's *Clyde Griffiths* was heavily criticized and closed after just nineteen performances at the Group Theatre.[27] Even amateur groups had distanced themselves from agitprop by 1933, when Herbert Kline declared in the left-wing periodical *New Theatre*: 'the day of the cliché and mechanical statement has gone by for the workers' theatre'.[28] Consequently, Brecht's insistence on replicating Neher's agitational aesthetic shows his limited sensitivity to the performance context in 1935.

[25] Cf. Lee Baxandall, 'Brecht in America, 1935', *TDR*, 12.1 (Fall 1967), 68–87; Joseph Dial, 'Brecht in den USA', *Weimarer Beiträge*, 24.2 (1978), 160–72; Morgan Y. Himelstein, 'The Pioneers of Bertolt Brecht in America', *Modern Drama*, 9 (1966), 178–89; James K. Lyon, *Bertolt Brecht in America* (Princeton: Princeton University Press, 1980), 6–12; Gerald Rabkin, *Drama and Commitment: Politics in the American Theatre of the Thirties* (Bloomington: Indiana University Press, 1964), 62–5; Mark W. Weisstuch, 'The Theatre Union, 1933–1937: A History' (unpublished doctoral thesis, City University of New York, 1982), 402–89; Jay Williams, *Stage Left* (New York: Charles Scribner's Sons, 1974), 179–83.

[26] Cf. Laura Bradley, ' "A Struggle of Two Styles": Brecht's *Mother* at the New York Theatre Union, 1935', in *Drama Translation and Theatre Practice*, ed. Sabine Coelsch-Foisner and Holger Klein (Frankfurt/Main: Peter Lang, 2004), 399–413.

[27] Malcolm Goldstein, *The Political Stage: American Drama and Theater of the Great Depression* (New York: Oxford University Press, 1974), 310.

[28] Rabkin, 48.

Although Brecht assumed that the Theatre Union was committed to Communism, it actually targeted both 'honest militant workers and middle-class sympathizers', 'particularly ... unorganized workers who are not yet class conscious'.[29] It could not afford to alienate any of its regular spectators, far less its financial backers, because it was already running at a high annual deficit.[30] Furthermore, even its own members could not be counted on to share Brecht's radical political views, for the advisory board included liberals like the dramatist Sidney Howard, and it soon transpired that Helen Henry, who played Wlassowa, had never even heard of a strikebreaker.[31] With productions like *Peace on Earth*, by Albert Maltz and George Sklar, the Theatre Union had earned a reputation for exciting and emotional theatre, and it wanted to keep to this winning formula—particularly because its only experiment, Maltz's *The Black Pit*, had incurred losses of over $7,000.[32] Thus, ideologically and aesthetically, the company had little in common with Brecht's actors in 1932.

3.2 Peters's Adaptation

3.2.1 Ideology

When the Theatre Union's members discovered that, contrary to their expectations, Brecht's play dispensed with the atmosphere, sentiment, and local colour of Gorky's novel, they commissioned Paul Peters, a graduate of the University of Wisconsin and writer for the Communist newspaper *New Masses*, to transform it into an ideologically and aesthetically safe version. Since Peters had co-written *Stevedore* for the Theatre Union, he knew exactly what the company and its audience expected.[33] So he replaced Brecht's references to Communism with allusions to Socialism and expunged all mention of Bolshevism. For example, in the closing demonstration 'hatten sie zu uns Bolschewiken getrieben' ('had driven them to us Bolsheviks') became 'brought them

---

[29] Goldstein, 60. For Brecht's attempts to use Victor Jerome, the head of the propaganda department of the US Communist Party, to force the Theatre Union to accept his proposals, see Elisabeth Hauptmann, 'Bericht an Gomez. Telefonisch in engl. Übersetzung durchgegeben', 3 Nov. 1935, BBA 341/52.

[30] Weisstuch, 581.   [31] Goldstein, 58–60; Kebir, 182.

[32] Albert Maltz and George Sklar, *Peace on Earth: An Anti-War Play* (New York: Samuel French, 1934); Albert Maltz, *The Black Pit* (New York: G. P. Putman, 1935); Weisstuch, 396.

[33] Paul Peters and George Sklar, *Stevedore* (New York: Covici Friede, 1934).

over to us'.[34] Peters also cut several potentially controversial passages, such as the speech in which Wlassowa equates religion with superstition, and shifted the focus from the public to the private. Significantly, the new title *Mother*—with no definite article—presented Wlassowa as a private individual rather than a representative figure, i.e. the mother of many. The Theatre Union's publicity showed her looking lovingly at her unarmed son carrying the flag, learning to read with a motherly smile, and as a tiny, frail figure on a bare stage. As a result of this shift from militancy to sentimentality, one critic described Wlassowa as 'really touching' and 'lovable', not as a spirited fighter.[35]

3.2.2 Dramaturgy

In order to adapt Brecht's epic play to the Theatre Union's usual repertoire, its actors' skills, and its audience's expectations, Peters transformed *Die Mutter* into a cathartic melodrama. He replaced the episodic structure with three acts, ignored the epic principle that each scene should stand in its own right, and rewrote the final third to provide an exciting climax. Then, to maximize the audience's involvement in the action, he cut the captions and transformed Wlassowa's stylized opening monologue into a naturalistic conversation with Pawel.[36] These changes led Hanns Eisler to conclude in disgust: 'man hat daraus einen Gerhart Hauptmann gemacht' ('they turned it into a Gerhart Hauptmann play'), a verdict that the Theatre Union would probably have taken as a great compliment.[37]

The effects of this theatrical and aesthetic appropriation are most striking in Act III, where Peters augmented and reshaped Brecht's material to furnish the action with a 'final spurt'.[38] After reading Brecht's version, he and the Theatre Union had 'felt the play stopped and became somewhat lost in this section', a view that reflects their preconceptions about the dramatic structure appropriate to a well-made play.[39] In Peters's adaptation, the tension mounts to a climax in Scene 3 before the triumphant demonstration and catharsis in Scene 4. Each scene opens with a dramatic revelation, then suspense mounts

---

[34] *BFA*, iii. 323; 'Die Mutter: englische Ausgabe' (Peters's adaptation), BBA 443/67.
[35] Gilbert W. Gabriel, 'Theatre Union Begins with a Musical Version of a Gorki Tale', *New York American*, 20 Nov. 1935.
[36] *BFA*, xxiv. 164–9.   [37] Bunge, *Gespräche*, 99.
[38] Brecht, draft article for the newspaper *New Masses*, BBA 341/14–18.
[39] James K. Lyon (ed.), 'Der Briefwechsel zwischen Bertolt Brecht und der New Yorker Theatre Union von 1935', *Brecht Yearbook*, 5 (1975), 136–55 (141).

until a temporary resolution is achieved at the end: in Scene 1 by Pavel's escape from a spy, in Scene 2 by his flight from prison, and in Scene 3 by his dramatic death.[40] Peters probably calculated that the introduction of a spy, a character who features in Gorky's novel but not in Brecht's play, would appeal to an audience well versed in the conventions of Hollywood gangster movies. He then tempered this excitement with more sentimentality: for example, the teacher selflessly donates his only suit to Pawel and then admits, 'his voice breaking', that he has tried to save Pawel's comrades by swallowing their addresses.[41]

To maximize the audience's identification with the characters, Peters replaced those introduced in the later scenes, like Jegor, the butcher, and the maid, with reassuringly familiar ones, like Iwan, Pawel, and Sostakowitsch. More importantly still, Pawel's survival until the penultimate scene transferred the dramatic interest from Wlassowa's political development to his fate. Brecht viewed this change as a cheap dramatic technique, a piece of emotional capitalism that pandered to the audience's expectations:

> Wie der Geschäftsmann
> Geld investiert in einen Betrieb, so, meint ihr, investiert der Zuschauer
> Gefühl in den Helden: er will es wieder herausbekommen[,]
> Und zwar verdoppelt.[42]

Furthermore, by transposing the 'Grabrede' into the future tense, Peters warned the audience of Pawel's imminent death and created further tension, replacing Brecht's epic 'Spannung auf den Gang' (tension focused on the course of the action) with the conventional 'Spannung auf den Ausgang' (tension focused on the outcome itself).[43]

The long-awaited climax arrived in the form of a melodramatic fight that ended in Pawel's death on stage—exactly the same technique as Peters and Sklar had used in *Stevedore*. But even Peters acknowledged that this scene was 'bad—bad because it is too naturalistic, too violent, and out of keeping with the style of the play'.[44] Pawel's death then inspires a desire for revenge in the other characters, whereas Brecht had used the landlady's insensitivity to Wlassowa's loss to provoke

---

[40] BBA 443/45–67.   [41] BBA 443/62, 65.

[42] 'As the businessman/Invests money in a firm, so, you think, the spectator invests/Emotion in the hero: he wants to have it returned/In fact doubled.' *BFA*, xiv (1993), 292–3.

[43] BBA 443/52; *BFA*, xxiv. 85.   [44] Lyon (ed.), 'Der Briefwechsel', 141.

productive indignation in the audience. In Peters's version, however, Wlassowa takes comfort from the knowledge: 'The workers will revenge you, Pavel [*sic*]. They won't forget. It won't be long now, Pavel. It won't be long.'[45] Again, this technique corresponded to *Stevedore*, where the black hero's death inspires black and white workers to unite and fight for their rights in the final scene.[46] By these means, Peters had transformed *Die Mutter* into exactly the sort of reassuringly cathartic drama that Brecht opposed.

3.2.3 Language and Style

Peters also made far-reaching changes to the play's style and language, which the Theatre Union believed were impoverished and unnatural. He replaced Brecht's 'kärgliche Sprache' ('frugal language') with colloquial, idiomatic phrases that were familiar to his audience, adding interjections like 'bingo' and 'huh' and Americanisms like 'not a red cent', 'I guess', and 'we got to hop to it'.[47] This drift towards colloquialism completely obscured the varied and contrasting registers of the original. In Brecht's version, for example, Wlassowa's stylized opening monologue contrasts with her gossipy tone when she talks her way past the factory porter in Scene 3.[48] Brecht had also used the heightened language with which 'man/Die Worte und Taten der Großen berichtet' ('one/Reports the words and deeds of the great') at moments of particular significance to invest the revolutionaries with dignity and present their activities as 'historische Vorgänge' ('historic events').[49] Thus, Anton tells Pawel:

> ANTON   … Genosse Wlassow, angesichts der besonderen Notlage und der schweren Gefährdung des Genossen sind wir dafür, das Angebot deiner Mutter anzunehmen.[50]

The casual tone of Peters's translation completely fails to convey this grave dignity:

> ANTON   All right, then, it's agreed. Pavel [*sic*], we're going to send your mother with the leaflets.[51]

---

[45] BBA 443/65.   [46] Peters and Sklar, *Stevedore*, 114–23.
[47] *BFA*, xiv. 290; BBA 443/14, 16, 18, 41.   [48] *BFA*, iii. 263, 272–3.
[49] *BFA*, xiv. 290.
[50] 'ANTON Comrade Wlassow, in view of the special emergency and the grave danger to our comrade we are in favour of accepting your mother's offer.' *BFA*, iii. 271–2.
[51] BBA 443/10.

Peters's colloquial register is particularly inappropriate when—in a line absent from Brecht's original—Pawel predicts that the revolution will succeed:

> PAVEL [*sic*] It won't be long now. We're going to come up. Up through the ground like a big horny fist. Look out you fat ones above![52]

Because of changes like this, Eisler characterized the adaptation as 'eine Mischung zwischen Tschechow und übelstem Jargongeschwätze, Slanggeschwätze, ohne alle Poesie'—a far more accurate assessment than Peters's assertion that he had 'caught the spirit of *Mother* and its style'.[53]

Further stylistic shifts abound in Peters's translations of the songs and verse. Uneven rhythms and fractured syntax are characteristic features of Brecht's unrhymed verse and foreground contradictions that make the listener think again.[54] The 'Lob der dritten Sache' is a typical example:

> DIE MUTTER   Immerfort hört man, wie schnell
> Die Mütter die Söhne verlieren, aber ich
> Behielt meinen Sohn. Wie behielt ich ihn? Durch
> Die dritte Sache.
> Er und ich waren zwei, aber die dritte
> Gemeinsame Sache, gemeinsam betrieben, war es, die
> Uns einte.
> Oftmals selber hörte ich Söhne
> Mit ihren Eltern sprechen.
> Wieviel besser war doch unser Gespräch
> Über die dritte Sache, die uns gemeinsam war[,]
> Vieler Menschen große, gemeinsame Sache!
> Wie nahe waren wir uns, dieser Sache
> Nahe. Wie gut waren wir uns, dieser
> Guten Sache nahe.[55]

Brecht's technique of breaking the syntax lends additional emphasis to the words at the start and end of each line: thus, by ending line 3

---

[52] BBA 443/62.

[53] 'A mixture of Chekhov and the worst kind of gossipy jargon, gossipy slang, without any poetry'. Bunge, *Gespräche*, 100; Lyon (ed.), 'Der Briefwechsel', 140.

[54] 'Über reimlose Lyrik mit unregelmäßigen Rhythmen', *BFA*, xxii.1. 357–64.

[55] 'THE MOTHER 'Constantly you hear how quickly/The mothers lose their sons, but I/Kept my son. How did I keep him? Through/The third cause./He and I were two, but the third/Common cause, pursued in common, was what/United us./Often I myself heard sons/Speak with their parents./How much better was our conversation/About the third cause, which we had in common/The great cause common to many people!/How close we were to each other, close/To this cause. How good we were to each other, close/To this good cause.' *BFA*, iii. 307.

on 'Durch', he draws attention to 'Die dritte Sache' which has saved Wlassowa's relationship with Pawel. But Peters destroyed this effect in the first eight lines of his translation by mapping the syntax largely on to the line structure and smoothing out Brecht's intentionally awkward rhythms:

THE MOTHER   You always hear
how mothers lose their sons;
but I've kept my son.
And how have I kept him?
By something we have in common.
He and I were two people, but this third thing
That we worked on together,
Brought us together.
Often I've heard children
Talk to their parents.
How much better were our talks
about this thing we have in common!
How close we were, when we were close
to this common thing.
And close to this thing we have in common
How we loved each other![56]

Peters also shifted the focus from the public to the private, so that his version prioritizes Wlassowa's personal relationship with Pawel over their relationship with Communism. He accomplished this by omitting the line 'vieler Menschen große, gemeinsame Sache' ('the great cause common to many people') and ending on the love between mother and son, rather than their closeness to the common cause and the mutual kindness that it promoted. These changes added considerably to the sentimentality of Peters's version and further diluted Brecht's ideology for the Theatre Union's audience.

3.3 The Shock of the Foreign: Brecht at the Theatre Union

When Brecht discovered that Peters had systematically destroyed the epic features of his play, he withdrew his authorization for the production. This came as an unpleasant shock to the Theatre Union, which had already spent the money raised through advance ticket sales and so could not afford to abandon the staging. So the company sent its

---

[56] BBA 443/43.

associate, the financial journalist Manuel Gomez, to negotiate with Brecht in Denmark. Gomez invited Brecht to New York, suggesting that he would be able to influence the production to his satisfaction, but without making any guarantees.[57]

When Brecht joined Eisler in New York on 15 October, rehearsals soon developed into a battle of wills between them and the director, Victor Wolfson. Aged just 25 and directing his first solo professional production, Wolfson resented this interference by a writer who was virtually unknown in America, and Brecht's confrontational approach and colourful language only made matters worse: indeed, Maltz remembers him chiefly as 'a screaming banshee'.[58] The increasingly hostile atmosphere and Brecht's inadequate command of English made productive dialogue impossible, so that his attempts to explain epic theatre fell on deaf ears. Sklar recalls that 'we were soon so embroiled in differences that we never could sit down and hear him out', and Maltz dismissed his ideas as 'a pretentious crock, contradictory within itself'.[59] The final straw came on 17 November, when Brecht accused the musical director, Jerome Moross, of performing 'Dreckmusik' ('filthy music'). Moross had just enough German to retort that he was trying to make 'Musik aus Dreck' ('music from filth') before threatening to 'break every bone in [Brecht's] body', whereupon Brecht and Eisler hastily left the theatre, never to return.[60] This fraught atmosphere and Brecht's vociferous criticism combined to destroy any enthusiasm that the cast had ever felt for the play, so that the stage-manager, P. A. Xantho, had to order them 'to stop saying "lousy"—"terrible"—etc.'.[61]

By this point, Brecht had changed the adaptation, line by line, until it respected the structure, style, and registers of his original text. The result was far closer to a literal translation: for example, 'ich glaube, daß es ihr gelingen kann' ('I believe that she can succeed'), translated by Peters as 'sure, I think it's a swell idea', became 'I believe she can do it'.[62] Similarly, 'der Marxismus an sich ist nicht schlecht', translated by Peters as 'Marxism in itself isn't to be sneezed at', was translated literally as 'Marxism in itself is not bad'.[63] Both the opening monologue and the final third of the play were restored, and Brecht persuaded the set designer, Mordecai Gorelik, to abandon his naturalistic design in favour

[57] Weisstuch, 422.   [58] Baxandall, 'Brecht in America', 74.   [59] Ibid. 75.
[60] Ibid. 74.   [61] Report dated 3 Dec. 1935, BBA Z50/309–68.
[62] *BFA*, iii. 271; BBA 443/10 and Z50/218.
[63] *BFA*, iii. 293; BBA 443/30 and Z50/264.

of a simple, plain structure based on Neher's sketches for the Berlin première. Accordingly, Gorelik placed the pianos on stage, in full view of the audience, and used slides and captions to interrupt the spectators' mechanical identification with the action. Some of the captions referred directly to American living conditions, references that Brecht accepted because they furthered the play's political effect.[64]

Brecht may have boasted to Weigel of having created a 'ganz hübsche kleine Diktatur' ('quite nice little dictatorship') at the Theatre Union, but his reliance on coercion seriously undermined the production.[65] Since the Theatre Union failed to grasp the function of the slides and captions, it used them as gimmicks or, as Brecht called them, 'spooks'. The lighting designer kept to his customary naturalistic approach, using dim lighting for the evening scenes and leaving the pianos in the dark. According to Brecht, this created the impression that they were on stage 'merely because there was no room for them elsewhere'.[66] In several scenes, the Theatre Union also cluttered the set with props that did not contribute directly to the action, like a washing-line, clothes on the settee, 'Russian Health Bread', and even an animal carcase in the butcher's scene.[67] Although similar naturalistic details had appealed to reviewers in the company's earlier productions, they were out of place in the new, anti-illusionist set.

The acting aggravated this stylistic confusion still further. Most of the Theatre Union's actors were trained in the Stanislavsky method, which the Group Theatre had introduced to New York, and so they attempted to maximize their identification with their roles.[68] Although this approach would have suited Peters's adaptation, it conflicted with the slides, captions, and particularly the chorus, which impeded identification and invited a more critical response. Indeed, an anecdote told by Michael Gordon, a member of the Executive Board, epitomizes the gulf between the different relationships that Brecht and the Theatre Union sought to establish with the spectators. Brecht showed Gordon a photograph of an enraptured audience, saying: 'They're intoxicated! It's disgusting. How can you teach them anything?', whereas Gordon recalled: 'I looked at it and all I could think was, *I* should only get that kind of response.'[69]

[64] *BFA*, xxiv. 153–5.   [65] *BFA*, xxviii (1998), 529.
[66] BBA 341/14–18.   [67] BBA Z50/200, 314–18.
[68] Morgan Y. Himelstein, *Drama Was a Weapon: The Left-Wing Theatre in New York 1929–1941* (New Brunswick, NJ: Rutgers University Press, 1963), 56.
[69] Williams, *Stage Left*, 181.

As Brecht subsequently argued, this stylistic confusion contributed to the production's generally negative reception. For instance, in the *New York Post*, Wilella Waldorf commented that 'the chants in unison to piano accompaniment ... seemed only to interrupt a story which was ... interesting and often very touching', while in *New Masses* Michael Gold highlighted 'the confusion of styles'.[70] But the failure to negotiate the ideological and cultural differences between the text and its new audience was even more important. This was confirmed by Elisabeth Hauptmann, who—unlike Brecht—had seen the finished production and judged it more positively: '... es kam dann zur Aufführung, die gar nicht schlecht war, die war dann sehr dünn und auch sehr durchsichtig und sehr deutlich. Und so deutlich, daß viele Kritiker fanden: es war zu deutlich, als wie für Kinder gemacht.... Aber setzen Sie das mal Leuten vor, die kein anderes Theater kennen außer dem kommerziellen New Yorker Theater!'[71] As the Theatre Union had always feared, reviewers perceived Brecht's didacticism as an insult to the intelligence of American workers. For example, in the *Brooklyn Daily Eagle* Arthur Pollock called the production 'a simple kindergarten for Communist tots', and in the *New York American* Gilbert W. Gabriel warned: 'Grown-up playgoers, beware.'[72] And whereas the Communist press in Berlin had—with some reservations—welcomed Brecht's play in 1932, the American Communist reviewer Michael Gold argued that *Mother* was completely inappropriate for the Theatre Union's audience: 'It is ... an agit-prop play, with a strongly German flavor, and as such I don't see how the Theatre Union directors misjudged their typical audience by presenting it.'[73] The irony, of course, was that Wolfson and Peters had never intended to present *Mother* in this manner. Unfortunately for the Theatre Union, the box office receipts confirmed Gold's verdict: according to the *Brooklyn Daily Eagle*, the production 'had the shortest

[70] Wilella Waldorf, '*Mother* Opens Theatre Union's Third Season', *New York Post*, 20 Nov. 1935; Michael Gold, 'Change the World!', *New Masses* (New York), 6 Dec. 1935.

[71] '... then the production was performed; it was not bad at all; it was very thin and also very transparent and very clear. So clear, in fact, that many critics felt it was too clear, as if it had been put on for children.... But you try serving that up to people who know no theatre besides the commercial New York theatre!' Kebir, 183.

[72] Arthur Pollock, 'Theater Union Opens its Season with *Mother*, a Play as Violent as a Zephyr', *Brooklyn Daily Eagle*, 20 Nov. 1935; Gilbert W. Gabriel, '*Mother*: Theatre Union Begins with a Musical Version of a Gorki Tale', *New York American*, 20 Nov. 1935.

[73] Michael Gold, 'Change the World!', *New Masses*, 5 Dec. 1935.

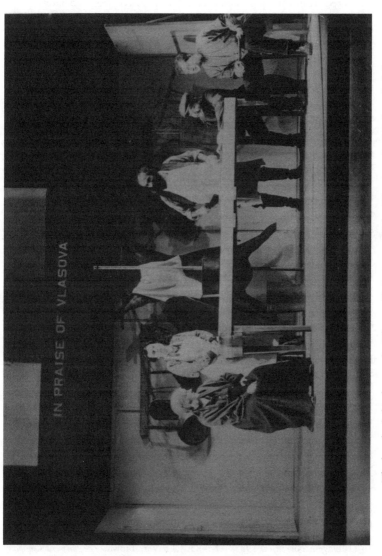

7. The butcher's kitchen at the Theatre Union, 1935. Helen Henry as the Mother, far left.

run of any of the labor group's plays'.[74] Indeed, the company never recovered from this spectacular failure and closed two years later.

3.4 Ideological and Aesthetic Appropriation in Glasgow

Even a brief glance at one other production, by the Citizens Theatre in Glasgow (1982), shows how the strategy of ideological and aesthetic appropriation has been applied successfully to *Die Mutter*. Much in the spirit of the Theatre Union's initial attempts, the director Giles Havergal used a predominantly naturalistic staging and augmented Steve Gooch's published translation with exciting direct action from Gorky's novel, such as Pawel's trial and execution. Like the Theatre Union, Havergal also increased the play's sentimentality, partly by re-introducing the love interest between Pawel and Mascha, and diluted Brecht's Communist arguments.[75] The resultant ideological shift towards a liberal humanist staging was epitomized in the opening and closing cry: 'Three cheers for freedom of speech! Three cheers for the heart of the mother!'[76]

Even so, there were significant ideological and theatrical differences between the adaptations that were prepared for the productions in New York and Glasgow. Whereas Peters retained Brecht's triumphant closing demonstration, Havergal cut it in the belief that historical developments had rendered Brecht's arguments unconvincing: 'The optimism, the sense of her marching in triumph, I felt utterly inappropriate. Alas the wages of revolution are not victory. In our version she was beaten up while handing out leaflets.'[77] Furthermore, although Havergal transformed many of the songs into naturalistic speeches, he—unlike Peters—also added some new reflective epic passages and used a narrator to set the scene by reading passages from Gorky's novel.[78] This suggests that by 1982 epic conventions had even entered into the naturalistic tradition, eroding some of the distinctions between the two

---

[74] Anon., 'The Theater Union's *Mother...*', *Brooklyn Daily Eagle*, 11 Dec. 1935.

[75] Citizens Theatre prompt script of *The Mother*, Scottish Theatre Archive (henceforth STA), E.p. Box 9/6. See also Claude Schumacher, 'The Glasgow Citizens Company Production of Brecht's *The Mother* (Nov.–Dec. 1982)', in *Das Drama und seine Inszenierung*, ed. Erika Fischer-Lichte, Medien in Forschung + Unterricht, series A, 16 (Tübingen: Niemeyer, 1985), 173–85; John Vere Brown, *The Citizens Company 1979–1985* (Glasgow: Citizens Theatre, 1985).

[76] Citizens Theatre prompt script, 1, 62.

[77] Margaret Eddershaw, *Performing Brecht: Forty Years of British Performances* (London: Routledge, 1996), 87.

[78] STA E.p. Box 9/6, e.g. 1–3, 6, 14, 30, 40, 48.

modes of production. So although the Citizens Theatre pursued the same overall strategy as the Theatre Union, the aesthetic results were significantly different.

4. INTERROGATING THE FOREIGN: *LA MÈRE* IN LILLE, 1979

In 1979 a production in Lille evinced a significantly more differentiated, nuanced understanding of cultural transference. In contrast to Wolfson and Havergal, the director Pierre-Etienne Heymann commented select-ively on French, German and Russian culture and history. Theatrically, he displayed far more detachment and freedom than directors had done in the first phase of the postwar reception of *Die Mutter*, and incorporated contemporary French techniques into his staging, which contrasted strikingly with Brecht's own productions.

4.1 Historical and Ideological Context

Heymann's staging was produced jointly by the Théâtre Populaire des Flandres and Théâtre de la Planchette, two regional companies which owed their existence to the decentralization of French theatre, a process encouraged by the cultural policy of successive postwar governments. Since both companies were committed to working closely with local audiences, their production opened in Lille and then toured towns throughout the Nord-Pas-de-Calais region.[79] Heymann, the manager of a theatre in neighbouring Villeneuve d'Ascq, had good reason to believe that *Die Mutter* would interest local spectators, because Lille, a traditionally left-wing town, was experiencing high levels of unemploy-ment as the local coal, steel and textile industries declined.[80] Even so, he—like Havergal—recognized that Brecht's optimistic assessment of the Russian Revolution would probably seem naïve to Western spec-tators in 1979, given Stalin's Purges, the atrocities in the Ukraine and the gulags, and the ongoing oppression in the Eastern bloc. Indeed,

---

[79] Laurence Arven, 'Les Intermittences de la révolution', *Témoignage Chrétien* (Paris), 9–15 Apr. 1979.

[80] Madeleine Duvinage, 'Un spectacle magistral', *Liberté* (Lens), 17 Mar. 1979; Jean-Marie Sourgens, '*La Mère*, de Brecht en coréalisation régionale', *La Voix du Nord* (Lille), 17 Mar. 1979.

the spectators might even regard such factors as proof that the revolutionaries' ideals had been fatally flawed from the start. Whereas Stein had evaded these problems at the Schaubühne, Heymann foregrounded them by engaging critically with Soviet history. Perhaps in order to placate the purists, he argued that this approach was entirely in the spirit of Brecht's pragmatism and 'pensée intervenante' ('eingreifendes Denken'/'interventionist thinking').[81]

4.2 Multiculturalism and the October Revolution

Heymann adopted a far more multicultural approach towards Brecht's text than any of his predecessors had done, either in Germany or abroad. Indeed, his notes refer to a wide range of background material, from Sergey Eisenstein's film *October* (1928) and essay on the 'Montage of Attractions' (1923), to Bernardo Bertolucci's film *Prima della rivoluzione* (*Before the Revolution*, 1962), Brecht's *Theaterarbeit* (1952), and Stein's *Regiebuch* (1971).[82] French influences also entered the staging in the form of allusions to the annual Bastille Day celebrations: thus the Greek-born set designer Yannis Kokkos scattered the stage with torn paper lanterns, cups, banners, and crumpled copies of the French Communist newspaper *L'Humanité Dimanche* and its Italian counterpart *L'Unità*—further evidence of multiculturalism.[83] These references were intended to evoke 'l'ambiance mélancolique d'une fin de fête populaire, à l'heure où les questions suivent les réponses' and to encourage the audience to reflect on the contemporary import of the action.[84] Heymann's juxtaposition of different layers and versions of history recalled Ariane Mnouchkine's *1789* (1971), a famous and even more complex spectacle that contrasted the common people's experience of the French Revolution with the traditional history-book version of events.[85]

[81] Pierre-Etienne Heymann, *Regards sur les mutations du théâtre public (1968–1998): La Mémoire et le désir* (Paris: L'Harmattan, 2000), 157.

[82] Ibid. 158, 208–9, 212.

[83] Fabienne Pascaud, 'A Lille', *Télérama* (Paris), 4 Apr. 1979; Anne Surgers, 'Les Dangers d'une fidélité absolue au passé', *Le Matin* (Paris), 10 Apr. 1979.

[84] 'The melancholy atmosphere of the end of a popular festival, at that time when the questions follow the answers.' Yannis Kokkos, 'Images pour *La Mère*', Lille 1979 programme. For Yannis Kokkos's designs, see *Obliques*, 20–1 (1979), 152, 159, 216, 222, 242–7.

[85] Lenora Champagne, *French Theatre Experiment since 1968*, Theater and Dramatic Studies, 18 (Michigan: UMI, 1984), 36–8; David Whitton, *Stage Directors in Modern France* (Manchester: Manchester University Press, 1987), 263–71.

Heymann and Kokkos interrogated Brecht's text and Soviet history almost exclusively through the set and props, without significantly altering Maurice Régnaut's translation.[86] In order to expose and indict the USSR's perversion of its founders' ideals, Kokkos set up the rectangular traverse (bifrontal) stage as 'un Musée de la Révolution d'Octobre' (a museum about the October Revolution) and lined it with glass cases containing artefacts from the revolutionary struggle, including flags, a printing press, leaflets, and megaphones.[87] Spectators were invited to examine the exhibits during the interval, and labels like 'pliant de la mère' ('the mother's folding chair') commented ironically on how the museum had created a cult around the characters' humble possessions.[88] Just before the play began, an effigy of Helene Weigel dressed as Wlassowa was carried on stage in a flamboyant cortège, decked with red flags, and placed in the remaining glass case.[89] This suggested that the BE had perpetuated the Soviet myth through its model production, which was still well known in French theatrical circles after the Parisian tours of 1960 and 1971. Kokkos then established a parallel between the BE's canonization of Wlassowa and Lenin's cult of personality by suspending immense effigies, photographs, and chromolithographs of the first Soviet leader from the walls. As one reviewer commented, the different media highlighted the contrast between 'la réalité et l'imagerie' ('the reality and the imagery'), a contrast that must have been equally evident from the dissimilarity between Weigel's effigy and Arlette Renard, who played Wlassowa on stage.[90]

Heymann distanced the production still further from the USSR's practice of Communism by alluding directly to oppression under the current Soviet regime: according to reviewers, three bodyguards in large coats and soft hats leant against the guardrail of the podium and presided over the demonstration in Scene 5.[91] This device demonstrated the bitter irony that the KGB and the Soviet Army now exercised the repressive

---

[86] Heymann, 211.

[87] Ibid. 209; Anne Surgers, *Le Matin*, 10 Apr. 1979; J.-M. de Montremy, '*La Mère* à Lille', *La Croix* (Paris), 29 Mar. 1979.

[88] Montremy, *La Croix*.

[89] Ibid.; Michel Boué, 'Le Chaud et le froid', *L'Humanité Dimanche* (Paris), [n.d.], BBA; Marc Perri, ' "Si les Mères sont révolutionnées, il n'y a plus rien à révolutionner" ', *Rouge* (Paris), [n.d.], BBA; Sourgens, *La Voix du Nord*, 17 Mar. 1979.

[90] Pascaud, *Télérama*, 4 Apr. 1979.

[91] Boué, *L'Humanité Dimanche*; Michel Cournot, '*La Mère* dans le Nord', *Le Monde* (Paris), 4 Apr. 1979; Sourgens, *La Voix du Nord*, 17 Mar. 1979.

function formerly performed by the Tsar's soldiers, even as the regime used the annual commemoration of Bloody Sunday to strengthen its hold on power. Thus, by distinguishing between the revolutionaries' ideals and their abuse by their Soviet successors, Heymann countered the potential charges that the ideals were fatally flawed and that Stalinism had been inherent in the 1917 Revolution.

4.3 The Play's Contemporary Relevance

The museum also provoked questions about the role and nature of Communism in contemporary France, by suggesting that the classic revolutionary struggle was now consigned to history. In his production notes Heymann argued that Brecht's depiction of revolutionaries wrapping leaflets around cucumbers would probably be perceived merely as a comic cartoon: 'Tintin fait la révolution' ('Tintin stages the revolution').[92] In order to challenge his spectators to redefine the means and ends of the contemporary struggle, Heymann displayed Lenin's question 'What are we to do?' in different languages on red banners around the auditorium. Since the production argued that the Soviet experiment in Communism had failed, these banners encouraged spectators to seek an alternative to both the capitalist and the Soviet systems. By these means, Heymann hoped to achieve 'une interrogation sur la fin, les moyens et le devenir d'une révolution socialiste revisitée à la lumière de l'histoire de l'URSS'.[93] As the term 'interrogation' suggests, Heymann refused to prescribe any answers to Lenin's question—an approach which often underpins post-Brechtian theatre.[94]

Heymann's refusal to endorse Brecht's solutions was criticized by Michel Cournot, the reviewer for the Paris-based left-liberal newspaper *Le Monde*, who called the production an 'embrouillis abstrait de contradictions, de propagandisme et de culpabilité' and argued that 'entre Brecht, qui caricature les personnages de Gorki, et Pierre-Etienne Heymann, qui tient à se laver les mains du militantisme de Brecht, on s'y perd'.[95] But other reviewers shared the enthusiasm of local audiences:

[92] Heymann, 209.
[93] 'An investigation of the ends, the means, and the development of a Socialist revolution revisited in the light of the history of the USSR.' Ibid. 156.
[94] Cf. sect. 5.2 and Ch. 5.
[95] 'An abstract muddle of contradictions, propaganda, and guilt'; 'between Brecht, who caricatures Gorky's characters, and Pierre-Etienne Heymann, who is set on washing his hands of Brecht's militancy, you get lost'. Cournot, *Le Monde*, 4 Apr. 1979.

Laurence Arven, for example, considered the production 'un travail théâtral remarquable d'acuité' ('a remarkably acute piece of theatre'), and Madeleine Duvinage called it 'un spectacle extraordinaire de vitalité, chaleureux et exaltant' ('an extraordinarily lively, warm and uplifting spectacle').[96] Indeed, Arven's review suggests that the staging aroused interest precisely because it departed from the play's agitational function: Heymann had highlighted the problems posed by recent Soviet history while resisting the temptation to satirize or dilute the politics of 1917. In addition, he had achieved a productive cultural exchange between Brecht's text, the BE's model production, Soviet history, and the domestic French context. This creative and open-ended approach contrasted with the production in New York, where Brecht had ignored local concerns and the Theatre Union had sought to satisfy existing expectations. Indeed, the positive reception of Heymann's production confirms the lessons of Brecht's stagings at the Theatre Union and the BE: that the decision how, and how far, to challenge the spectators' expectations is the key to the success or failure of cultural transference.

5. POST-1968 POLITICAL THEATRE: *THE MOTHER* IN LONDON, 1986, AND NEW YORK, 1997

Although the emphasis which Heymann and Stein placed on reflection indicates the caution of certain strands of political theatre after 1968, the 1970s and 1980s actually witnessed a re-assertion of direct agitation in British political theatre. During this period left-wing companies performed *Die Mutter* and even used it as a model for new political plays. Their direct, unashamedly political productions contrasted with the approaches which US companies have adopted towards *Die Mutter* since 1968: both the San Francisco Mime Troupe, one of the USA's foremost alternative companies, and the Irondale Ensemble Project cultivated a far more playful performance style and relationship with their audiences. This fundamental difference in approach was rooted in the performance contexts: whereas left-wing theatre in Britain could capitalize on industrial discontent and, as time went on, opposition to the right-wing policies of Margaret Thatcher's Government, alternative companies in the USA have continued to face the same kinds of prejudice against Communism and didactic theatre as the Theatre Union did in 1935.

---

[96] Arven, *Témoignage Chrétien*, 9–15 Apr. 1979; Duvinage, *Liberté*, 17 Mar. 1979.

In her informative survey of British productions of Brecht's plays, Margaret Eddershaw argues that the growth of socially committed alternative theatre after 1968 provided an appropriate cultural context for strong, radical productions of Brecht's plays, a thesis that is supported by stagings of *Die Mutter* in both England and Scandinavia during the 1970s and 1980s.[97] Eddershaw also distinguishes between the alternative and mainstream reception of Brecht during this period, arguing that in mainstream theatre 'it became the fashion to adopt what was perceived as a Brechtian "style" and to ignore the fundamental principles and intentions of his working method'.[98] Even so, a production of *Die Mutter* by one of England's foremost establishment theatres, the National, adhered far more closely to Brecht's methods than Eddershaw's comments suggest.

In England, the abolition of theatre censorship in 1968 facilitated the growth of alternative theatre. Besides which, endemic industrial action, the international oil crisis, and the Left's disappointment at Labour's modest reforms created a ready market for Steve Gooch's translation of *Die Mutter*, both amongst professional theatres and militant alternative groups. After the translation had been premièred at London's Half Moon Theatre in 1973, it was performed on tour by Belt & Braces in 1978 and by M6 in 1981, by which time economic recession and Margaret Thatcher's radical programme of denationalization had enhanced its appeal for the Left.[99] As the Conservative Government's cuts in arts spending accelerated the politicization of theatre, the boundary between the alternative and mainstream sectors became blurred.

Industrial unrest and economic crisis also explain why *Die Mutter* was popular during the 1970s in Scandinavia, where it was staged by professional theatres like Copenhagen's Fiolteatret (1972), Oslo's Nationaltheatret (1972), and Malmö's Bruksteatern (1973), and by amateur groups in Malmberget (1974), Malmö (1978), and Lejre (1981). Like the English alternative companies, Scandinavia's amateur groups were committed to performing political drama for working-class

[97] Eddershaw, 90. I refer to England deliberately: there were no known productions in Wales and only one in Scotland (at the Citizens Theatre) during this period.

[98] Ibid. 117.

[99] Catherine Itzin, *Stages in the Revolution: Political Theatre in Britain since 1968* (London: Eyre Methuen, 1980), 162, 373; Bertolt Brecht, *The Mother*, trans. Steve Gooch (London: Eyre Methuen, 1978); personal letter from Joy Westendarp of the International Copyright Bureau, 21 Nov. 2000. For brief comments on Gooch's translation and the Belt & Braces production, cf. Eddershaw, 73–4.

audiences; in Malmö, for example, the Studioteatern's links with schools, trade unions, and residents' associations enabled it to attract a wide audience to its production in 1978.[100] Again like the English companies, these groups were keen to learn from Brecht's political theatre, but used his methods selectively and only for their own, context-specific purposes.

5.1 The National Theatre, 1986

In 1986, the NT's agitational production of *Die Mutter* marked a culmination of the aforementioned trends. The decision to tour schools and colleges with Brecht's most pro-Communist play showed not only how the reaction against Thatcherism had politicized even mainstream professional theatre, but also how alternative theatre's outreach work had stimulated the Theatre-in-Education movement. Thus, before the production finished in the Cottesloe Theatre on London's South Bank, it toured small-to-medium-scale venues around England and Northern Ireland, including colleges and community centres.[101] Even though it was overtly Communist and confrontational, the production was sponsored by the corporate giant BP—a sign that funding constraints were forcing even politicized companies to rely on commercial sponsorship.[102]

The NT production was directed by Di Trevis, who had acted and directed at the Citizens Theatre before becoming, in 1985, the first female guest director of the RSC tour.[103] The set was designed by Bunny Christie, who had staged *Die Mutter* with Trevis in February 1986 at Manchester's Contact Theatre—which sued the NT for allegedly giving insufficient credit to the earlier production.[104] Although Trevis made only minimal changes to Gooch's translation, she confirmed its political arguments by ending with Eisler's 'Solidarity Song'.[105]

---

[100] Anon., 'På gårdsfest med Brecht', *Den Hialöse* (Malmö), 1 May 1978; Annika Gustafsson, 'Studioteatern spelar *Modern* på gården', *Sydsvenska Dagbladet* (Malmö), 12 Apr. 1978; Claes Sturm, 'Brecht blir gårdsteater', *Dagens Nyheter* (Stockholm), 13 Apr. 1978.

[101] 'The Mother Tour 1986', National Theatre Archive (henceforth NTA), Bibed 4 F2.

[102] Publicity leaflet, NTA, Bibed 4 F2.

[103] Christine Eccles, 'Naked Ambitions', *Time Out* (London), 12–18 Sept. 1985, 10; Angela Wilkes, 'Company Director', *Sunday Times* (London), 25 Aug. 1985.

[104] Leslie Geddes-Brown, 'The Question Is: Whose Mother Is It?', *Sunday Times* (London), 9 Nov. 1986.

[105] Prompt script, NTA, Bibed 4.

Christie's functional set and props grounded the action in the domestic sphere: for example, the red flag was stitched together from rags, and white sheets pegged to a washing-line functioned as a backdrop. Smaller pillowcases were draped over the sheets, with slogans or dates on the reverse so that they could be flipped over as necessary. According to the critic Michael Billington, this resourceful approach redirected spectators' attention from the outcome to the course of the action, exactly as Brecht had intended: 'I also noticed at Battersea, for one of the few times in my life, Brecht's narrative technique working. When a charcoal-inscribed sheet announced the death of Pelagea's son, a woman on my left uttered a devastated sigh: she then leant forward in her seat to discover what effect the news would have.'[106] But whereas the Contact set had included television footage of Thatcher, Arthur Scargill, and the 1984 miners' strike, Christie cut these overt contemporary references at the NT.[107] This move allowed the spectators to spot the topical connections themselves and so experience the 'Lust am Erkennen' ('joy of recognition') that was central to Brecht's political theatre.[108]

Reviewers in the centre and left-wing press were positively surprised by the politics and aesthetics of both stagings. For instance, Erlend Clouston wrote in the *Guardian*: 'Contact's production of Brecht's revolutionary parable overturns all expectations. It provides an evening of theatre that is sharp, shrewd, and beautifully engineered.'[109] Also writing in the *Guardian*, Michael Billington called the NT staging 'one of the strongest things to have emerged from the South Bank all year', a view that Helen Rose endorsed in *Time Out*.[110] In the *Independent*, meanwhile, Andrew Rissik praised Trevis's 'admirable economy and visual flair', and in the Communist *Morning Star* Tom Vaughan told his readers: 'You must bend all your energies and if necessary rob a bank to see this play.'[111] But in the pro-Thatcher *Daily Telegraph* Stella Flint conceded only that '*The Mother* emerges as vivid theatrical history'—as if the production had no topical relevance.[112] Thus, the largely enthusiastic reception of the productions reflected not only the energy, wit, and resourcefulness of

[106] Michael Billington, 'Mother Cunning', *Guardian* (London), 21 Nov. 1986.

[107] Alan Hulme, 'Contact', *Manchester Evening News*, 1 Mar. 1986.

[108] *BFA*, xxv. 418.

[109] Erlend Clouston, 'The Mother', *Guardian* (Manchester), 28 Feb. 1986.

[110] Billington, *Guardian*, 21 Nov. 1986; Helen Rose, 'The Mother', *Time Out* (London), 10–17 Dec. 1986.

[111] Andrew Rissik, 'Naiveté to Please', *Independent* (London), 21 Nov. 1986; Tom Vaughan, 'Brecht's Mother of Invention', *Morning Star* (London), 1 Dec. 1986.

[112] Stella Flint, 'The Mother', *Daily Telegraph* (Manchester), 28 Feb. 1986.

Trevis's stagings, but also the Centre and Left's appetite for oppositional theatre at the height of the Thatcher era.

5.2 The Irondale Ensemble Project

Even though the Irondale Ensemble Project presented itself as a radical theatre, its staging of *Die Mutter* involved far less agitation than the production at the middle-class National Theatre. Indeed, Irondale diluted Brecht's ideology, included multiple references to contemporary popular culture, and established a far more playful relationship with its audience. These strategies corresponded broadly to the use of circus tricks, jazz, and domestic references to Helen Keller and Richard Nixon in a staging by the San Francisco Mime Troupe in 1973, at the height of the Watergate Affair.[113] In both stagings, the emphasis on entertainment was designed to overcome the American public's endemic suspicion of far left-wing politics and didactic theatre, the selfsame problems that the Theatre Union had faced in 1935.

Irondale's production of *The Mother* ran from 26 November to 20 December 1997 at the Theater for the New City in New York. Whereas the Mime Troupe had frankly admitted that it was interested only in Brecht's ideology, Irondale professed a commitment to his staging methods too: indeed, according to one of its founders, Terry Greiss, it even 'considers Brecht to be its touchstone playwright'. Yet although Greiss claimed that Brecht's 'style of acting and ... techniques of theatrical production ... are at the core of Irondale's performance vocabulary', the company's production of *The Mother* owed far more to postmodern notions of performance.[114] Geraldine Harris defines postmodern productions as follows:

They are eclectic in terms of borrowing from other, past texts and performances, employ irony, parody and pastiche, paradox and contradiction, and while they deliberately play upon intertextuality, they are also self-reflexive and self-referential. They eschew linear narratives, operating through juxtaposition and collage, and resist the production of fixed or single meanings or reading positions.[115]

[113] Cf. Mel Gordon, 'The San Francisco Mime Troupe's *The Mother*', *TDR*, 19.2 (June 1975), 94–101.

[114] Terry Greiss, 'A Brecht-Free Environment', <http://www.irondale.org/news-letters/FALL97.PDF>.

[115] Geraldine Harris, *Staging Femininities: Performance and Performativity* (Manchester: Manchester University Press, 1999), 7.

8. A political washing-line: the National Theatre's set, 1986 © Michael Mayhew. Yvonne Bryceland as the Mother, centre.

In contrast, Brecht's use of irony, parody, and contradiction in *Die Mutter* was firmly harnessed to his critical analysis of sociopolitical reality. Furthermore, his use of juxtaposition and montage did not involve a rejection of linear narratives, since he paid close attention to the *Fabel* in both 1932 and 1951. Instead, Irondale's director Jim Niesen subverted Brecht's argument that Communism was a positive alternative to capitalism and shifted the staging ideologically towards anarchism.

Irondale's theatrical style borrowed heavily from vaudeville performance, which consists of unconnected musical, dance, and comedy acts, throughout which the performers maintain a direct relationship with the audience. These techniques were adapted for cinema in the 1920s and 1930s by the Marx Brothers, to whom Irondale alluded directly in *The Mother*: one worker was seen studying the screenplay of *Why a Duck?*, and the teacher was made up to look like Groucho Marx, a reference to the anarchist slogan of Paris 1968: 'Je suis marxiste, tendance Groucho.'[116] Like vaudeville performers, Irondale's actors frequently ad-libbed and encouraged audience participation, an approach which went far beyond the occasional direct addresses in Brecht's text. Indeed, the actors even paraded their irreverent treatment of the text by asking each other 'Is that in the translation?'.[117]

Whilst Irondale's production contained more domestic references than any other staging short of a rewrite, they did not always serve a clear political purpose. For example, although the backdrop depicted a front page of *The New York Times* headlining the end of Prohibition in 1933, this reference was not developed in any way. This contrasted with the political import of the opening scene, in which 'a stout black man ... wearing a blond wig and sexy evening dress, makes his entrance and tells the audience he is J. Edgar Hoover'.[118] Here, by cross-dressing an Afro-American actor, Irondale alluded comically both to rumours about the former FBI chief's sexuality and to his persecution of Martin Luther King. The same reviewer reported that Hoover 'has come to close down the show because the cast is singing "You Can't Fool Me, I'm Sticking with the Union." When he demands that they sing a patriotic American song instead, they respond with "This Land is your Land, This Land is my Land," and our Hoover says, "Well, that's more like it!".' [119] Thus,

---

[116] 'I'm a Marxist, of the Groucho variety.' <http://www.irondale.org/newsletters/FALL97.PDF>.

[117] Leonard J. Lehrn, 'The Good Fight against a Brecht-Free New York', *Aufbau* (New York), 2 Jan. 1998.

[118] Dan Isaac, 'The Mother', *Backstage* (New York), 12 Dec. 1997.   [119] Ibid.

having discredited Hoover's prejudice against Afro-Americans, Irondale also hoped to discredit his prejudice against the Left—particularly since the unofficial American anthem 'This Land is your Land' was, just like 'Union Maid', written by the left-wing folk-singer Woody Guthrie. Like the Mime Troupe, Irondale also introduced left-wing American songs into the performance, such as Arlo Guthrie's 'Santa Claus Has a Red Suit—He's a Communist!' (1968), which satirized the irrational prejudices of McCarthyism.[120] In the programme Irondale again related the production to domestic politics and popular culture, this time by quoting Woody Allen alongside information about American labour history. Nevertheless, the production also invoked the struggles of the international Left: for instance, the actors sang the 'Internationale' in the original French.[121]

Irondale included so many domestic references and cut the 'Lob des Kommunismus' because it feared that, in America, 'Communism has become synonymous with totalitarianism and capitalism with democracy.'[122] But although the domestic allusions related Brecht's subject-matter to the USA's cultural heritage and political history, the failure to integrate them into a socially critical analysis frustrated Irondale's objective of staging *Die Mutter* as 'a parable about revolutionary change in a society dominated by the interests of large corporate power'.[123] In fact, this aim was entirely incompatible with Irondale's postmodern approach, which rejected the metanarrative of the parable in favour of eclecticism and irony. Furthermore, the humorous use of cross-dressing and pop culture risked implying that Irondale did not take Brecht's politics seriously, giving the audience little incentive to penetrate the surface. So instead of encouraging a first principles analysis, as Irondale had hoped, many spectators perceived the production as pastiche. Thus, in *The New York Times* Bruckner commented: 'How seriously Irondale ever takes its radical thinking is hard to gauge,' and in the transatlantic Jewish newspaper *Aufbau* Leonard Lehrn concluded: 'Whatever "Irondale" means, it obviously stands at least in part for irony.'[124] Irondale's failure to communicate its intentions provides some indication why, as we shall

---

[120] Lehrn, *Aufbau*, 2 Jan. 1998.   [121] Ibid.

[122] Jim Neisen [*sic*], 'Eight Questions from the Acting Company to Jim', <http://www.irondale.org/newsletters/FALL97.PDF>.

[123] 'Irondale Ensemble Project Revives Rare Brecht Play', press release, Billy Rose Collection, New York Public Library.

[124] D. J. R. Bruckner, 'Not your Typical Russian Revolution', *New York Times*, 27 Nov. 1997; Lehrn, *Aufbau*, 2 Jan. 1998.

see in Chapter 5, left-wing practitioners resisted postmodern approaches when staging *Die Mutter* in the reunified Germany.

5.3 Differences in the Practice of Political Theatre since 1968

These productions point to clear differences in the practice of far left-wing theatre in England and the USA since 1968. Whilst political commitment drew alternative companies in both England and the USA to *Die Mutter*, it was only in England that theatres—including even the NT—opted for stark, confrontational stagings. In the USA, where the Left was traditionally weaker and suspicion against anything perceived as Communism was still endemic, Irondale never took its spectators' political support or interest for granted. Just like the Theatre Union, it feared that Brecht's subject-matter would be too remote, too didactic, and too radical for its audience. So, like the San Francisco Mime Troupe, it opted for a more playful relationship with its spectators, incorporated elements of popular culture, and referred to the acceptable face of American left-wing protest: the folk-songs that had been revived by singers like Woody Guthrie. But this technically subversive approach diluted Brecht's overtly critical arguments and allowed the audience to consume the performance simply as a piece of light entertainment.

6. RADICAL ENGLISH AND IRISH REWRITES FROM THE 1970S AND 1980S

In addition to being performed by politicized theatres in the 1970s and 1980s, *Die Mutter* inspired several new texts by English and Irish playwrights.[125] These left-wing rewrites addressed contemporary domestic politics directly, almost always using the vernacular of popular culture as the Mime Troupe and Irondale had done.

Since Brecht's text depicts the conversion of a strong female protagonist to Marxism, rewriting the play offered dramatists an ideal opportunity to tackle feminist issues from a left-wing perspective—even

---

[125] In addition to the texts discussed here, *Die Mutter* inspired the Belt & Braces production *England Expects*, while *US*—Peter Brook's controversial production about Vietnam—used the techniques from Scene 5 to describe the 1945 August Revolution in Hanoi. See Gavin Richards, *England Expects: A Musical Entertainment for All Those Sick with Sacrifice* (London: Journeyman and Belt & Braces Roadshow, 1977); Peter Brook et al., *US: The Book of Royal Shakespeare Theatre Production US* (London: Calder and Boyars, 1968), 42–8.

though feminist critics would soon criticize Brecht's depiction and use of female characters, including Wlassowa. One such critic was Sara Lennox, who argued that Brecht's 'conception of women as figures willing, to the neglect of their own subjective concerns, to be used by a cause in which they are totally subsumed, remains a male fantasy projection which fails to take women's own needs into account'.[126] In similar vein, Sue-Ellen Case criticized Brecht for failing to challenge gender roles and stereotypes in *Die Mutter*, arguing that his presentation of Wlassowa was 'a petrification of political possibilities'.[127] Furthermore, Michelene Wandor argued that 'there is no space here for any feminist critique of the world in which [Wlassowa] lives', and 'her femaleness is only useful insofar as its qualities can be harnessed to political activism outside the home. Once that has happened, the qualities themselves have no personal application, and the home itself is no longer relevant to the action, separating the female and the domestic from the political.'[128]

Even so, *Die Mutter* indicates in several respects that, as feminists were to argue in the 1960s, 'the personal is political'. Although Wandor accuses Brecht of separating 'the domestic from the political', the agitation in the factory, in the countryside, and on the street actually alternates with political activity in the home, where Wlassowa promotes education and campaigns against superstition and rent increases. Indeed, Brecht suggests that politicization most frequently begins at home: in Scene 1 Wlassowa attributes Pawel's political engagement to his dissatisfaction with his poor nourishment: 'das Essen war ihm nie gut genug' ('the food was never good enough for him'), and in Scene 6 she declares proudly that he opens people's eyes to their domestic suffering: 'als eng wird erkannt die Kammer' ('the room is recognized as too small').[129] More significantly still, in Scene 9 Brecht actually reverses the gender roles of Scene 1: whereas previously Wlassowa had prepared Pawel's soup, now she prints while he cuts his own bread.[130] As early as 1932, Walter Benjamin highlighted the importance of this

---

[126] Sara Lennox, 'Women in Brecht's Works', *New German Critique*, 14 (1978), 83–96 (89).

[127] Sue-Ellen Case, 'Brecht and Women: Homosexuality and the Mother', *Brecht Yearbook*, 12 (1983), 65–74 (72).

[128] Michelene Wandor, 'Women Playwrights and the Challenge of Feminism in the 1970s', in *The Cambridge Companion to Modern British Women Playwrights*, ed. Elaine Aston and Janelle Reinelt (Cambridge: Cambridge University Press, 2000), 53–68 (62); idem, *Look Back in Gender: Sexuality and the Family in Post-War British Drama* (London: Methuen, 1987), 151.

[129] *BFA*, iii. 263, 292. [130] Ibid. 263, 306.

brief reversal: 'die Notdurft des Lebens [hat] aufgehört, die Menschen nach Geschlechtern zu kommandieren' ('the bare necessities of life have ceased ordering people about according to their gender').[131] In 1977 Laureen Nussbaum wrote that the scene 'must ... bring joy to anybody who is in favor of woman's [*sic*] liberation,' and in 1974 Mary Cronin argued that Wlassowa's political engagement involves 'a movement away from the bonds of the housewife'.[132] By exploring the domestic ramifications of female politicization more fully, two rewrites of *Die Mutter* addressed specifically feminist issues and argued that change at home must accompany change at work.

The first English rewrite was written and directed collectively in 1974 by Red Ladder, a militant group founded in 1968 as the AgitProp Street Players.[133] The pun in the title, *Strike while the Iron Is Hot*, highlighted the play's dual concern with the home and the workplace, while the subtitle focused on its feminist agenda: *A Woman's Work Is Never Done*. When Helen, a bored and disillusioned full-time mother, goes out to work, she quickly outstrips the male union members' lessons on political struggle and even persuades the factory's female canteen workers to strike until the male trade unionists support their demands for equal pay. Red Ladder also explored the conflict between Helen's desires to care for her family and to lead a fulfilling life outside the home, and showed how this conflict and inadequate social provision culminate in her decision to terminate her pregnancy. Significantly, Helen's political Odyssey at work is paralleled by her husband Dave's educational Odyssey at home: when the final scene opens, he has fed the children and is doing the ironing while Helen attends her union meeting.[134] And whereas Brecht had depicted the change in Wlassowa's and Pawel's relationship by showing them printing leaflets together, Red Ladder showed Helen and Dave jointly folding a sheet.[135] But Red Ladder also showed the limits of their new partnership, for at the end of the play Dave's insistence on attending a football match provokes an

---

[131] Walter Benjamin, 'Ein Familiendrama auf dem epischen Theater', in *Versuche über Brecht*, ed. Rolf Tiedemann (Frankfurt/Main: Suhrkamp, 1967), 39–43 (42).

[132] Laureen Nussbaum, 'The Image of Woman in the Work of Bertolt Brecht' (unpublished doctoral thesis, University of Washington, 1977), 373; Mary J. Cronin, 'The Politics of Brecht's Women Characters' (unpublished doctoral thesis, Brown University, 1974), 129.

[133] Itzin, 39–47; Red Ladder, 'Strike while the Iron Is Hot: A Woman's Work Is Never Done', in *Strike while the Iron Is Hot: Three Plays on Sexual Politics*, ed. Michelene Wandor (London: Journeyman, 1980), 17–62.

[134] Red Ladder, 58–9.   [135] *BFA*, iii. 306–7; Red Ladder, 59.

argument with Helen, who has signed him up to help with the union playgroup.[136] Thus, by avoiding a saccharine ending, the group showed how much remained to be done, both at home and in the factory.

The second left-wing feminist version was written in 1975 by John McGrath for 7:84 (England) and entitled *Yobbo Nowt*.[137] From the 1970s until his death in 2002, McGrath was one of Britain's leading practitioners and theorists of political theatre, and in 1971 he founded 7:84 with his partner, the actress Elizabeth McLennan. The group's name alluded to a statistic published that year in *The Economist*, according to which 7 per cent of the English population owned 84 per cent of the nation's wealth.[138] In 1973 the goal of working more closely with regional audiences led 7:84 to split into English and Scottish branches, both of which McGrath continued to oversee. One of his plays for the Scottish group, *Little Red Hen* (first performed in 1975), also borrowed the learning journey and Noh-style introduction from *Die Mutter*, but *Yobbo Nowt* drew more heavily on Brecht's play and acknowledged it as its main source.[139]

Like Red Ladder, McGrath focused far more on female experience than Brecht by showing his heroine's unfulfilling life as a housewife and then her struggles as a single working mother. Like Helen, Marie takes the initiative: she launches her political journey by deciding to seek employment and throws her husband out of their home after discovering his infidelity. Thus, whereas Wlassowa is simply the widow of a worker, Marie becomes a single mother by choice.[140] At the end of the play, McGrath tackles male chauvinism head-on: when Marie's husband re-appears, he dismisses her new-found independence as 'unnatural' and accuses her of being 'hard' and 'bitter' for refusing to welcome him back.[141] But McGrath also explores how a different division of domestic responsibility might work: thanks to Marie's training, her son is happy to cook and help out at home.[142] So although the play ends before Marie calls on her union to strike, she—like Helen—has already transformed her life at home.

---

[136] Red Ladder, 59–60.

[137] John McGrath, *Yobbo Nowt* (London: Pluto, 1978).

[138] John McGrath, *Naked Thoughts that Roam About: Reflections on Theatre 1958–2001*, ed. Nadine Holdsworth (London: Nick Hern, 2002), 48.

[139] John McGrath, *Little Red Hen* (London: Pluto, 1977), 3–4; *idem*, *Yobbo Nowt* [n.p.].

[140] *BFA*, iii. 263; McGrath, *Yobbo Nowt*, 12.   [141] McGrath, *Yobbo Nowt*, 62.

[142] Ibid. 40.

These rewrites were designed for the moment and recast *Die Mutter* in the modern working-class vernacular, using forms and techniques from popular culture. So although their aggressive politics contrasted with the American productions discussed in section 5, they shared the American emphasis on popular entertainment. After all, as McGrath points out in his aptly titled book *A Good Night Out*, when companies like 7:84 performed in community halls and working men's clubs, they had to compete with the bar and the snooker table.[143] Consequently, the companies used familiar styles of modern music to attract their listeners' attention and introduce them to the less familiar territory of political debate. For example, Red Ladder added new songs to *Strike* when it extended its tour from politicized trade union audiences to tenants' associations, women's groups, working men's clubs, schools, and colleges.[144] *Yobbo Nowt* also used more reflective songs to express its characters' inner thoughts and feelings, a technique that would have been familiar to spectators from popular musicals.[145]

Both rewrites retained only those Brechtian features which served their context-specific purposes. For instance, Red Ladder used placards to summarize the theme of each scene, while McGrath directly echoed some of Brecht's arguments.[146] Moreover, their productions were structured for an audience accustomed to cinema and television: the opening scene of *Yobbo Nowt* included a flashback, and the first scene of *Strike* featured a sharp, cinema-style cut from the heroine's wedding to her life as the mother of three squabbling children.[147] The rewrites also alleviated their didacticism through humour; Red Ladder updated Brecht's explanation of Marxist economics by using pints of beer to explain the need for parity and equal pay.[148]

In contrast, a new Anglo-Irish version adhered much more closely to the structure of Eisler's cantata, which had first been performed in Austria in 1949 and consisted of the songs, linked by short texts which set the scene and summarized the action. This new version was written in 1983–4 by the English dramatist John Arden and his Irish partner Margaretta D'Arcy, both of whom vehemently opposed the British

[143] John McGrath, *A Good Night Out: Popular Theatre: Audience, Class and Form*, 2nd edn (London: Nick Hern, 1996), 73–4.

[144] Red Ladder, 19.   [145] McGrath, *Yobbo Nowt*, 6, 41.

[146] e.g. Red Ladder, 28, 30; McGrath, *Yobbo Nowt*, 16; *idem*, *Little Red Hen*, 8–9, 36; *BFA*, iii. 274, 278–9, 296.

[147] McGrath, *Yobbo Nowt*, 4–7; Red Ladder, 26.

[148] *BFA*, iii. 277–81; Red Ladder, 38–43.

presence in Northern Ireland and supported Communism. Although they left the songs in Gooch's translation, they wrote a new parallel text that transposed the events to Northern Ireland, substituted a daughter for Pawel, and followed the action from the civil rights campaigns in 1968 through to the contemporary anti-nuclear movement.[149] The musical director John Tilbury also substituted modern bass and electric guitars for the original double bass and banjo, so that Eisler's music would not seem simply 'a fascinating relic of bygone times'.[150]

Arden and D'Arcy made major, controversial changes to the setting, subject-matter, and ideology of Brecht's text. Their new heroine, Maire Doherty, is a Catholic working-class widow from Derry, whose daughter Mairead joins the IRA. Instead of delivering leaflets like Wlassowa, Maire 'makes tea and sandwiches for the beleagured [*sic*] people behind the barricades, and helps to prepare petrol bombs'. Whereas Pawel is imprisoned for participating in a peaceful demonstration, Mairead is arrested for her involvement with the IRA, 'interrogated in Castlereagh, tortured and convicted by a non-jury court … sentenced to Armagh Gaol and labelled a criminal'. Instead of learning to read, Maire learns to type and operates an illegal Republican radio station, the modern equivalent of Brecht's illegal printing press. Then, instead of supporting strikes in the countryside, she 'takes part in the militant actions of the H-Block/Armagh Committees, blocking roads, occupying buildings, supporting strikes north and south of the border'. When Mairead, who has been on hunger strike, is assassinated in hospital by four masked men, her mother fights on, 'to mobilize the people for socialism and national liberation against capitalism and nuclear war'. Finally, the narrator asks: 'Who can say that this will not happen again? That as in Russia the people will have had enough and will take the world into their own hands, changing it according to their interests…?'[151]

By relocating Brecht's action and radicalizing the political activities, this adaptation tackled some of Northern Ireland's most topical and controversial issues, including terrorism, imprisonment without trial, Loyalist intimidation, and the pro-Unionist sympathies of the RUC and the British Army. But its support for terrorist violence prevented it from provoking a serious debate in London, particularly since the cantata was performed only weeks after the IRA bombing of Harrods had killed five and wounded eighty. So in *The Financial Times* Dominic Gill dismissed

[149] Parallel text printed in the Eisler Collective's programme, 4–11, BBA.
[150] Eisler Collective, 2.   [151] Ibid. 5–11.

the new text as 'a naïve and contemptible reduction to partisan cliché of one of the most complex political stories of the postwar years'.[152] Similarly, in *The Sunday Times* David Cairns wrote: 'I can understand the organisers' wish to update Brecht's spoken text and make it apply to Northern Ireland; but John Arden and Margaretta D'Arcy did the job crudely, not at all in the spirit of Brecht's shrewd idealism.'[153]

Nevertheless, the Northern Ireland version was far closer to the structure and radicalism of the cantata than either of the English rewrites had been to Brecht's play. This was because Nationalists in Northern Ireland, unlike far-left groups in England, could identify with a mass political movement. Indeed, according to Peter Ansorge, practitioners like McGrath viewed 'the policies of the Labour Party as only slightly less evil than those practised by the post-1970 ruling Conservative Government'.[154] So, recognizing that imminent revolution was unlikely, Red Ladder and 7:84 (England) used their rewrites to demand the more modest, reformist goals of parity, equal pay, and improved working conditions. They also campaigned for change within the home and suggested how domestic relations might work differently, thus using their spectators' political sympathy to challenge their acceptance of gender stereotypes both at work and at home.

It is no coincidence that these rewrites were all produced by militant alternative groups. They, far more than most mainstream theatres, used *Die Mutter* as Brecht had intended: as a means of intervening in contemporary political debates. But in order to do so, they assimilated the play to the domestic context by adopting the modern vernacular of popular culture, focusing on topical issues, and relocating the action to a domestic setting. In the full-length rewrites this process removed all obvious traces of the 'foreign' and dispensed entirely with Brecht's techniques of *Historisierung* and *Verfremdung*.

7. CONCLUSION

The international performance history of *Die Mutter* conforms to the pattern of the play's postwar German reception in two important

---

152 Dominic Gill, 'Eisler Collective/Elizabeth Hall', *Financial Times* (London), 20 Jan. 1984.

153 David Cairns, 'How to Communicate with the Aliens', *Sunday Times* (London), 22 Jan. 1984.

154 Peter Ansorge, *Disrupting the Spectacle: Five Years of Experimental and Fringe Theatre in Britain* (London: Pitman, 1975), 60.

respects. First, it demonstrates that the BE influenced foreign-language productions of *Die Mutter* just as strongly as it shaped stagings in the GDR. Second, it shows that the BE's model restricted the scope for culturally specific interpretations and approaches until the 1970s, when directors began to design new stagings for their own political and cultural contexts. The universal nature of this delay suggests that the model's prolonged hegemony was closely related to the problem of 'Einschüchterung durch die Klassizität' ('intimidation through classic status'),[155] not just to the GDR's conservative approach towards Brecht's legacy. By the 1970s, however, more practitioners were beginning to understand Brecht's theatre in terms of methods rather than styles, and this development enabled directors like Heymann and Trevis to use the methods selectively and pursue their own context-specific interpretations, just as Berghaus and Stein were doing in East and West Berlin. As a result, stagings of *Die Mutter* soon became politically and theatrically far more diverse, both in Germany and abroad.

The production history of *Die Mutter* actually contradicts Kohlmayer's thesis that foreign directors are more likely to adapt a text when it is in translation. Indeed, when a published translation was already available, most directors simply treated it as they would an original. When companies like the Theatre Union, Citizens Theatre, and Irondale did make significant changes, this was because they tended to adapt all their texts for performance, irrespective of their original language. What does emerge, however, is that American theatres have consistently opted for a strategy of appropriation, often for political reasons. This trend indicates that, as Lefevere suggests, dominant cultures may well be more likely to appropriate texts because they view their own practice as 'natural'.

Overall, this investigation indicates that ideology is more important than nationality in the cultural transference of overtly political texts. Staging *Die Mutter* in politically tense situations, like the aftermath of the miners' strike in England, posed relatively few problems because the text's confrontational politics were so topical. In other contexts, however, ideological shifts were a major feature of foreign-language productions and were often accompanied by a drift towards colloquialism. Such ideological and linguistic changes correspond to the desire for commercially 'safe' productions that satisfy the audience's

---

[155] *BFA*, xxiii. 316.

expectations, and thus tend towards the 'culinary' theatre that Brecht opposed. Nevertheless, Heymann's French production demonstrates how theatres can win over spectators by exploiting historical, political and cultural difference, instead of seeking to erode or conceal it. After the fall of the Berlin Wall, three German directors would adopt the same broad strategy in their productions of *Die Mutter*, to which I shall now turn.

5

Die Mutter and German Reunification, 1988–2003

1. INTRODUCTION

In Chapter 3, we saw how political theatre was being redefined in the early 1970s in both East and West Germany. During the next two decades, the movement away from agitation accelerated as even politically committed dramatists challenged the notion that theatre could communicate a clear message, a challenge that was spearheaded by Heiner Müller. After 1989 this literary and theatrical trend became even stronger, as conservative commentators like Ulrich Greiner and Frank Schirrmacher advocated an end to the politicized aesthetics of the Cold War.[1] Even in the former GDR, socially committed theatres increasingly conveyed their concerns—as distinct from a coherent message—through the fragmented postmodern aesthetic that had become so fashionable in the West. At the Volksbühne in 1997, for instance, Frank Castorf interrupted Hauptmann's *De Waber* (*The Weavers*) with quotations from film, advertising, and such diverse artists as Brecht, Busch, Bob Marley, and Quentin Tarantino in order to invoke the themes of Western cultural imperialism, materialism, and the end of the Socialist Utopia.[2]

The problems that now face *Die Mutter* are particularly acute because it, more than any of Brecht's other works, had been used to affirm the GDR. Its reputation as a *Staatsfeststück* explains why an advertisement for the GDR's final production, at the BE in 1988, is currently displayed alongside other GDR memorabilia in Berlin's *Ständige Vertretung*,

---

[1] Ulrich Greiner, 'Die deutsche Gesinnungsästhetik', *Die Zeit* (Hamburg), 2 Nov. 1990; Frank Schirrmacher, 'Literatur und Kritik', *FAZ*, 8 Oct. 1990; Hans J. Hahn, ' "Es geht nicht um Literatur": Some Observations on the 1990 "Literaturstreit" and its Recent Anti-Intellectual Implications', *GLL*, 50 (1997), 65–81.

[2] Comments based on a performance seen in Sept. 1999.

previously the FRG consulate and now a Cold War theme pub, and why Castorf ironically quoted Brecht's 'Lob des Kommunismus' in his aforementioned production. Indeed, when the East German director and former BE member Hans-Joachim Frank decided to stage *Die Mutter* in 1998, his actors were horrified: 'Um Gottes willen, machen wir nicht das, und so kurz nach der Wende.'[3] Even so, these problems have actually provoked the most interesting new interpretations of the text, when directors have used it to confront the political and cultural legacies of Marxism and state Socialism.

After examining what the 1988 production reveals about the play's role as a *Staatsfeststück* and East Germany just before the collapse of the GDR, I consider three productions in the reunified Germany: in 1998 by theater 89 in Berlin, in 2002 by the Stadttheater in Konstanz, and in 2003 by the BE. These stagings provide contrasting perspectives on both the reunified Germany and the *Wende* (a term that means 'change' and refers to the fall of the Berlin Wall, the collapse of the GDR, and the period leading up to reunification on 3 October 1990). This is because theater 89 was exclusively East German, whereas the cast of the Stadttheater came from southern Germany and, in the case of one actor, Switzerland, and the BE included actors from both East and West, led by Claus Peymann, a West German director who had experienced the *Wende* from the safe distance of Vienna's Burgtheater. I investigate how, and how far, their contrasting productions engaged with history and the present; how they treated Brecht's Marxist ideology; and how they compared to earlier productions in and beyond Germany. This investigation reveals how *Die Mutter* has, against the odds, survived the demise of the political system that it came to uphold.

2. THE APOTHEOSIS OF THE *STAATSFESTSTÜCK*: THE BERLINER ENSEMBLE, 1988

2.1 Context

When Manfred Wekwerth staged *Die Mutter* in 1988, unrest was mounting across the Eastern bloc. Since Gorbachev had been elected General Secretary of the USSR's Communist Party in 1985, his policies

---

[3] 'For God's sake, we're not doing that, especially not so soon after the fall of the Wall.' Hans-Joachim Frank, personal interview, 10 Aug. 2001.

of *glasnost'* and *perestroika* had seemed to transform the Soviet Union from political reactionary to pioneer of change, suggesting that it would no longer block reform as it had done in Hungary in 1956 and in Prague in 1968. This impression was confirmed in May 1989, when Gorbachev renounced the Brezhnev Doctrine and thus guaranteed that the USSR would no longer intervene militarily in the internal affairs of its allies.

The East German public learnt of the reforms in the USSR, Czechoslovakia, Hungary, and Poland through travel and, more importantly, the press and Western television. Edited but highly revealing translations of Gorbachev's speeches were published in *Neues Deutschland*, and more detailed analysis could be found in the Soviet periodical *Sputnik* until the SED prohibited it in November 1988. News of Gorbachev's policies stimulated the growth of an East German reform movement which demanded unrestricted travel, freedom of assembly, and an end to censorship. Yet, instead of making political concessions, the *Politbüro* prohibited the press from even mentioning *perestroika*. Its intransigence was epitomized by the ideological chief, Kurt Hager, who famously asked: 'Würden Sie ... wenn Ihr Nachbar seine Wohnung neu tapeziert, sich verpflichtet fühlen, Ihre Wohnung ebenfalls neu zu tapezieren?'[4] By completely refusing to countenance change, Hager and his colleagues only increased the population's frustration and resentment.

2.2 The Directors: Manfred Wekwerth and Joachim Tenschert

The 1988 production was directed by Manfred Wekwerth, who had succeeded Ruth Berghaus as the BE's manager in 1977, and his dramaturge Joachim Tenschert. Wekwerth's political views, artistic practice, and public standing exercised a crucial influence on the staging.

In his public statements Wekwerth argued that reform from within was essential for the survival of Socialism.[5] He took a keen interest in Gorbachev's reforms and even published extracts from his most recent speech—on the seventieth anniversary of the October Revolution—in

---

[4] 'If your neighbour was redecorating his apartment, would you ... feel obliged to redecorate your apartment too?' 'Kurt Hager beantwortete Fragen der Illustrierten *Stern*', *ND*, 10 Apr. 1987.

[5] Manfred Wekwerth, 'Entdeckungen und Spaß', *Sonntag* (East Berlin), 25 Apr. 1977; 'Der Durst nach Sinn', interview with Dieter Kranz, *notate*, 1/87, 10; 'Nachdenken—politisch wie poetisch', *Der Morgen* (East Berlin), 11 Oct. 1989.

the programme for *Die Mutter*.[6] But Wekwerth was also a prominent member of the GDR's political establishment: he became President of the Academy of Arts in 1982, joined the Central Committee in 1986, received the GDR's top honour, the Order of Karl Marx, in 1984, and was awarded the National Prize for Art and Literature, First Class, in 1989. These offices and accolades compromised Wekwerth's public credibility as an advocate of reform, even though it was not yet known that he had been working for the Stasi since 1969.[7]

Although Wekwerth had introduced more modern staging methods to the BE in the 1960s, by the late 1970s and the 1980s he had a reputation for producing clear, technically precise stagings that lacked creative spark.[8] This was partly because of comparisons with Berghaus's more radical approach during the early 1970s, partly because of the contrast with recent experiments by younger directors like Castorf, and partly because Wekwerth had secured the post of theatre manager in alliance with Brecht's heirs, who strongly opposed aesthetic experimentation with Brecht's works. Indeed, Western journalists heralded his appointment as the return of the old guard and the reinstatement of Weigel's 'Brecht museum'.[9] So although Wekwerth disputes the charge of aesthetic conservatism,[10] theatre critics believed that his involvement would guarantee a politically and aesthetically safe production. Thus, Sibylle Wirsing argued in West Germany's *FAZ*: '*Die Mutter* ging einer bombensicheren Aufführung entgegen.'[11]

2.3 Wholesale Revolution?

Wekwerth's ambivalent position as representative of the establishment and advocate of *perestroika* resulted in contradictions throughout his staging. He explained that he intended to use *Die Mutter* as a parable about change and the need for 'neues Denken' ('new thinking'), a term closely identified with *perestroika*: '*Die Mutter* ist nicht nur ein "Bericht

---

[6] Programme for the 1988 production, BEA.

[7] Hoffmann *et al.*, *Wer war wer*, 904–5.

[8] e.g. anon., 'Ein neuer Prinzipal und ein altes Programm', *Neue Zürcher Zeitung*, 7 June 1977.

[9] Ibid.; Benjamin Heinrichs, 'Aufhaltsamer Abstieg', *Die Zeit* (Hamburg), 27 May 1977.

[10] Wekwerth, 13 Dec. 2000.

[11] '*The Mother* was heading for a production as safe as houses.' Sibylle Wirsing, 'Ein Verdienst-Orden für Pelagea Wlassowa', *FAZ*, 13 Feb. 1988.

aus großer Zeit", sie ist ebenso das Hohe Lied der "Umwälzung von Grund auf".'[12] He then continued: 'wie sehr könnte [der unbestechliche Realismus der Mutter] helfen, die Lehren (und die Lehrer) davor zu bewahren, sich von der Realität zu entfernen und ins Dogma zu retten'.[13] Almost certainly, these comments were an oblique criticism of the authorities' dogmatism and a warning to heed the growing pressure for reform. Yet they were diametrically opposed to the state ceremony at the première, which was staged on 10 February 1988 to mark Brecht's ninetieth birthday, just hours after leading dignitaries like Honecker and Hager had unveiled Fritz Cremer's new statue of Brecht at the BE. So even though Wekwerth intended to advocate internal reform, the performance context confirmed the play's retrospective designation as an affirmative *Staatsfeststück*.

Wekwerth's publicity failed to communicate his production concept sufficiently clearly and consistently. In the programme he combined topical material with texts that had traditionally featured in the programmes of GDR productions of *Die Mutter*: thus, in addition to the extracts from Gorbachev's speech, it contained Brecht's poem to the Theatre Union and his essay about Gorky's influence on literature, and Benjamin's piece about the 1932 production. It also included Brecht's 1932 poem, 'Keinen Gedanken verschwendet an das Unänderbare!',[14] which suggested contradictory and almost certainly unintended parallels with the present. Thus, although the poem's title could be interpreted as an injunction for spectators to resign themselves to their rulers' intransigence, the lines 'Dem, was nicht zu retten ist/Zeigt keine Träne' could be read as a message not to mourn the moribund GDR.[15] In contrast, the poster clearly signalled that the production would advocate radical change, for it quoted Brecht's 'Lob der Dialektik', including the crucial line 'Die Besiegten von heute sind die Sieger von morgen'.[16] Yet this prophecy conflicted with Wekwerth's

---

[12] '*The Mother* is not only a "report from a great epoch", it is equally the Song of Songs to "wholesale revolution".' Manfred Wekwerth, '*Die Mutter* 1988: Gedanken während der Arbeit', in *Theater nach Brecht: Baukasten für eine Theorie und Praxis des Berliner Ensembles in den neunziger Jahren*, ed. Wekwerth (East Berlin: Sonderausgabe der Theater Arbeit, 1989), 124–9 (127).

[13] 'How much [the Mother's incorruptible realism] might help to save our teachings (and our teachers) from losing touch with reality and taking refuge in dogma.' Ibid. 127.

[14] 'Waste no thought on what cannot be changed!' *BFA*, xiv. 154–5.

[15] 'For what cannot be changed/Shed no tears.'

[16] 'The conquered of today are the conquerors of tomorrow.' Dieckmann and Drescher, 161.

commitment to state Socialism and his characterization of the production as 'den Versuch, Leute für Veränderungen im Sinne des Erhaltens
sozialistischer Verhältnisse zu interessieren'.[17] This crucial contradiction
suggests that the poster promised spectators more than the staging would
deliver.

The 1988 script contained only two significant concessions to the
contemporary situation, and even these had only a limited political
impact. First, Wekwerth and Tenschert softened Brecht's critique of
religion by cutting the Bible scene and adding lines which acknowledged that Christ had worked towards positive social goals.[18] This
was because the Church had become a popular focus for the reform
movement within the GDR, as Wekwerth subsequently explained
to me: 'Die Kirchen waren Orte, wo sich Leute versammelten, die
diesen Staat nicht abschaffen, sondern verändern wollten. Sie stell-
ten gerade die Fragen, die die Sozialisten eigentlich hätten stellen
müssen.'[19] But by using Russian Orthodox Church music to suggest the 'Dunkelheit und Enge' ('darkness and claustrophobia') of
Wlassowa's situation in the opening scene, Wekwerth and Tenschert
reinforced the text's original argument that religion was the opium of
the masses and confused their overall presentation of religion.[20] The
second significant change was that the Party members took the teacher's
reservations about Marxism more seriously. Tenschert explained that
Lapkin 'heute, 1988, eher Haltungen vertritt und Argumente äußert,
denen wir ... unsere Zustimmung schwerlich versagen können'.[21]
Nevertheless, the new script still gave the final word to the Party's
representatives:

DER LEHRER   ... Wo bleibt das Einzelwesen in eurer Lehre?

SEMJON   Eine Assoziation, in der die freie Entwicklung eines jeden die
Bedingung für die freie Entwicklung aller ist.

[17] 'The attempt to interest people in changes designed to preserve the Socialist system.'
Wekwerth, 13 Dec. 2000.
[18] 'Soufflierbuch', 71–9, in 'Die Mutter', box file 132, BEA; audio recording of the
preview performance on 6 Feb. 1988, Wekwerth's personal copy.
[19] 'The churches were meeting-places for people who did not want to abolish this
state, but to change it. They asked precisely those questions which the Socialists should
really have asked.' Wekwerth, 13 Dec. 2000.
[20] 1988 audio recording; Joachim Tenschert to the actors playing the revolutionaries,
11 Mar. 1988, in 'Die Mutter', file 1988, BEA.
[21] 'Today, in 1988, actually holds views and expresses arguments with which we ...
can hardly refuse to agree.' Joachim Tenschert to Michael Gerber, 11 Mar. 1988, in 'Die
Mutter', file 1988, BEA.

DER LEHRER Richtig.
SEMJON Marx.[22]

Overall then, the new version still suggested that the Party knew better than its critics—a view that was unlikely to appeal to the SED's opponents.

Wekwerth's production aesthetic failed to communicate the idea of wholesale revolution because its simple, muted clarity was far tamer than either Berghaus's 1974 staging or contemporary avant-garde productions. Crucially, the programme did not explain that Matthias Stein's set was inspired by Paul Klee's political paintings, especially 'Revolution des Viaduktes' ('Revolution of the Viaduct') and 'Brückenbögen treten aus der Reihe' ('Arches of the Bridge Break Ranks'), both from 1937.[23] Klee's images of arches breaking free from a viaduct symbolized assertion of individuality and rebellion against fixed structures. But because this reference was not immediately apparent, it eluded all the reviewers, and so the set failed to realize its politically critical potential.

The production was rendered even less dynamic by Wekwerth's sanitized presentation of the characters and emphasis on emotional identification. With the aid of the costume designer Christine Stromberg, he presented Brecht's workers as attractive, well-heeled proletarians who bore little resemblance to the worn-down, oppressed characters of the earlier productions: indeed, the elegantly coiffeured maid looked positively glamorous. The modified script courted the audience's sympathy for the equally well-dressed Wlassowa by revealing that she had suffered domestic abuse, a detail present in Gorky's novel but not in Brecht's play.[24] This emphasis on feeling corresponded to Brecht's approach in 1951, which explains why Ernst Schumacher perceived the production as a return to the model.[25] Although Wekwerth disputed Schumacher's view, citing the visual contrast between Stein's quasi-constructivist set and Neher's realistic one, he still identified his approach with Brecht's aim in 1951, 'dem einzelnen die Revolution ... "liebenswert"

---

[22] 'THE TEACHER What place is there for the individual in your doctrine? SEMJON An association in which the free development of each individual is the prerequisite for the free development of everyone. THE TEACHER Correct. SEMJON Marx.' 'Soufflierbuch', 48.

[23] Wekwerth, 13 Dec. 2000. Cf. <http://www.architetturamoderna.com/klee/Immagini/Viaduct%20Revolution,%201937.jpg>; <http://www.guggenheimcollection.org/site/artist_work_md_75_7.html> [both accessed 24 Feb. 2005].

[24] 'Soufflierbuch', inserted after 42; Gorky, *Die Mutter*, 119.

[25] Ernst Schumacher, 'Der Besuch der alten Mutter', *Berliner Zeitung* (East Berlin), 20–1 Feb. 1988.

9. Well-heeled proletarians at the BE, 1988 © Vera Tenschert. Renate Richter as
Wlassowa and Kirsten Block as the maid.

zu machen': '[Es geht] um eine Rückverlagerung der Revolution in den einzelnen, in seine Gefühle, Gedanken, Hoffnungen, Utopien, um das Herausarbeiten zutiefst menschlichen Verhaltens, um die Chancen der Individuen in ihren vielen Möglichkeiten und Schwächen, um die unendliche Geduld, die das 70 Jahre nach dem Oktober kostet.'[26] The frequency with which Wekwerth and his colleagues referred to 'Geduld' ('patience') in the rehearsal notes reinforces the argument that their production was anything but dynamic. Indeed, reviewers actually perceived it as a reverent treatment of an old story, and Schumacher even cited Brecht's criticism of the Theatre Union's staging: 'Die Kühne wird brav, das Historische alltäglich.'[27]

Even so, the rehearsal notes and script also testify to a sense of beleaguerment and crisis that belies both Wekwerth's bold production concept and his reverential staging. In the late 1980s proponents of moderate internal reform faced opposition on two fronts: from citizens who demanded more radical measures and from hard-liners who refused to countenance any form of *perestroika*. Consequently, both Wekwerth and his dramaturgical assistant Holger Teschke identified strongly with Wlassowa's desperation when the workers ignore her urgent warnings against the war. For instance, on 16 October 1987 Teschke noted 'der aktuelle Aspekt nicht nur der Unbekanntheit, sondern auch der Unbeliebtheit des Soldaten der Revolution bei der eigenen Klasse'.[28] In 2000 Wekwerth made a similar point: 'In der DDR hörten sie auf nichts mehr, wie die Arbeiter sagen in der Szene: "Geh nach Hause, es bleibt wie es ist, man kann nichts verändern." Das bezog sich auf die sozialistischen Vorschläge.'[29] But whereas Wekwerth identified Brecht's workers with GDR workers who were indifferent to internal reform, Teschke compared them with Gorbachev's hard-line opponents:

---

[26] 'To "endear" … the Revolution to the individual'; 'we need to bring the Revolution back to the individual, to his feelings, thoughts, hopes, Utopian dreams; we need to bring out profoundly human behaviour, the opportunities of individuals with their many capabilities and weaknesses, the infinite patience which this costs seventy years after the October Revolution.' Manfred Wekwerth, 'Gegenbesuch', 23 Feb. 1988, in 'Die Mutter', file 1988, BEA.

[27] 'The bold woman becomes well-behaved, the historic everyday.' Schumacher, *Berliner Zeitung*, 20–1 Feb. 1988; cf. *BFA*, xiv. 292.

[28] 'The topical point that the revolutionary soldier is not only unknown to his own class, but also unpopular with them.' Holger Teschke, '4 Punkte zur MUTTER', in 'Die Mutter', file 1988, BEA.

[29] 'In the GDR they no longer listened to anything, just as the workers say in the scene: "Go home, things will stay as they are, nothing can be changed." That applied to the Socialists' suggestions.' Wekwerth, 13 Dec. 2000.

Nicht Klassensolidarität, sondern Mitleid rettet die Mutter.... Der Moment, in dem die Mutter das begreift, ist der Moment ihres größten Entsetzens, das nicht als Verzweiflung, sondern als Moment des Hasses gegen jene gezeigt werden sollte, die 'nicht lernen wollen', die man in ihre Zukunft prügeln muß. Im Moment dieses Hasses könnte der Fall des Mannes Stalins aufblitzen, der zum Problem des Mannes Gorbatschow geworden ist. Was tun, wenn die Einsicht in die Notwendigkeit ausbleibt?[30]

Whilst Teschke's comments indicate his frustration at the hard-liners' blindness to the need for reform, his phrase 'in ihre Zukunft prügeln' ('beaten into their own future') also implies the disturbing practice of enlightenment by force, indicating how far the regime's repressive intolerance had permeated the language and thought-processes of even those who favoured moderate reform.

The script testifies in a similar way to the reformers' sense of beleaguerment, for Tenschert and Wekwerth cut the final demonstration because they, like Berghaus, felt that its triumphalism was no longer convincing. In 2000, Wekwerth explained to me:

Wir [haben] die Schlußszene nicht mehr gespielt als Demonstration, als Sieg, sondern wir haben sie gespielt als kleine Szene zwischen dem Dienstmädchen und der Mutter, und das Dienstmädchen, völlig entnervt, desillusioniert, sagt: 'Es ist aus.' Das war der Zustand in der DDR damals. Und da hat die Mutter dem Dienstmädchen ganz privat, persönlich das 'Lob der Dialektik' gesagt, aber nicht als Sieg, sondern als letzte Möglichkeit.[31]

Although both the audio recording and the photograph of the copper collection scene suggest reticence rather than disillusionment or despair, this reticence still coexisted uneasily with both the official ceremony at the première and the poster's demands for change. This contradiction again demonstrates how far artistic conservatism and the constraints

---

[30] 'Not class solidarity but pity saves the Mother.... The moment when the Mother realizes this is the moment when she experiences the greatest horror; this should not be shown as despair, but as a moment of hatred of those who "do not want to learn", who have to be beaten into their own future. In this moment of hatred, the example of Stalin could flash up, which has turned into the problem facing Gorbachev. What are we to do, when people fail to recognize what is necessary?' Teschke, '4 Punkte', in 'Die Mutter', file 1988, BEA.

[31] 'We no longer performed the final scene as a demonstration, as a victory; instead we performed it as a short scene between the maid and the Mother, and the maid, disillusioned and at her wits' end, says: "It's over." That was the situation in the GDR then. And then the Mother spoke "In Praise of Dialectics" to the maid, quite privately and personally, but not as a victory, rather as a last chance.' Wekwerth, 13 Dec. 2000.

of high political office compromised the credibility and consistency of Wekwerth's attempt to advocate *perestroika*.

2.4 The Press and Audience Response

In 1988, only Gerhard Ebert toed the Party line by calling *Die Mutter* 'überzeugender denn je' ('more convincing than ever') in the SED newspaper *Neues Deutschland*.[32] Even so, he inadvertently betrayed how far Wekwerth's production had deviated from the aesthetic techniques inscribed in the play, for he referred to Brecht's 'revolutionäre Romantik' ('revolutionary romanticism') and distanced his practice from Piscator's epic techniques: 'die "Hausmittel" Erwin Piscators ... waren nicht die Brechts'.[33] But other GDR critics considered the production unexciting: Ingrid Seyfarth deemed it unspectacularly clear, and Schumacher discerned 'bewährtes handwerkliches Können ... aber kaum irgendeine Innovation'.[34] Christoph Funke referred to Wekwerth's 'achtungsvolle Vorsicht', 'vorsichtiges Fragen', 'Fleiß', 'Sorgsamkeit', and 'Zuverlässigkeit', but argued that his reverential, tentative approach precluded topicality: 'Es ist der Bericht aus einer anderen Zeit, der uns übermittelt wird, Fragen an diesen Bericht sind ausgespart. Text und Lieder werden behandelt, als seien sie leicht zerbrechlich—diese bewahrende Vorsicht hat durchaus ästhetischen Reiz, ... beläßt [die Anfänge revolutionären Geschehens] allerdings auch ganz in den Zusammenhängen der damaligen Zeit.'[35] Dieter Kranz, Manfred Nössig, and Jürgen Schebera all argued that Wekwerth had not solved the—admittedly difficult—problem of how to present *Die Mutter* to a contemporary audience.[36] Schebera was disappointed that

[32] Gerhard Ebert, 'Rationale Kraft und poetische Frische Brechtscher Gedanken', *ND*, 12 Feb. 1988.

[33] 'Erwin Piscator's "trademarks" ... were not those of Brecht.'

[34] Ingrid Seyfarth, 'Variationen zu Brecht', *Sonntag* (East Berlin), 28 Feb. 1988. 'Proven craftsmanship ... but scarcely any innovation.' Schumacher, *Berliner Zeitung*, 20–1 Feb. 1988.

[35] 'Respectful caution', 'cautious questioning', 'diligence', 'carefulness', 'reliability'; 'it is the report from another epoch which is conveyed to us; this report goes unquestioned. The text and songs are treated as if they could break easily—this protective caution certainly has an aesthetic charm, ... but it also leaves [these early revolutionary activities] entirely in their historical context.' Christoph Funke, 'Aufbruch am Jahrhundertbeginn', *Der Morgen* (East Berlin), 11 Feb. 1988.

[36] Dieter Kranz, 'Das Berliner Ensemble...', Berliner Rundfunk, 14 Feb. 1988, transcript, in 'Die Mutter', file 1988, BEA; Manfred Nössig, 'Erneuter Versuch nach 56 Jahren', *Theater der Zeit*, Apr. 1988, 14–15; Jürgen Schebera, 'Bericht aus großer Zeit', *notate*, 4/1988, [n.p.].

the directors had failed to provide a consistently topical interpretation using the theatrical methods of the 1980s, and Schumacher was even more forthright: 'Die Not- und Zweckmäßigkeit, dieses Stück auf die heutige Bühne zu bringen, wurde nicht erwiesen.'[37]

East German reviewers' frank criticism of this latter-day *Staatsfeststück* suggests that they were emancipating themselves from the Party line, a process that had already been evident in 1974. Consequently, the gap between reviews in the East and West was much narrower than in 1968. Like their colleagues in the GDR, reviewers in West Germany and Switzerland argued that Wekwerth's production was excessively reverential and lacked topical relevance. In the *Rheinische Post* Michael Stone stated: 'Man hätte sich zur Feier des Tages vielleicht doch ein anderes Stück von Brecht vornehmen sollen', and in the *Neue Zürcher Zeitung* Horst Wenderoth concluded simply: '[*Die Mutter*] widerstand diesem Wiederbelebungsversuch'.[38] Meanwhile, in the conservative *FAZ*, Sibylle Wirsing summed up the staging as 'ein nachträglicher Verdienst-Orden für die längst verstorbene Pelagea Wlassowa'—a telling indictment of a production that had been intended to promote change.[39]

Nevertheless, Wekwerth's publicity and production concept ensured that the staging remained ambivalent, and there is some evidence that Brecht's text resisted the affirmative function that was suggested by the performance context. This was because the unintended parallels between Tsarist Russia and the GDR created space for topical criticism of the SED, including Wekwerth. For instance, the audio recording of the preview performance and Western reviews of the première indicate that some spectators applauded or laughed at lines that criticized Tsarist repression and the Bolshevik press. In the *Neue Zürcher Zeitung* Wenderoth noted:

Als der Gefängniswärter mit Blick auf ihren inhaftierten Sohn sagt: 'Weine nicht. Er kommt frei. Ist kein Platz mehr. Sind zu viele', gab es sofort Beifall. Auch als der ... Lehrer Lapkin den Revolutionären zuruft: 'Könnt ihr eure Zeitung nicht etwas unterhaltsamer machen', lachten viele Leute und

---

[37] 'The necessity and advisability of putting this play on today's stage were not proven.' Schumacher, *Berliner Zeitung*, 20–1 Feb. 1988.

[38] 'Perhaps they should have chosen a different Brecht play to celebrate the occasion after all.' Michael Stone, 'Revolution ohne Ende', *Rheinische Post* (Düsseldorf), 19 Feb. 1988. '[*The Mother*] resisted this resuscitation attempt.' Horst Wenderoth, 'Transit in die Vergangenheit', *Neue Zürcher Zeitung*, 18 Feb. 1988.

[39] 'A posthumous order of merit for the long since deceased Pelagea Wlassowa.' Wirsing, *FAZ*, 13 Feb. 1988.

klatschten. An solchen Stellen bricht Aktualität in die museale Darbietung ein, doch vermutlich eine andere als die beabsichtigte.[40]

Similarly, the *FAZ* reported 'daß … eine Zuschauerin ihrem Unwillen schließlich mit der lautstark vorgebrachten Frage freien Lauf ließ: "Wo leben wir eigentlich?" ', and the *Süddeutsche Zeitung* mentioned 'einen Buhruf gegen Wekwerth'.[41] More serious disturbances followed at four subsequent performances, and although the BE tended to attribute the cat-calls, noise, and lack of interest to pupils' indiscipline, on 8 March 1989 Teschke argued that they testified to serious political problems:

Wenn nicht binnen kürzester Zeit in unserer Bildungs-[,] Kultur- und Informationspolitik eine spürbare Veränderung in Richtung auf die drängenden, alltäglichen Fragen und Probleme eines Großteils unserer Bevölk[e]rung erfolgt, dann wird jenes Desinteresse und jene Unwissenheit, die sich gestern abend artikulierten, zum Normalfall…. Das Schrecknis der Zukunft ist die Eskalation der Gewalt *und* der Apathie—Thema der *Mutter*…[42]

This confirms the impression suggested by Heiner Müller's anecdote in Chapter 3: although Brecht's subversive text could resist its retrospective designation as a *Staatsfeststück*, the play's public reputation led many spectators to reject it as yet more propaganda about the Russian Revolution.

2.5 Conclusion

Although wholesale revolution was an interesting and topical production concept, Wekwerth failed to communicate it sufficiently clearly

---

[40] 'When the prison guard says, looking at her imprisoned son: "Don't cry. He'll be let out. No room left. Too many of them," there was immediate applause. Similarly, when the … teacher Lapkin calls to the revolutionaries: "Can't you make your newspaper a bit more entertaining", many people laughed and clapped. At such points contemporary relevance breaks into the museum-like performance, but presumably a different kind of relevance from that which was intended.' Wenderoth, *Neue Zürcher Zeitung*, 18 Feb. 1988.

[41] 'That … one female spectator finally gave full vent to her displeasure by asking loudly: "Where are we living then?" ' M. Z., 'Armer B. B.', *FAZ*, 10 Feb. 1988. 'Wekwerth was booed once.' Jürgen Beckelmann, 'Mal historisch, mal ungestüm-heutig', *Süddeutsche Zeitung* (Munich), 20 Feb. 1988.

[42] 'Unless an imminent and tangible change takes place so that our education, culture, and information policies begin to address the urgent, everyday questions and problems of a large section of our population, then the disinterest and the ignorance articulated yesterday evening will become the norm…. The terrifying prospect for the future is the escalation of violence *and* of apathy—the theme of *The Mother*… ' Holger Teschke, 8 Mar. 1989. Cf. reports of performances by Gabriele Jander, 4 Mar. 1988; Gisela Stoll, 16 June 1988 and 23 Feb. 1989. All in 'Die Mutter', file 1988, BEA.

and consistently. Indeed, his assumption that spectators would approach his production without prejudice shows how removed he was from the political realities of 1988. This reality gap was also reflected in the contrast between the BE's internal assessments of the production and the responses of many reviewers and spectators: only *Neues Deutschland* shared Teschke's view that the production was extremely topical.[43] This gulf widened as public demands for change became increasingly insistent, and the production was finally removed from the BE's repertoire in March 1989.

The timing of the production did not, however, make its failure inevitable. Since Gorbachev's reforms had already lent a new, subversive meaning to the SED slogan 'von der Sowjetunion lernen heißt siegen lernen',[44] Brecht's use of Russia as a model for Germany could have had a topical, revolutionary relevance. But Wekwerth's ambivalent position and aesthetic conservatism made him ill-suited to such a task, and by 1988 the play held few attractions for more radical, outspoken directors who might have taken the artistic and political risks that were needed to transform a *Staatsfeststück* into a revolutionary staging.

3. ARCHAEOLOGICAL SELF-DISCOVERY: THEATER 89, 1998

3.1 Theater 89

In 1998 *Die Mutter* returned to the theatrical fringe when it was staged by theater 89, a professional off-company that had been founded in 1989, shortly before the *Wende*. Its manager, Hans-Joachim Frank, and dramaturge, Jörg Mihan, both came from the BE, and they had assembled a group of actors who wanted to preserve the East German theatrical traditions of hand-crafted aesthetics and social criticism.[45] Theatrically, this involved a commitment to an aesthetic free from postmodernism and the modern media, to the Brechtian *Fabel*, and to revealing the social significance of behaviour through acting. Politically, theater 89 adopted a critical and inquiring attitude towards both past and present, as Mihan explained:

---

[43] Teschke to Wekwerth, 4 Feb. 1988, in 'Die Mutter', file 1988, BEA.

[44] 'Learning from the Soviet Union means learning to win.'

[45] Martin Linzer, 'Berlin: Theater zwischen Berliner City und Brandenburger Provinz', *Theater der Zeit*, Sept./Oct. 1998, 58–9.

Our theme is history, ... from a point of view from below. We didn't want to follow the changes in [a] mindless way, not to jump into new times just to join the mainstream blindly.... We decided for our way of change by questioning the development of society and ourselves. We take time to research and publish the results. Doing this, we find out less answers than questions. Then we bring these questions into focus and share them with the audience.[46]

Frank believed that *Die Mutter* would allow the members of theater 89 to examine the GDR and their role in it, and that it would enable Mihan and himself to re-assess their involvement in Berghaus's 1974 production. He also chose the play because he disliked the mainstream productions that were being staged in 1998 to mark Brecht's centenary: in his view, they falsified the politics of Brecht's works.[47] So by staging one of the most classic and political pieces of epic theatre, theater 89 sought to 'find out what [the] political Brecht could tell us today'.[48]

3.2 The Archaeological Approach

Frank and Mihan used the metaphor of archaeology to express their desire to examine their own past and recover *Die Mutter* from the GDR's affirmative performance tradition. Frank explained: 'wir haben versucht, es wieder auszubuddeln', 'DDR-Ideologie wegzuschaufeln', and Mihan argued: 'es könnte wie das Vorführen einer Entdeckung, einer Ausgrabung werden, wobei das Entdeckte in ein würdiges und angemessenes Licht gerückt wird, damit es frei und kritisch zur Kenntnis genommen werden kann, damit ein Echo entsteht, Erinnerung möglich ist und Auseinandersetzung stattfinden kann'.[49] Their caution and concern with objectivity indicate their determination neither to replace one set of dogmas with another, nor to resort to postmodernist irony

---

[46] Jörg Mihan, talk on theater 89's production of *Die Mutter* at the CPR, Aberystwyth, 27–9 Nov. 1998. Video recording held by the CPR.

[47] Frank, 10 Aug. 2001. Similarly, Mihan argued that only three productions since 1989—all at the BE—had shown 'a really new and exciting way of performing [Brecht]': Heiner Müller's *Arturo Ui* (1995), Einar Schleef's *Puntila* (1996), and Klaus Emmerich's *Die Maßnahme* (1997). Mihan, 27–9 Nov. 1998.

[48] Mihan, 27–9 Nov. 1998.

[49] 'We tried to dig it up again', 'to shovel away the GDR ideology'. Frank, 10 Aug. 2001. 'It could turn into something resembling the presentation of a discovery, of an excavation, where what has been discovered is placed in a worthy and appropriate light so that it can be appraised freely and critically, so that an echo sounds, remembrance is possible, and a debate can take place.' Mihan, 'DIE MUTTER—2. Hauptprobe am 24. April 1998', Mihan's personal copy.

and pastiche. Thus, Mihan called for 'eine werk- und autorentreue, jeden äußerlichen arroganten Kommentar vermeidende Inszenierung', arguing: 'Der Gestus der Vorsicht: das könnte so und so gewesen sein, ist besser als der Gestus der Behauptung: das war so und so.'[50]

Nevertheless, an interpretation from the perspective of 1998 did emerge during rehearsals: namely, that *Die Mutter* depicted a lost Utopia, a failed historical possibility. Seeing it as 'ein Stück über die nicht stattgefundene deutsche Revolution', Frank painted quotations from one of the leaders of this failed revolution, Rosa Luxemburg, on the theatre's walls.[51] This enabled theater 89 to show its respect for the struggles and failures of the early German Communists even as it acknowledged that yesterday's answers could not solve today's problems. Thus Mihan explained: 'The ideological instruments they trusted in were either the wrong ones or not strong enough. The play works now as a kind of memorial, like a requiem, and shows a platform from which to start again and again.'[52] The decision to commemorate Luxemburg was particularly significant, because her theory of spontaneous revolution contradicted the Party-led view to which Lenin and Stalin had both subscribed. Whilst this meant that the KPD and the SED had always regarded her with ambivalence, it made her an ideal figurehead for those who, like Frank and Mihan, opposed the SED but advocated Socialism.

As rehearsals progressed, the actors overcame their initial prejudices and discovered parallels between Brecht's text and the reunified Germany. Frank recalled: 'Es gibt nur dieses Klischee: *Mutter*, Scheiß-Ideologie. Stimmt alles nicht mehr. Und stellt sich heraus, es stimmt sehr viel mehr, als man denkt.'[53] In 1998 German unemployment rose to a new postwar high of 12.6 per cent (21.1 per cent in the East), and it became increasingly clear that Kohl's Christian Democratic Government was heading for electoral defeat after failing to deliver the promised economic miracle.[54] According to Frank, this socio-economic

---

[50] 'A production that is faithful to the work and the author, that avoids all superficial, arrogant commentary.' Mihan, 'DIE MUTTER—Durchlauf am 20. April 1998'. 'The *Gestus* of caution: it could have been like this, is better than the *Gestus* of assertion: it was like this.' Mihan, 'DIE MUTTER—2. Hauptprobe', both Mihan's personal copies.

[51] 'A play about the German Revolution which did not take place.' Frank, 10 Aug. 2001.

[52] Mihan, 27–9 Nov. 1998.

[53] 'There is only this cliché: *The Mother*, ideological shit. None of it's true any more. And it transpires that far more is true than people think.' Frank, 10 Aug. 2001.

[54] <http://www.eiro.eurofound.ie/print/1998/02/feature/DE9802148F.html> [accessed 10 Jan. 2003].

context enabled theater 89 to understand some aspects of the play for the first time, such as the butcher's courage in risking his job or the landlady's power over her tenants: 'Das war auch eine Überraschung, … was die für eine Macht bekommt jetzt. Sie war in der BE-Inszenierung eine Witzfigur, weil man gar nicht verstand, welche Macht sie besitzt, als Hausbesitzerin.'[55] Since there had been full employment in the GDR, such points had previously been lost on most of the cast and audience.

3.3 Set Design and Music

Although the 1998 production took place only two streets away from the BE, theater 89 was worlds away from the BE's opulence. After crossing the backyard of a building in Torstraße and climbing two dingy flights of stairs, spectators reached the dark, windowless theatre which Frank likened to an underground car park.[56] Theater 89 further emphasized its distance from establishment theatre by releasing the performance from the traditional proscenium stage. Instead, the audience was seated at an angle towards an open performance space, and the musicians were seated in an area at the far end that was also used for 'epic' episodes like Smilgin's death.[57] Like Berghaus, Frank replaced Eisler's choir with a soloist whose powerful, clean and clear delivery was free from any trace of nostalgia, melancholy, or militancy. Mihan related this change directly to the failure of the Socialist project: 'There doesn't exist a collective hero in reality any longer, so we decided to leave the collective hero in the scenes and make the musical element a more objective one, sung by one singer, like the evangelist in a Bach oratorio.'[58]

The set, lighting, and special effects reinforced the improvised appearance of the performance venue. A staircase led up from a makeshift platform to the actors' entrance, suggesting an underground location—an apt metaphor for the revolutionaries' illegal activity. The set was made from untreated wooden planks which Frank explained as an attempt to illustrate the world of work using the material substance of the set.[59] Instead of representing the different locations realistically,

---

[55] 'That was a surprise too, … how much power she has now. In the BE production she was a figure of fun because people did not understand at all how much power she wields as a landlady.' Frank, 10 Aug. 2001.

[56] Ibid.

[57] This and further comments on the performance are based on an amateur video recording of theater 89's production, loaned from the CPR.

[58] Mihan, 27–9 Nov. 1998.   [59] Frank, 10 Aug. 2001.

as Brecht had done in 1951, Frank used sparse, symbolic props as if they were quotations of, or excerpts from, reality. For instance, a large armchair and piles of books, placed on top of the platform, sufficed as indications of the teacher's profession and higher social status. The factory scene, on the other hand, recalled Berghaus's solution, for workers crawled out of small holes—this time in the walls—to attend the illegal meeting. During this scene, darkness and smoke created a negative impression of industrial capitalism that contrasted sharply with the light, space, and clarity which Wekwerth had used in 1988 to identify industrialization unambiguously with human progress.

3.4 Trauma and Repression

The prison scene was central to theater 89's investigation of the GDR and its legacy. Through the acting and delivery, the company emphasized the effects of state repression, the older generation's complicity in the SED's crimes, and the lack of value that was now attached to experience and knowledge inherited from the GDR. This made Scene 7 both menacing and moving, so that it had much more in common with Berghaus's presentation than with either the model staging or the 1988 production, which had emphasized Wlassowa's serene superiority and skill in outwitting the guard. In Frank's version, Wlassowa and Pawel stood on opposite sides of a semi-transparent curtain, with Wlassowa on the same side as the audience. As the guard paced up and down behind him, Pawel spoke loudly, slowly, and clearly, as if Wlassowa were far away. At one point, he cried out in pain, and Wlassowa turned away, afraid and upset, before hurrying back to the curtain. She then delivered the following lines slowly, quietly, and seriously:

> DIE MUTTER ... Ach, Pawel, was bleibt uns alten Leuten schon übrig, als uns zu verkriechen, damit man uns nicht mehr sehen muß, denn wir sind zu nichts mehr nütze.... Man läßt es uns merken, unsere Zeit ist um. Vor uns liegt nichts mehr. Was wir wissen, ist vergangen ... und unsere Erfahrungen betreffen nichts mehr. Unser Rat ist schädlich, denn zwischen uns und unseren Söhnen ist eine Kluft, unüberbrückbar.[60]

---

[60] 'THE MOTHER ... Oh, Pawel, what is left for us old folk to do, except crawl away so that people no longer have to see us, for we are no longer good for anything.... People let us see that our time is over. We no longer have anything ahead of us. Our knowledge belongs to the past ... and our experiences are no longer relevant. Our advice is harmful, for between us and our sons lies an unbridgeable abyss.' *BFA*, iii. 295; CPR video recording.

10. Scene 7 at theater 89, 1998 © Beate Nelken. André Zimmermann as Pawel and Gabriele Heinz as Wlassowa.

In most previous productions these lines had provided the humour that Brecht had intended, but in 1998 Gabriele Heinz allowed them to be interpreted as a comment on the way in which the new Republic did not value the experiences of spectators who had lived through the GDR.

3.5 The Press and Audience Response

To theater 89's surprise, most reviewers responded sympathetically to its aims and approach. Only one former West German newspaper, Springer's right-wing *BZ*, dismissed the production as ideally suited to the pensioners' coffee club of the PDS, the political party which had succeeded the SED.[61] Reviewers from the former GDR particularly appreciated theater 89's critical but sensitive approach, and in the PDS organ, *Neues Deutschland*, Hans-Dieter Schütt wrote: 'Hans-Joachim Franks Inszenierung, die aufgebrochenen Brücken und mit gebrochenen Gefühlen einen vorsichtigen Vormarsch versucht, stellt das Stück vor. Sie stellt die Illusionen des Stücks nicht aus, stellt den Irrtümern seiner Ideologie nicht nach und stellt den Autor nicht bloß.'[62] Unlike in 1988, critics accepted that the production had a valuable message for its contemporary audience, notably about the Socialist ideals that were current during the Weimar Republic but had been perverted during the GDR. Thus, Ernst Schumacher, who had criticized Wekwerth's staging so strongly, highlighted the parallels between repression in Tsarist Russia, the Soviet Union, and the GDR, arguing that the 'Grabrede' was now doubly tragic since the revolutionaries—like the Tsar's firing squads—had turned against their comrades during Stalin's Purges.[63] Martin Linzer also saw the production as an investigation of the failed Socialist project, explaining in *Theater der Zeit*: 'Der kämpferisch-optimistische Schluß wird nicht behauptet, aber zur Diskussion gestellt, was in greifbarer Nähe schien, ist wieder in utopische Ferne gerückt.'[64] Such comments suggest that theater 89's production had succeeded in

---

[61] Matthias Heine, 'Eine *Mutter* fürs Seniorenkränzchen', *BZ* (Berlin), 2 May 1998.

[62] 'Hans-Joachim Frank's production, which attempts to advance cautiously across fractured bridges, with fractured feelings, introduces the play. It does not flaunt the play's illusions, does not trace the errors of its ideology, and does not expose the author.' Hans-Dieter Schütt, 'Schwerer, leichter Gang', *ND*, 5 May 1998.

[63] Schumacher, 'Denn die Besiegten von heute sind die Sieger von morgen', *Berliner Zeitung*, 2–3 May 1998; 'Noch Glut im Kraterherde?', 1 May 1998, unabbreviated typescript of Schumacher's article, Frank's personal copy.

[64] 'The aggressively optimistic ending is not asserted but put up for discussion; what seemed within our grasp has receded once more into a distant Utopia.' Linzer, *Theater der Zeit*, Sept./Oct. 1998, 58–9.

provoking at least some former citizens of the GDR to question the past more critically than had been possible a decade earlier.

Theater 89's post-show discussions indicate how strongly spectators' personal experiences influenced their responses to the staging. Nine years after the fall of the Berlin Wall, younger spectators were unaware of the play's problematic performance history in the GDR, and this explains why students from the berliner schule für schauspiel [*sic*] 'haben niemals das Stück ideologisch angezweifelt, sondern naiv gelesen, geglaubt und geschaut'.[65] Some of them were even disappointed by theater 89's preoccupation with the past and reliance on a more traditional aesthetic: 'Das Stück ist aktuell—Arbeitslosigkeit. Die Inszenierung wirkt antiquiert, kein Bezug zu heute.'[66] On the other hand, older spectators with strong memories and personal experience of the former GDR—and perhaps more conservative aesthetic expectations—praised the production and its aesthetic, but criticized the text's ideology. For instance, the playwright Christoph Hein called it one of the best productions, and Elisabeth Seidel asserted that it was wonderfully performed but found the agitation and ideology unbearable.[67] In contrast, spectators from the West could not identify with either theater 89's distinctively East German perspective or Brecht's depiction of revolutionary activity. For instance, an unnamed author from West Berlin commented: 'Ich bleibe eigenartig draußen … ich suche, woran es mich erinnern sollte: RAF, Meinhof, Baader vielleicht, warum habt ihr das Stück gemacht?'[68] Such a sense of exclusion testifies both to the long-term politico-cultural legacy of Germany's division and to the mental obstacles that hinder West Germans from empathizing with East Germans' experience of reunification—both of which mean that the new task of *Vergangenheitsbewältigung* (coming to terms with the past) risks being regarded as a purely East German problem. These difficulties would be clearly exemplified when the Stadttheater in Konstanz staged *Die Mutter* in October 2002.

---

[65] 'Never doubted the play's ideology, but interpreted it naively, believed, and watched.' Mihan, 'Beobachtungen der Studenten der berliner schule für schauspiel', 22 Apr. 1998, Mihan's personal copy.

[66] 'The play is topical—unemployment. The production seems antiquated, has no relevance to today.'

[67] Mihan, 'DIE MUTTER—Voraufführung am 27. April 1998', Mihan's personal copy.

[68] 'In a quite curious way, I remain an outsider … I am searching for what it is meant to remind me of: the RAF [Red Army Faction], Meinhof, Baader, perhaps; why did you stage the play?' Ibid.

4. AN OUTSIDER'S PERSPECTIVE: THE STADTTHEATER IN KONSTANZ, 2002

4.1 *Die Mutter*—in Konstanz?

Die Mutter was an unlikely choice for a theatre in Konstanz, as both the actors and the spectators pointed out.[69] The conservative Christian Democrats (CDU) have won every general election in Baden-Württemberg since the Second World War, and in five of the fifteen elections they secured over 50 per cent of the votes cast.[70] The region's conservative outlook reflects its economic prosperity: in October 2002, Baden-Württemberg had the lowest unemployment rate in Germany (5.5 per cent compared to the East German average of 16.9 per cent).[71] Furthermore, Konstanz's proximity to neutral Switzerland sheltered it from the worst traumas of the Second World War, and the city actually has far more in common with its Swiss neighbour, politically, economically, and culturally, than with the comparatively remote states in the East. Indeed, the Stadttheater's production is of interest precisely because it offers an entirely different perspective on *Die Mutter* from the stagings in the reunified Berlin.

Although the Stadttheater devoted its 2002–3 season to the question 'Handeln oder Nichtstun?' ('Act or do nothing?'), it opted for an abstract approach instead of relating this motto to contemporary politics.[72] For instance, the in-house director of *Die Mutter*, Wolfram Apprich, planned to stage *Die Gerechten* (*The Just*) by Camus and *Mauser* by Müller in order to question the limits of revolutionary expediency: 'Wie weit darf politisches Handeln gehen, um eine überkommene Gesellschaft zu verändern?'[73] The manager, Dagmar Schlingmann, decided to stage Gorky's *Sommergäste* (*Summer Guests*) in parallel with *Die Mutter* because these works provided contrasting snapshots of Russian society

---

[69] Dramaturge Ursula Thinnes and spectators at the post-performance discussion, 10 Dec. 2002.

[70] <http://www.election.de> [accessed 24 Feb. 2005]. This statistic refers to *Zweitstimmen*, the votes cast for party lists rather than for local candidates.

[71] <http://www.arbeitsamt.de/hst/services/statistik/200210/iiia4/s034l.pdf> [accessed 11 Jan. 2003].

[72] Anon., 'Die Theatersaison steht unter dem Motto… ', *Akzent*, Nov. 2002, [n.p.].

[73] 'How far can political activity legitimately go to change an outmoded society?' <http://stadt.konstanz.de/kultur_freizeit/theater/stadttheater_kn/vorschau/inhalt/index.htm> [accessed 24 Feb. 2005].

before the Revolution. Thus, Apprich explained: 'Wo *Die Sommergäste* von Gorki voller Dekadenz einer saturierten Gesellschaft sind, gibt es in der *Mutter* den Glauben an die Veränderung, an die Möglichkeit des Handelns.'[74] But even though the stagings were conceived as a contrast, the company's scepticism regarding Brecht's Marxism ensured that they had far more in common than the texts themselves.

4.2 Nostalgia and Scepticism

The Stadttheater presented *Die Mutter* as a memory of a bygone era, describing it as 'erfüllt von einem revolutionären Geist, der uns heute unmöglich geworden scheint'.[75] The key difference from theater 89's approach was that Apprich and his predominantly south German cast did not regard *Die Mutter* as part of their own history: their primary reference point was the 'foreign' history of the GDR, not the 1968 protests or the far left-wing culture of the Weimar Republic. Furthermore, whereas theater 89 had treated Brecht's Marxist ideology with critical respect, Apprich was frankly sceptical of revolutionary activity in general, and of Marxism in particular. So instead of using the play to explore a lost Utopia, Apprich used it to question political engagement and ironize nostalgia, an approach that implied criticism of *Ostalgie*, nostalgia for the former GDR.

Apprich conveyed his scepticism towards revolutionary activity by opting for a set that evoked a sense of leisure, idleness, and stagnation and that also featured in Schlingmann's production of *Sommergäste*.[76] It consisted of white plastic sun-loungers on a green baize carpet, with a backdrop depicting rampant tropical green foliage—a static, hermetic environment that contradicted the notional progression of Wlassowa's political education. Furthermore, by projecting a film at the start of *Die Mutter* showing the *Sommergäste* reclining on the sun-loungers, Apprich suggested that although the revolutionaries had ousted the bourgeoisie in the Eastern bloc, they still shared their narrow horizons and aspirations.

In order to foreground memory and nostalgia, Apprich cast older actors as the revolutionaries. He explained: 'Sie kommen in das Stück

---

[74] 'Where Gorky's *Summer Guests* are full of the decadence of a sated and self-satisfied society, in *The Mother* there is the belief in change, in the possibility of action.' Ibid.

[75] 'Filled with a revolutionary spirit which seems to us today to have become impossible.' Ibid.

[76] These, and other comments are based on the performance of 10 Dec. 2002.

wie eine Art Wiedergänger. Das sind keine euphorischen Revolutionäre mehr, sondern Menschen mit einer Geschichte, in deren Verhalten sich auch ihr Scheitern erkennen lässt.'[77] The three down-at-heel revolutionaries, clad in faded blue denim and grey coats, spent most of the production reclining on the sun-loungers. Thus, instead of printing leaflets in Scene 2, they merely discussed the need to do so, giving the impression that they—just like Gorky's *Sommergäste*—'tun nichts und reden unerträglich viel'.[78] They were accompanied by a young champagne Socialist, played by Gertrud Kohl, who was fashionably dressed in a fur coat, mini-skirt, cream jumper, and sun-glasses, and together they sang Eisler's songs as if they were familiar old tunes which had long since lost their revolutionary impetus. As a result, the behaviour of the older revolutionaries suggested that, with time, the naïve enthusiasm and energy of Wlassowa and Pawel would probably fade too.

4.3 The Price of Political Engagement

Apprich was of the firm opinion that all ideology has a negative, dehumanizing effect: 'Letztlich zwängt jede Form von Ideologie den Menschen in ein starres Korsett.'[79] This view was conveyed through Kohl's performance of the 'Lob des Kommunismus', when her increasingly insane delivery and strumming on the double bass contradicted Brecht's lyrics about the rationality of Communism. In similar vein, Apprich characterized Pawel as a fanatic whose aim was to indoctrinate rather than educate his mother. In Scene 2 he stood with his clenched right fist raised, and in Scene 4 he delivered the lesson on Marxist economics *ex cathedra*, from the top of a step-ladder—a solution which also ironized Brecht's didacticism. Most significantly, where Brecht had emphasized that personal relationships grow stronger through shared political commitment, Apprich showed that they suffer by presenting Pawel as single-minded and unfeeling. Accordingly, when he returned

---

[77] 'They enter the play rather like people returning from the dead. They are no longer euphoric revolutionaries but human beings with a history, and their behaviour also allows us to recognize that they have failed.' Conversation between Wolfram Apprich and Ursula Thinnes, Konstanz programme (own copy).

[78] 'Do nothing and talk an unbearable amount.' Maxim Gorky, *Sommergäste*, trans. August Scholz (Berlin: Ladyschnikow, 1906), 149. The Stadttheater translated this line as 'wir tun nichts und reden entsetzlich viel' ('we do nothing and talk a dreadful amount').

[79] 'In the final analysis every form of ideology forces humans into a straitjacket.' Konstanz programme.

from exile, he ignored Wlassowa's questions and sang 'Die Partei' so aggressively that the teacher confiscated his banjo. Similarly, after bidding Wlassowa farewell, Pawel turned away and left her standing alone behind him.

The new ending of the Konstanz version also emphasized the personal cost of political engagement. Whereas Brecht's text begins with a personal, domestic scene and ends with a public demonstration, Apprich opened the play with the public 'Lob der Dialektik', cut the last four scenes, and ended on a personal note, with Wlassowa singing the last three of Brecht's and Eisler's 'Wiegenlieder' ('Lullabies') to Pawel's corpse. Although Wlassowa performed the first two songs softly, she sang the third one strongly and mechanically while walking away from Pawel. By the line 'daß du eines Nachts nicht im Stacheldraht hängst', she sounded angry, and then, by the line 'daß es nicht zweierlei Menschen gibt', desperate.[80] In themselves, the 'Wiegenlieder' issue a powerful call for class solidarity, indicating that matters need to change if people have to struggle for bare essentials like coal, bread, towels, and milk. But because they were performed after Pawel's death, they lost their revolutionary impetus. Instead, they reminded viewers that Wlassowa's domestic struggle for survival and her political struggle for change had failed to achieve their main objective, to protect her son, and thus supported the conservative thrust of Apprich's staging.

4.4 Reception

The Konstanz production was reviewed by four local theatre critics, three of whom reacted positively to Apprich's approach. So although 'Bami' concluded that the text was beyond redemption for the stage, Wolfgang Bager argued that the production was an absolute must.[81] Brigitte Elsner-Heller believed that the interpretation worked because it was surprisingly multi-layered, and Udo Berenbrinker argued that Apprich's use of irony and comedy had made the play bearable for a modern audience.[82] The most striking aspect of the reviews is that the critics were

---

[80] 'So that you will not be caught hanging in the barbed wire one night', 'so that there will not be two classes of people', *BFA*, xi (1988), 206–9.

[81] Bami, 'Die Fallstricke des B. B.', *Schwäbische Zeitung* (Friedrichshafen), 15 Oct. 2002; Wolfgang Bager, 'Revolution mit dem Filzstift', *Südkurier* (Konstanz), 14 Oct. 2002.

[82] Brigitte Elsner-Heller, 'Wiegenlied für die Revolution', *Thurgauer Zeitung*, 14 Oct. 2002; Udo Berenbrinker, 'Leben einer Revolutionärin', *Singener Wochenblatt*, 6 Nov. 2002.

completely unfamiliar with the play, in total contrast to their colleagues elsewhere in Germany. Bager, for instance, argued that at first glance Apprich seemed to have staged the pure, unvarnished Brecht of 1931 [*sic*], and Elsner-Heller criticized Brecht—rather than Apprich—for ending with the 'Wiegenlieder'. This unfamiliarity highlights not only the differences between the quality of criticism in the national and regional press but also the cultural legacies of Germany's division and regionalism: reviewers in Konstanz, on the country's southern border, were completely unfamiliar with a play that had been an important part of the GDR's establishment culture and had also been staged by the FRG's best-known politicized theatres like the Schaubühne in West Berlin and the Schauspielhaus in Bochum. Indeed, *Die Mutter* was as foreign to the reviewers as it had been to the Stadttheater itself.

5. OPPOSING THE WAR: THE BERLINER ENSEMBLE, 2003

5.1 Context

In January 2003 *Die Mutter* was staged at the BE by Claus Peymann, one of Germany's leading postwar directors. Peymann began his career in the early 1960s in the student theatre movement and co-founded the Schaubühne with Peter Stein in 1970. But, unlike Stein, Peymann was firmly convinced that collective decision making should not extend to artistic matters.[83] This view contradicted the Schaubühne's entire ethos and created conflict with the actors, with the result that Peymann left the company in 1971. After directing as a guest in various cities, he finally acquired his own theatre in 1974, when he became the manager of the Württemburgisches Staatstheater in Stuttgart. There, he succeeded in creating a permanent ensemble, an achievement inspired by Brecht's work at the BE and matched in West Germany at that time only by the Schaubühne. One sign of Peymann's success is the loyalty of his actors, many of whom followed him when he moved to Bochum's Schauspielhaus in 1978, then to Vienna's Burgtheater in 1986, and to Berlin in 2000 when he became the BE's new manager.

---

[83] Jörg W. Gronius and Wend Kässens, *Theatermacher: Gespräche mit Luc Bondy, Jürgen Flimm, Hansgünther Heyme, Hans Neuenfels, Peter Palitzsch, Claus Peymann, Frank-Patrick Steckel, George Tabori und Peter Zadek* (Frankfurt/Main: Hain, 1990), 119–20. For further details of Peymann's career, see Koberg.

Peymann still holds the classical German conviction to which the SED and the SPD had both subscribed: namely, that theatre is a place of moral education. In 2001, he explained: 'Ich empfinde mich in der Tat als jemand, der mit seiner Arbeit aufklären will. In der Tradition von Lessing, Schiller und Brecht.'[84] In practice this has involved a commitment to left-wing theatre, but Peymann's radicalism has varied in response to the political climate. When leading terrorists from the Red Army Faction (RAF) were sentenced to life imprisonment in 1977, for instance, his production of *Die Gerechten* controversially compared the RAF with the Russian revolutionaries of 1917, but he is still best known for directing the classics and plays by Thomas Bernhard and Peter Handke. Since the 9/11 attacks, however, Peymann's productions have again addressed the most topical political issues. For instance, in January 2002 his new staging of Lessing's *Nathan der Weise* (*Nathan the Wise*) alluded to the debate about responses to 9/11:

Das Stück handelt von einem Juden, der seinen persönlichen Holocaust erlebt.... Und dieser Nathan übt keine Vergeltung, keine Rache, sondern die Vernunft kehrt wieder. Und über die Vernunft das Vergeben. Und das ist die Botschaft, die dieses helle Stück in dunklen [*sic*] Zeit vermitteln kann. Ich denke, das muß man heute predigen, damit es alle Ohren hören.[85]

In July 2002 the prospect of German involvement in a war against Iraq led Peymann to advocate 'erheblich härtere und grundsätzlichere Positionen am Theater'.[86] He explained: 'Es ist ja nicht so, dass alles so gut läuft in Deutschland. Wir werden sogar noch den Krieg mit nach Bagdad tragen.... Da habe ich schon die Vorstellung, dass ich etwas tun müsste.'[87] But by the time *Die Mutter* was premièred in

---

[84] 'I do indeed perceive myself as someone who wants to enlighten people through his work. In the tradition of Lessing, Schiller, and Brecht.' Claus Peymann, 'Wir leben im Übergang', interview with Wolfgang Höbel and Joachim Kronsbein, *Der Spiegel*, 8 Jan. 2001, 161–3 (162).

[85] 'The play is about a Jew who experiences a Holocaust of his own.... And this Nathan does not seek retaliation or revenge; instead, reason returns. And through reason, forgiveness. And that is the message which this bright play can spread in dark times. I think that we have to preach this today so that all ears can hear it.' Peymann, publicity leaflet for *Nathan der Weise*. The programme for *Nathan* included a photograph of Ground Zero.

[86] 'Considerably tougher, more principled positions in theatre'. Peymann, 'Nichts ist, wie es bleibt', interview with Christine Dössel, *Süddeutsche Zeitung* (Munich), 31 July 2002.

[87] 'After all, it is not as if everything were going particularly well in Germany. We are even going to help take the war to Baghdad.... That makes me feel I ought to do something.' Ibid.

January 2003, the gap between Peymann's position and government policy had narrowed, because Chancellor Schröder had pledged not to involve German forces in any such war. So instead of challenging the government's policy, Peymann's production actually articulated public opposition to a US/British-led conflict.

By choosing *Die Mutter* for his first Brecht production at the BE, Peymann also signalled his determination to confront the company's political role during the GDR and the play's performance tradition. But because the participants originally came from theatres in both East and West, the production actually marked the intertwining of two strands of the postwar performance history of *Die Mutter*: on the one hand, the BE's three stagings, and on the other, the three West German productions that Peymann had witnessed in West Berlin in 1970, in Stuttgart in 1978, and in Bochum in 1983. This suggests why the West German tradition of using *Die Mutter* to comment on contemporary politics influenced his production just as much as the play's problematic reputation in the GDR. Indeed, the pre-performance publicity made a strong case for the play's topical relevance: 'voller Aktualität und Brisanz. Ein Theaterstück, eine Utopie, ein Traum von einer besseren Welt. Vielleicht heute wichtiger denn je?'[88]

Although Peymann now advocates a return to a more radical and principled mode of theatre, he admits that it is far harder to depict clear ideological fronts than it was in the Kohl era.[89] For whilst he vehemently opposed the ruling red–green coalition's support for NATO intervention in Kosovo in 1999 and in Afghanistan in 2002, he recognizes that he shares the coalition's political background of involvement in the student movement of 1968. Furthermore, because the failure of state Socialism has undermined Peymann's confidence in left-wing ideology, he actually opts for ambivalent solutions in theatre. For instance, his production of *Nathan* ended on a note of historical pessimism, with a reading from Müller's 'Lessings Schlaf Traum Schrei' ('Lessing's Sleep Dream Scream') which includes the Dantonesque image: 'Die Geschichte reitet auf toten Gäulen ins Ziel.'[90] Correspondingly, although Peymann's

---

[88] 'Full of topical relevance and explosive force. A play, a Utopia, a dream of a better world. Perhaps more important today than ever before?' <http://www.berliner-ensemble.de/index_repertoire.htm> [accessed 24 Feb. 2005].

[89] 'Wir leben im Übergang', *Der Spiegel*, 8 Jan. 2001, 162–3.

[90] 'History is charging on dead horses towards its goal.' Performance of *Nathan der Weise* at the BE on 20 Sept. 2002; Heiner Müller, 'Lessings Schlaf Traum Schrei', in *Herzstück* (West Berlin: Rotbuch, 1983), 34–7.

production of *Die Mutter* projected a strong anti-war message, it also evinced his ambivalence towards the ideological solutions proposed by Brecht.

5.2 History, Politics, and Ideology

In order to show that history and contemporary politics were the production's twin reference points, Peymann published photographs of Bloody Sunday in 1905 and Grozny in 1994 in the programme.[91] Like theater 89, Peymann used references to Rosa Luxemburg to remind his audience that the play's intellectual origins lay in the far left-wing culture of the Weimar Republic, long before the GDR. Indeed, he presented the entire staging as a homage to Luxemburg by holding the première on 15 January, the eighty-fourth anniversary of her murder, displaying her image on flags flying from the theatre's roof and on the stage curtain, and publishing Brecht's poetic epitaph to her in the programme.[92] But his most striking innovation was the addition of a documentary historical commentary: between the scenes Therese Affolter appeared as Luxemburg and delivered extracts from her speeches and writings in place of Brecht's scene captions.

Even though the failure of state Socialism made Luxemburg's faith in revolution sound impossibly dated, her anti-war propaganda was still topical. For example, her analysis of the uneasy peace before the First World War had a strong resonance with the Left's analysis of the international situation since the Second World War:

Der Wahn vom Hineinwachsen in den Frieden ist heute zerronnen. Die auf 40 Jahre europäischen Frieden hinwiesen, vergaßen die Kriege, die außerhalb Europas sich abspielten, und in denen Europa die Hand mit im Spiel hatte.... Die Regierenden glauben, sie hätten das Recht, in einer so lebenswichtigen Frage über das gesamte Volk zu entscheiden. Ich frage Sie nun: dürfen wir uns Krieg, den wir nicht gewollt haben, ungestraft gefallen lassen?[93]

Even though, by the time of the première, the German government had pledged not to participate in a war against Iraq, prolonged and

[91] Programme for *Die Mutter*, BE 2003.

[92] This and subsequent comments are based on performances seen on 15, 16, and 17 Jan. 2003.

[93] 'The delusion of moving forwards into peace has now dissolved. Those who pointed towards forty years of peace in Europe forgot the wars which were waged outside Europe and in which Europe had a hand.... Our rulers believe they have the right to decide for the entire people in such a life-and-death question. Now I ask you: can we put up with this war, which we did not want, with impunity?' 2003 programme, 50.

enthusiastic applause greeted Luxemburg's final sentence on the first two nights, suggesting that it articulated the opinions of many of the spectators.

The contemporary economic context made the relevance of Brecht's arguments about wage cuts so self-evident that spectators on the first three nights laughed spontaneously at Karpow's line: 'wir [stehen] vor einer der größten Wirtschaftskrisen, die unser Land je durchgemacht hat'.[94] This reflected their concern at the state of the German economy, which was heading for the longest recession since the Second World War: on the day after the première, new statistics showed that GDP had risen by just 0.2 per cent in 2002.[95] The theme of wage negotiations was particularly topical in Berlin, where the Senate's budget deficit of some 40 billion euros had just forced the SPD Mayor, Klaus Wowereit, to withdraw from nationwide pay negotiations and propose a public sector wage freeze.[96] But the fact that the new commentary did not explicitly endorse Brecht's socio-economic criticism suggests that its relevance was a fortuitous by-product of the performance context, and that anti-war opposition was Peymann's main concern.

Even while Peymann endorsed Brecht's anti-war arguments, he also acknowledged that state Socialism had brought Marxist solutions into disrepute. For instance, he followed Brecht's 'Lob des Kommunismus' with Luxemburg's assertion of the need for humanity and tolerance:

Rücksichtsloseste Tatkraft und weitherzigste Menschlichkeit. Dies allein ist der wahre Odem des Sozialismus.

Eine Welt muß umgestürzt werden, aber jede Träne, die geweint wurde, auch wenn sie abgewischt werden konnte, ist eine Anklage. Und ein zu einem wichtigen Tun eilender Mensch, der aus roher Unachtsamkeit einen armen Wurm zertritt, begeht ein Verbrechen.

Freiheit nur für die Anhänger und Mitglieder einer Partei—mögen sie noch so zahlreich sein—ist keine Freiheit. Freiheit ist immer Freiheit der Andersdenkenden.[97]

---

[94] 'We are on the brink of one of the greatest economic crises which our country has ever experienced.' 2003 programme, 25; *BFA*, iii. 275.

[95] Andreas Krosta and Mark Schieritz, 'Deutschland trudelt auf Rekordflaute zu', *Financial Times Deutschland* (Hamburg), 17–19 Jan. 2003.

[96] Ulrich Zawatka Gerlach, 'Wowereit: Wir stehen einen Streik durch', *Der Tagesspiegel* (Berlin), 17 Jan. 2003; Stefan Schulz, 'Opposition spricht von Versagen des rot-roten Senats', *Berliner Morgenpost*, 17 Jan. 2003.

[97] 'The most ruthless energy and the most generous humanity. These alone are the true essence of Socialism. / A world must be overturned, but every tear that was shed, even if it could be wiped away, is an indictment. And any man rushing to complete an

This quotation suggested that the Left needed to regroup around Luxemburg's humanitarian values—just as East German demonstrators had argued by adopting the final line as a slogan in 1989. So Peymann distanced himself from orthodox Party solutions by portraying the revolutionaries with chalk-white faces, in clothes caked with the dust of history. The musical director Michael Gross added new dissonances to Eisler's score and replaced the choir's strident, uniform voice in 'Die Partei' with a gentle, two-part harmony. Most significantly of all, the bloodstained edges of a small white triangle jutted out from Karl-Ernst Herrmann's set, alluding to the human sacrifices in and beyond the action. But because Centre-Right critics had expected Peymann to repudiate Brecht's 'schlimmes Lehrstück' ('harmful *Lehrstück*') explicitly and unreservedly, they were dissatisfied with his approach.[98] Fourteen years after the *Wende*, sensitivities regarding the Communist cultural heritage still ran so high that Eckhard Fuhr accused Peymann of turning the BE into a 'demagogische Anstalt' ('demagogic institution')—prompting Peter Kümmel to argue that Fuhr appeared to have suffered a flashback to the days of the Cold War.[99]

The endings of both the programme and the production indicated that although Peymann was sceptical of the ideological solutions that Brecht propagated in this, one of his most overtly and unequivocally Communist works, he still believed that the problems identified by Brecht needed urgent attention. Towards the end of the programme Peymann included 'Laßt eure Träume fahren' ('Let Go of your Dreams') from Brecht's *Lesebuch für Städtebewohner* (*Reader for City-Dwellers*). Significantly, the speaker of this poem destroys the addressee's illusions one by one, only then to add in parentheses: 'Aber das soll euch/Nicht entmutigen!' ('But that should/Not discourage you!').[100] After the poem, statistics on the current distribution of wealth returned readers to the present, and thence to a headline published in the *Süddeutsche Zeitung* on 8 January 2003: 'London und Paris bereiten sich auf Krieg vor' ('London and Paris are preparing for war'). On stage, the action ended

important task, who crushes a poor worm underfoot through rough carelessness, is guilty of a crime. / Freedom only for the supporters and members of one party—however numerous they may be—is not freedom. Freedom is always freedom for those who think differently.' 2003 programme, 35.

[98] Eckhard Fuhr, 'Ein brünstiger Akt politischer Regression', *Die Welt* (Berlin), 17 Jan. 2003.

[99] Ibid; Peter Kümmel, 'Nachtgespenster', *Die Zeit* (Hamburg), 5/2003.

[100] 2003 programme, [n.p]; *BFA*, xi. 163–4.

11. Caked with the dust of history: revolutionaries and workers at the BE, 2003 © Monika Rittershaus. Carmen-Maja Antoni as Wlassowa, second from left.

208 Die Mutter *and German Reunification*

with the failure of Socialist opposition to the First World War, as a wounded and disorientated Wlassowa staggered around, muttering the final lines of the 'Lob der Dialektik' until the orchestra drowned her out. Nevertheless, her final message was delivered not to the characters on stage, but to the audience: 'Bedenkt, wenn ihr versagt.'[101]

5.3 Performance Aesthetics

Like Wekwerth and Frank, Peymann resisted the postmodern trend towards fragmentation and pastiche, and instead foregrounded the Brechtian *Fabel*. He explained: 'Ich stehe für die ureigensten Werte des Theaters, für erzählte Geschichten und Zusammenhänge. Das ist im Moment zwar nicht das, was die Feuilletons … wünschen, aber ich spüre beim Publikum ein tiefes Interesse an dieser Art Theater, in dem die Figuren auf der Bühne … nicht gleich ironisiert … werden.'[102] Peymann further increased the emphasis on direct action by removing many of the epic elements, including the scene captions, Wlassowa's self-introduction in Scene 1, Pawel's third-person speech in Scene 9, and the sections of elevated verse in Scene 10 and the street corner scene.[103] He also removed the epic report in Scene 5, keeping only the sections in direct speech and replacing Eisler's music with Heiner Goebbels's more contemporary 'Berlin - Q-Damm'.[104] The shift towards direct action was accompanied by a strong reliance on identification, partly because Wlassowa was played by Carmen-Maja Antoni, a popular comic actress who had trained at the BE and the Volksbühne and is now famous for her appearances in the television crime series *Rosa Roth*. Antoni quickly built up a rapport with the audience by displaying her down-to-earth wit: in Scene 2 she showed her frustration at not being able to hear the revolutionaries' whispered plans, and during her entrance in Scene 8b her exaggerated 'Oh' of pain turned into an 'Oh' of recognition and understanding when she saw the strikebreakers. She also foregrounded Wlassowa's affection for Pawel by tugging his hair on her way out in Scene 2, giving him his cap at the start of Scene 5, keeping it

---

[101] 'Remember what will happen if you fail.'

[102] 'I stand for the oldest intrinsic values of theatre, for story-telling and coherence. At the moment that may not be what the arts sections of the newspapers … want, but I sense that the audience is deeply interested in this kind of theatre, in which the characters on stage … are not immediately treated ironically…' 'Wir leben im Übergang', *Der Spiegel*, 8 Jan. 2001, 162.

[103] 2003 programme, 15, 53, 58, 60.   [104] Ibid. 31–3.

safe in Scene 6, and returning it to him when they were reunited in Scene 9. But this emphasis on identification and direct action did not involve a return to the realism of the 1951 model, or to the patient reverence of Wekwerth's production. None of the minimalist props suggested the play's Russian setting: Wlassowa poured the tea from a plain white teapot instead of the traditional samovar, while Karl-Ernst Herrmann's set, consisting of a large white sloping triangle, with a smaller, bloodstained triangle jutting out from the front edge into the audience, teased viewers to decipher its figurative meaning. Although several reviewers likened it to a Soviet star, Detlef Friedrich pointed out that its shape had just as much in common with the horizontal cross-section of an American fighter jet.[105] Furthermore, its colours recalled the photograph of bloodstained snow in Grozny in the programme.

Peymann also used the new musical accompaniment, striking visual sequences, and entertainment to create a refreshing staging and thus counter the perception that *Die Mutter* was an old-fashioned propaganda piece. In Scene 3, for instance, loud metallic thuds set the pace for seventeen workers who were walking clockwise in a circle, making two steps forwards before leaning back and drinking their soup on the third. This stylized solution suggested a parallel between the factory and a prison yard, showing that the rhythm of the machines dictated the workers' every movement, even during their free time. The pattern was disrupted when some of the workers paused to read the revolutionaries' leaflets, and then the entire group stopped to listen to Karpow, who placed himself at the centre of the circle. What they heard united them in anger, causing them to throw their spoons into their soup-pots and turn outwards in disgust, ignoring Karpow. When he argued that there was no alternative but to accept the wage cut, the workers threw down their soup-pots and folded their arms, then evicted Karpow from their midst and formed a new, tight circle around the revolutionaries, surrounded by the larger circle that was now marked out by the soup-pots. The new brass accompaniment to the chorus of 'Das Lied vom Flicken' sounded cheerful, and the musicians clapped rhythmically as Karpow slumped to the ground, loosened his tie, and opened his collar, visibly uncomfortable in defeat.

---

[105] e.g. Irene Bazinger, 'Wenn Rosas Fahnen wieder blühen', *FAZ*, 17 Jan. 2003; Detlef Friedrich, 'Ostwestrevolutionsmärchenposse', *Berliner Zeitung*, 17 Jan. 2003; Hartmut Krug, 'Das politische Theater lebt', *Deutschlandfunk*, 16 Jan. 2003 (<http://www.dradio.de/cgi-bin/es/neu-kulturheute/624.html> [accessed 19 Jan. 2003]); Reinhard Wengierek, 'Rote Fahne ohne Blutspur', *Die Welt* (Berlin), 17 Jan. 2003.

The end of Scene 8b shows most clearly how Peymann and Gross injected entertainment into the performance. Peymann borrowed a sequence from a staging directed at Bochum's Schauspielhaus in 1983 by Manfred Karge, who played Smilgin and the butcher in 2003.[106] The musicians performed a fast, jazzed-up instrumental, while the kitchen staff fanned out in a line in front of the stage, passing plates from the middle to both ends, from where they were thrown diagonally into the stage space and—mostly—caught and set down on a table for the strikebreakers. This sequence transformed the washing-up chain into a celebration of the kitchen staff's new-found solidarity and ended the first half of the performance on a high note. It elicited enthusiastic applause from the audience and from one spectator the verdict: 'Also, doch kein langweiliger Brecht!'[107]

5.4 Critical Response

The audience's positive response to the first three performances contrasted with the reviews published in most newspapers, and this disparity owed at least as much to Peymann's uneasy relationship with the press as to hostility towards Brecht's ideology. Prejudice in favour of élite, avant-garde theatre has led some reviewers to dismiss Peymann's more conservative aesthetic as populist and therefore sub-standard, and his success in defending the BE's large subsidy has generated envy and mistrust, particularly because other theatres in Berlin are fighting for their very survival.[108] In a vitriolic article in *Der Spiegel* Matthias Matussek attacked Peymann and Daniel Barenboim, the conductor of the Deutsche Staatsoper, as follows: 'Die Diven des deutschen Kulturbetriebs arbeiten stets mit der gleichen Überhebung: Ich, Peymann, Barenboim, Müllermeierschulze, bin Weltkultur. Jede Mark weniger für mich ist ein Schritt ins provinzielle Elend.... Mein Gott Peymann.... Wer Goethe unterstützt, muss doch deshalb noch lange keinen Peymann fördern!'[109] Matussek also cited Peymann's commercial success

---

[106] Ulrich Schreiber, 'Bedenkt, wenn ihr versagt', *Frankfurter Rundschau*, 15 Oct. 1983; 1983 Bochum programme, SW.

[107] 'Not a boring Brecht play after all!' Overheard at the performance on 16 Jan. 2003.

[108] e.g. Detlef Friedrich, 'Lob der Großmäuligkeit', *Berliner Zeitung*, 5 May 2000; Rola, 'Was macht eigentlich ... Claus Peymann?', *Die Tageszeitung* (Berlin), 15 Mar. 2002.

[109] 'The divas of German cultural life always operate with the same arrogance. I, Peymann, Barenboim, Tom-Dick-or-Harry, am world-class culture. Every pound less for

as evidence that, politically, he is simply a professional rebel.[110] In August 2002, Peymann returned this hostility by declaring: 'die Kritiker sollen mich—entschuldigen Sie bitte—am Arsch lecken.... Ich werde in Berlin seit drei Jahren verrissen und die Bude ist brechend voll.'[111]

Most reviewers acknowledged that Peymann had related *Die Mutter* to the political issues of the day. For instance, the Associated Press critic declared: 'Offensichtlich kann politisches Theater angesichts eines drohenden Kriegs und steigender Arbeitslosigkeit auch mehr als sieben Jahrzehnte später funktionieren.'[112] But the *Tagesspiegel* argued that the production's political relevance was merely a substitute for artistic merit: 'Was du als Kunst nicht hast, das macht zur Not die Botschaft. Die rote Rosa als Deutschlands bleiche Mutter, das rührt, wenn unser Kapitalismus draußen kriselt und kriegelt, allemal ans Gemüt.'[113] Critics across the political spectrum agreed that Brecht's solutions were simplistic: for instance, in the *Financial Times Deutschland* Willy Theobald likened them to the attempt to survive atom bomb explosions under tin foil mats.[114] Ironically, however, Centre-Right reviewers failed to perceive the subtleties of Peymann's critique of Brecht's ideology even as they attacked his production as simplistic. Thus, the production was deemed well and truly mendacious by *Der Tagesspiegel*, still full of blind faith by the *FAZ*, shamelessly forgetful of history by *Die Welt*, and lacking any sense of irony or distance from the work by the *Sächsische Zeitung*.[115]

---

me is a step towards provincial misery.... My God, Peymann.... Anyone who supports Goethe does not automatically have to sponsor a Peymann, not by a long shot!' Matthias Matussek, 'Goldhamster mit Löwenpranke', *Der Spiegel*, 10 Apr. 2000, 46–9 (46–7).

[110] Ibid. 47.

[111] 'The critics can—excuse my language—kiss my arse.... I've been panned in Berlin for the last three years and the place is full to bursting.' Claus Peymann, 'Im Unruhestand', interview with Volker Corsten, *Die Welt am Sonntag* (Hamburg), 4 Aug. 2002.

[112] 'Obviously political theatre can work more than seven decades later, given an impending war and rising unemployment.' Anon. (AP), 'Ein Brecht-Abend im Zeichen Rosa Luxemburgs', *Yahoo! Schlagzeilen Deutschland* (<http://de.news.yahoo.com/030116/12/366r3.html> [accessed 19 Jan. 2003]).

[113] 'What you lack in art, you can make up for with your message if necessary. Red Rosa as Germany's pale mother, that never fails to tug at the heartstrings when our capitalism is undergoing another little crisis or war outside.' Peter von Becker, 'Rosa Rot', *Der Tagesspiegel* (Berlin), 17 Jan. 2003. 'Germany's pale mother' alludes to the first line of Brecht's 1933 poem 'Deutschland'. See *BFA*, xi. 253–4.

[114] Willy Theobald, 'Claus Peymann kauft sich eine Mütze', *Financial Times Deutschland* (Hamburg), 17–19 Jan. 2003.

[115] Becker, *Der Tagesspiegel*, 17 Jan. 2003; Bazinger, *FAZ*, 17 Jan. 2003; Wengierek, *Die Welt*, 17 Jan. 2003; Valeria Heintges, 'Schwarzweiß-Malerei mit blutroten Flecken', *Sächsische Zeitung* (Dresden), 17 Jan. 2003.

But Peter Kümmel, writing in the more liberal *Die Zeit*, had little patience with such criticism: 'Ach *Welt*, warum so viel Schaum vor dem Mund? Das leuchtende Aschfahl, das knallige Schwarzweiß, das wilde Grau, die intensive Leichenblässe dieser Inszenierung verweisen deutlich genug auf alles, was noch kommen sollte.'[116] Furthermore, in the tabloid *Bild-Zeitung*, Stefan Peter directly attributed the Centre-Right's reaction to ideological prejudice: 'Ein Stück von rührender Naivität, von der Zeit überholt, voll mit Propaganda. Könnte man sagen. Man könnte freilich auch ohne Vorurteile ins Theater gehen und feststellen: *Die Mutter* ist nicht nur ein Klassiker von Bertolt Brecht, sondern ein herausragendes Stück.'[117] The fact that ideological prejudice blinded so many reviewers to Peymann's criticism of Marxist dogma indicates just how wary theatre historians need to be when using reviews as evidence of performance rather than reception.

5.5 Conclusion

The 2003 production went beyond the GDR, the archaeological approach employed by theater 89, and the ironic treatment of *Ostalgie* in the Konstanz staging. Although Peymann problematized Marxist ideology, he was primarily concerned with present-day problems rather than the past trauma of state Socialism. It was precisely this contemporary relevance which, together with vibrant visual and musical entertainment, elicited a far more enthusiastic response from the audience than the preceding three productions. But because many reviewers expected Peymann to focus exclusively on the folly of Brecht's ideology, the press response was considerably less enthusiastic.

The disparity between the audience's and the critics' reception of *Die Mutter* raises the question for whom theatre is staged. Peymann adopted a more populist aesthetic than avant-garde directors, and articulated popular opposition to the war. Even if this makes him less radical than his public pronouncements suggest, the charge that he appeals to the lowest common denominator reflects only the élitist prejudice that art

---

[116] 'Oh *Welt*, why foam so much at the mouth? The glowing ashen pallor, the striking black and white, the wild grey, the intensive corpse-like paleness of this production point clearly enough towards everything that was to follow.' Kümmel, *Die Zeit*, 5/2003.

[117] 'A touchingly naïve play, overtaken by time, full of propaganda. You could say. Of course, you could also go to the theatre without any prejudice and discover: *The Mother* is not only a classic by Bertolt Brecht, but an excellent play.' Stefan Peter, 'Peymann inszeniert *Die Mutter*', *Bild* (Berlin), 17 Jan. 2003.

cannot be good if it is commercially successful and popular. Indeed, the audience's enthusiastic response to this production and the BE's consistently high ticket sales actually suggest that there is a need and a market for Peymann's more populist, accessible approach to drama.[118]

6. POLITICAL THEATRE, THE *WENDE*, AND THE BERLIN REPUBLIC

The reaction against the politicization of art during the Cold War has affected not only affirmative theatre but political theatre in general. Whilst Wekwerth failed to recognize the difficulties facing affirmative theatre in 1988, the three post-*Wende* productions of *Die Mutter* responded to the challenges facing political theatre in different ways. In Konstanz, Apprich's ostensible rejection of ideology actually amounted to the right-wing argument that Socialism was futile and incompatible with ethics. In Berlin, Frank and Peymann retained a qualified commitment to left-wing theatre by acknowledging that crimes had been perpetrated in the name of Marxism but still upholding the ideals of the early Socialists. Yet, whilst Frank conceived of political theatre solely in terms of reflection on the past and its legacy, Peymann used it to address the present too. Thus, whereas Frank evaded the question of whether political theatre could influence contemporary reality, Peymann assumed that the question did not even arise.

All three Berlin directors sought to preserve the older theatrical tradition of story-telling and clear communication against the irony and pastiche of the Konstanz staging and the disintegration and fragmentation of productions, for example, at Castorf's Volksbühne. The audience's enthusiastic response to Peymann's production suggests that there is a demand for this approach in mainstream theatre, particularly if it is combined with a strong emphasis on entertainment. In fact, since the late 1990s there have been signs that this traditional approach is re-emerging and is practised not only by directors like Wekwerth and Peymann who began their careers before the advent of postmodernism, but also by directors like Thomas Ostermeier who began to direct professionally in the 1990s and now works at the Schaubühne. One

---

[118] Claus Peymann, 'Hier herrscht der Kannibalismus', interview with Henryk M. Broder and Wolfgang Höbel, *Der Spiegel*, 25 Feb. 2002, 210–12 (210); Stefan Kirschner, 'Quotenkönig Peymann', *Berliner Morgenpost*, 10 July 2002.

might even speculate that, to some extent at least, the artistic practice of the BE and the Schaubühne is still informed by the traditions that were established by their respective founders.

The three Berlin stagings also show that performances of *Die Mutter* have become increasingly intertextual since the 1970s. Interestingly, whilst the 1988 and 1998 productions were both distinctively East German, the differences between them indicate that there were actually two East German performance traditions of the play. Thus, Wekwerth's 1988 production was ideologically and aesthetically closer to the dominant tradition established by the affirmative model production, whereas theater 89 incorporated political questions and performance techniques from Berghaus's subversive staging. Although this contrast partly reflected Wekwerth's personal involvement in the revivals of the model and Frank's and Mihan's participation in Berghaus's production, it also reflected their two sets of ideological and aesthetic preferences. Peymann's approach, however, was more eclectic: he borrowed techniques from the model and from West German stagings; he emphasized the direct action and identification with Wlassowa; but he resisted realism and added a new historical commentary. In Konstanz, meanwhile, the lack of performance allusions in the Stadttheater's staging simply reflected the participants' unfamiliarity with the earlier productions.

The fact that Frank and Peymann both used *Die Mutter* to confront the political and cultural legacies of Marxism and state Socialism indicates that the text can still provoke productive new interpretations, even though Brecht's agitation is no longer theatrically or politically fashionable. Together with Apprich's staging, their productions suggest how, and how far, different groups are coming to terms with these complex legacies. Whereas theater 89 used *Die Mutter* to investigate its members' past as East Germans and the problems that they faced in the reunified Germany, the Stadttheater in Konstanz turned the play into a critique of Socialism. Indeed, the Stadttheater's approach suggests that there is a strong tendency in prosperous, provincial parts of former West Germany to regard the new task of *Vergangenheitsbewältigung* as a distinctively East German problem. This almost certainly reflects the regionalized nature of Germany and the way in which the former GDR was simply incorporated into the FRG, without any re-negotiation of the West German legal and political systems. Then again, Peymann's production aroused critical controversy because it deviated from accepted West and East German approaches to the Socialist cultural heritage by intervening in the present rather than exclusively exploring the past. The reception of his production suggests that although far left-wing art from the Weimar Republic has the potential to survive the *Wende*, memories of its affirmative role in the GDR are still too strong for Cold War critics to welcome a re-assertion of its earlier agitational function.

Conclusion

Although *Die Mutter* was premièred in an agitational, topical staging, it has subsequently been performed in imaginative and sometimes surprising new ways: as a historical drama, *Lehrstück*, tragedy, anti-war play, and postmodern pastiche. As I explain in section 1 below, these interpretations relate partly to the text, partly to the contexts in which it has been performed, and partly to changes in theatrical conventions. Brecht's own stagings of *Die Mutter* reveal important continuities and changes in his theatrical practice between 1932 and 1951, which I identify in section 2. I then explore in section 3 what the SED's attitudes towards *Die Mutter* and the BE indicate about developments in GDR cultural politics, and in section 4 I show what stagings since 1970 reveal about post-Brechtian theatre. Finally, I suggest in section 5 how this kind of detailed, analytical production history can contribute to the future study of theatre, drama, and Brecht.

1. *DIE MUTTER*: THE TEXT AND ITS PERFORMANCES

Die Mutter was extremely topical in 1932, but it dealt only indirectly with Weimar Germany, through the form of a parable. Both of these factors contributed significantly to the political effect of the première. By highlighting the similarities between contemporary Germany and pre-revolutionary Russia, Brecht's topical allusions encouraged spectators to believe that a German revolution was both imminent and practicable. Yet this approach succeeded only because Brecht addressed themes whose relevance went beyond the historical Russian setting—such as poverty, industrial unrest, political education, and anti-war opposition. These enduring left-wing concerns subsequently facilitated the play's transference to contexts where spectators were unlikely to understand the allusions to the Germany of 1932. So, because *Die Mutter* also deals with political struggle in the wider sense, it has attracted new directors with their own priorities, not just in Germany, but worldwide.

International developments since 1932 have also created new challenges for directors staging *Die Mutter*, stimulating them to engage in new ways with Brecht's provocative text. At the première, Brecht correctly calculated that Communist spectators would offset the tragic deaths of Smilgin and Pawel with their jubilation at the revolutionaries' subsequent victory. This positive assessment was more difficult to sustain when the longer-term ramifications of the Russian Revolution became apparent. Even before 1989, knowledge of Stalin's Purges, the atrocities in the gulags, and repression in the Eastern bloc encouraged spectators to see Wlassowa as tragic—or even deluded—for trusting completely in Socialism. So, from 1974 onwards, most German directors cut the final two scenes and ended their productions at the street corner, where workers ignore Wlassowa's desperate warnings. Far from creating the tragic interpretation of *Die Mutter*, these cuts acknowledged how historical change had already affected its reception. Indeed, the text's changing reception indicates the risks of turning such recent events into a parable—risks that Brecht avoided in his other history plays.

The complex, hybrid form of *Die Mutter* is one reason why it has generated such different theatrical interpretations, ranging from an agitprop play to a modern tragedy. Since it combines forms and genres, directors have been able to construct new interpretations by emphasizing different generic aspects. In 1951, for example, Brecht presented *Die Mutter* as a historical drama by using a realistic aesthetic and adding historical references to the text and the programme. Whilst such an approach may generate stylistic and generic tensions that only further textual revisions can overcome, the extent to which audiences tolerate such tensions depends on historically and culturally contingent conventions. So, whereas critics argued that Brecht's epic devices were incompatible with his realistic aesthetic in 1951, the epic narrator in the Citizens Theatre's otherwise naturalistic production elicited no such comments in 1982.[1]

The dialectic between Brecht's 'epic' and 'dramatic' techniques is the second reason why *Die Mutter* has supported a wide range of

---

[1] Cf. Ch. 2, sect. 4.2; Mary Brennan, 'The Mother', *Glasgow Herald*, 27 Nov. 1982; J. Farrell, 'Brecht Well Served', *Scotsman* (Edinburgh), 29 Nov. 1982; Joyce McMillan, 'Communism in 14 Easy Lessons', *Sunday Standard* (Glasgow), 28 Nov. 1982; Cordelia Oliver, 'The Mother', *Guardian* (Manchester), 7 Nov. 1982.

interpretations in performance. Even though there is a common mis-
conception that Brecht's theatrical theory and practice consistently
prioritize the epic over the dramatic, *Die Mutter* actually combines
dramatic cohesion and montage, identification and distance, emotional
arousal and *Verfremdung*, in order to achieve its political impact. This
applies not just to the text but also to the music, which both comments
critically on Brecht's lyrics and encourages emotional responses at certain key points, such as the report of Pawel's death. So, even though
Brecht's epic devices are particularly prominent in *Die Mutter*, they still
achieve their effects through a dialectical interplay with more traditional
'dramatic' techniques. This interplay has allowed directors and actors to
shift the balance in favour of the epic or the dramatic, in line with their
chosen interpretation.

Although the performance theorist Fernando de Toro argues that a
dramatic text 'provides only one structure', the dialogue, and that 'the
rest is the job of the performance', Brecht's productions of *Die Mutter*
show that the dialogue can guide the blocking, line delivery, and set
design.[2] Nevertheless, since 1974 directors have frequently used the non-
verbal and para-lingual aspects of performance to contradict the dialogue
as well as the stage directions. So, although the dialogue mentions the
sofa, mirror, chest of drawers, and clean curtains in Wlassowa's home,[3]
Berghaus presented the action in an industrial wasteland, Heymann set
it in a museum, and Apprich used sun-loungers and jungle scenery. Postmodern directors have gone further still, by treating the dialogue as raw
material—an approach that Jim Niesen pursued at Irondale in 1997. So,
according to current conventions, the 'proof of the pudding'[4] is whether
the interpretation, script, and aesthetic work on stage, not whether they
can be justified with reference solely or even primarily to the text.

These conclusions suggest that the ideology and form of *Die Mutter* bring aspects of the relationship between text and performance into
sharp relief. The meanings of this text are particularly sensitive to contextual change because its politics and historical judgements are so explicit
and provocative, and its combination of different forms, genres, and
techniques stimulates different aesthetic approaches. Even so, since the
early 1970s changes in theatrical conventions have encouraged directors

---

[2] Fernando de Toro, *Theatre Semiotics: Text and Staging in Modern Theatre*, trans.
John Lewis, rev. and ed. Carole Hubbard (Toronto: University of Toronto Press,
1995), 57.

[3] *BFA*, iii. 268–9.   [4] *BFA*, xxvi. 395.

to subvert the text and provoke an even wider range of associations and meanings. In particular, they have used abstract sets to encourage spectators to question the text and actively interpret the staging. Yet, even though the text has lost its automatic hegemony in performance, productions of *Die Mutter* have still engaged with the same broad problems and themes, albeit from different angles and in contrasting ways.

2. BRECHT'S THEATRICAL PRACTICE

2.1 Staging Methods and Theatre Aesthetics

Brecht's own productions of *Die Mutter* reveal continuities in his staging methods but important differences in his aesthetic approaches. In 1932, 1935, and 1951 he attended closely to the *Fabel*, *Gestus*, and blocking, and used captions and photographs to highlight the political significance of the action. Nevertheless, the aesthetic of the 1951 production indicates that Brecht had shifted significantly away from the austere epic theatre of 1932. This aesthetic change was closely related to his new audience, the SED's cultural policy, and the transition from subversive to predominantly affirmative theatre.

The set designs, props, and costumes reveal major differences between the 1932 and 1951 productions. In 1951 Brecht and Neher rejected their earlier austere, makeshift aesthetic, and foregrounded craftsmanship, elegance, and beauty. They included substantial social detail in the props and costumes, not just the acting and blocking, and used projected paintings to illustrate the setting. This emphasis on visual pleasure corresponded to a declaration that Brecht had made in the *Kleines Organon* in 1948: 'Widerrufen wir also, wohl zum allgemeinen Bedauern, unsere Absicht, aus dem Reich des Wohlgefälligen zu emigrieren, und bekunden wir, zu noch allgemeinerem Bedauern, nunmehr die Absicht, uns in diesem Reich niederzulassen.'[5] If due allowance is made for Brecht's irony, this statement suggests that the 1951 production was part of a larger shift in his theatre aesthetics, and that he expected his new approach to prove popular.

In 1951 the need to re-invent *Die Mutter* for the GDR governed Brecht's aesthetic decisions. He hoped that his postwar productions at

---

[5] 'Let us renounce, no doubt to most people's regret, our decision to emigrate from the realm of the pleasurable, and declare, to even more people's regret, our intention of taking up residence there henceforth.' *BFA*, xxiii. 66.

the Berliner Ensemble would attract a socially more inclusive audience than *Die Mutter* had done in 1932. To achieve this, Brecht was even prepared to sacrifice some of his principles and approve measures that he had strongly opposed in 1935—such as the Russian costumes, detailed set, and increased identification. But his strenuous efforts to distance *Die Mutter* publicly from the proletarian revolutionary tradition suggest that his new aesthetic was also designed to pre-empt charges of Formalism from the SED. So, although Brecht's basic staging methods remained the same, his aesthetic changes were so far-reaching and so closely related to the politico-cultural situation that it is incorrect to claim that political constraints made no 'decisive impact on the essential core of his theatre work' in the GDR.[6]

Brecht's flexibility and pragmatism at the BE contrast with his earlier dogmatism at the Theatre Union: by 1951 he had become far more sensitive to political and cultural realities, and was therefore prepared to make substantive changes to the text and its staging. Since these changes served his strategic objectives, they should not be viewed as a capitulation either to his audience or to the SED. Indeed, although Brecht acted on the SED's political criticisms because he shared the regime's long-term objectives, he robustly defended the production's remaining epic features.[7] Even so, his concessions came at a price, because the realistic aspects of the aesthetic conflicted with the anti-illusionistic captions, songs, half-curtain, and projected photographs. Given the conservative expectations of spectators in 1951, the new set and costumes might better have suited less 'epic' plays like *Die Gewehre der Frau Carrar* and *Die Tage der Commune*. Yet, because Neher's crafted aesthetic presented a sanitized, idealized vision of working-class life, it is questionable whether it was really appropriate for any of Brecht's socially critical plays. After all, by the 1960s the realistic aspects of the aesthetic had allowed *Die Mutter* to become a self-congratulatory *Staatsfeststück*—which explains why Berghaus and Reinhardt instead used such a bleak, fractured landscape when they sought to promote self-criticism and change in 1974.

2.2 Theatre Pedagogy

Brecht's day-to-day practice at the BE reveals that he valued the establishment of a permanent ensemble as highly as his finished productions.

---

[6] Rouse, 60.   [7] Cf. Ch. 2, sect. 4.2.

In the early 1950s he promoted practical training and political education, conducted lengthy discussions with his assistants, and arranged for rehearsals and meetings to be documented for the benefit of the company and future practitioners and scholars.[8] He also encouraged self-reflection and analysis by instructing his assistants to file nightly reports on performances and suggest how they might be improved. By these means, Brecht established an apparatus that would—in time—function without him. After his death in 1956, his assistants were able to take over the BE's artistic management and stage new, context-specific productions using his methods and insights from his archive. As a result, the theatre's influence and renown continued to spread.

Brecht also worked assiduously to disseminate his staging methods beyond the BE. Whereas he had previously promoted his methods mainly through his theoretical writings, in the GDR he focused attention on his practice by including hundreds of photographs and sketches in *Theaterarbeit* and the model books—probably to correct the misleading impressions generated by his more polemical theories. Nevertheless, by presenting only one way of performing each play, the model books made it harder for directors to distinguish between Brecht's methods and his aesthetics—which was particularly unfortunate in the case of *Die Mutter*, because the model production contained so many aesthetic compromises. Similarly, even though Berlau acknowledged in *Theaterarbeit* that *Die Mutter* had been staged differently in 1932, 1935, and 1950, the book still presented the 1951 production as the definitive interpretation for the GDR.[9]

Brecht's insistence that directors should copy every detail of the model contradicted his theatrical practice and theoretical statements. At the BE, he consistently advocated context-specific interpretations of plays and, in an essay of 1954, warned directors against being intimidated by the classic status of certain plays and performance traditions: 'Es gibt eine Tradition der Aufführung, die gedankenlos zum kulturellen Erbe gezählt wird, obwohl sie das Werk, das eigentliche Erbe, nur schädigt.... Es fällt sozusagen durch Vernachlässigung mehr und mehr Staub auf die großen alten Bilder, und die Kopisten kopieren mehr oder minder fleißig diese Staubflecken mit.'[10] The fact that he none the less required other theatres to copy his own productions indicates the ambivalence

---

[8] Cf. *BFA*, xxiii. 310–11. [9] *Theaterarbeit*, 333–7.
[10] 'There is a performance tradition which is counted automatically as part of the cultural heritage, even though it only damages the work, the actual heritage.... You

that derived from his dual role as writer and director. As a director, Brecht was excited by the possibility of adapting plays for performance, particularly because he possessed the creative ability to revise texts; but as a writer, he was anxious to prevent mediocre theatre practitioners from riding roughshod over his plays. Whilst Brecht's anxiety was understandable, given the Theatre Union's staging in 1935 and the SED's readiness to accuse him of Formalism in the GDR, it had serious long-term repercussions for stagings of *Die Mutter*. By encouraging directors to imitate his achievements uncritically, the model production soon became a source of stagnation more than inspiration.

2.3 Impulses and Attitudes

The 1951 production of *Die Mutter* reveals some of the impulses and attitudes behind Brecht's work in the early years of the GDR, before the uprising of 17 June 1953. His commitment to in-house political education and to outreach work with trades unions demonstrates his genuine enthusiasm for the new social order. Whilst this enthusiasm helped to reconcile him to the need for tactical concessions, the SED's increasingly dogmatic cultural policy still caused him considerable frustration, particularly when the BE was targeted in the campaign against Formalism. Even so, the early 1950s were a period of immense energy and productivity for Brecht. Having his own, state-funded ensemble gave him unprecedented opportunities to test his methods, produce his plays, and develop his theatre pedagogy. Given the attractions of these opportunities after writing 'für die Schublade' ('for the bottom drawer')[11] in exile, it is not surprising that Brecht devoted most of his attention to theatre in the GDR, instead of recreating the symbiosis between writing and directing that had characterized his dramatic practice in the Weimar Republic.

3. GDR CULTURAL POLITICS

The SED's attitudes towards *Die Mutter* and the BE offer significant insights into changes in cultural politics and the company's status in the

---

might say that more and more dust falls on the great old masters through neglect, and the copyists copy the dust marks too, more or less diligently.' *BFA*, xxiii. 316.

[11] *BFA*, xxvi. 332.

GDR. In 1951, the members of the *Politbüro* rated theatre's ideological importance so highly that they discussed *Die Mutter* in person and asked Brecht to make changes. Furthermore, cultural politicians like Oelßner and Rodenberg were so suspicious of Brecht's ideology and aesthetics that they publicly criticized the production at the conference on Formalism on 17 March. Like the official ban on *Das Verhör des Lukullus* just five days earlier, this criticism indicates that the risk of adverse international publicity did not deter the SED from openly interfering with the work of its leading artists. It may also explain why directors' enthusiasm for *Die Mutter* soon abated in the GDR: after being performed at five theatres besides the BE in 1950–2, it was not staged again until 1957. In contrast, between 1946 and 1956 thirty-six theatres staged *Die Gewehre der Frau Carrar*, a realistic drama that respected the three unities.[12]

The SED's initial reactions to *Die Mutter* contrast sharply with the play's subsequent status as a GDR propaganda piece. In 1957 four theatres restaged the model to mark the fortieth anniversary of the October Revolution, and in 1967 another six theatres followed suit to commemorate the Revolution's fiftieth anniversary. In 1988 Wekwerth's production was even announced in a front-page headline in *Neues Deutschland*, above a photograph of the GDR's political élite. The play's transition to a *Staatsfeststück* was facilitated by Brecht's positive depiction of Russian history, the aesthetic concessions that he had made in 1951, and the less stringent enforcement of Socialist Realism after Khrushchev criticized Stalin in 1956. Yet it also indicates how the SED gradually came to regard both Brecht and the BE as national status symbols. After all, by winning prestigious awards at international theatre festivals in Paris in 1954 and 1960, the BE had presented the GDR as the real home of the German cultural heritage—which even the SED now deemed to include Brecht.[13]

Whilst the BE's role as a status symbol bolstered its position, it also created problems for the company and the SED. Most importantly, it increased the international and domestic pressure on the BE to fulfil its two functions: to preserve Brecht's methods and productions, and to remain at the cutting edge of world theatre by developing new stagings and techniques. As experiments and styles proliferated at

---

[12] *BFA*, iv (1988), 517.
[13] The 1960 award was particularly important because the BE won first prize for all its productions.

other leading European theatres, the incompatibility of these functions became increasingly evident. But the BE's enhanced status also made the authorities reluctant to intervene in its internal affairs for fear of causing an international scandal, particularly while Weigel was still alive. After all, she was not only Brecht's widow but a world-renowned actress who had represented the GDR by playing Mother Courage in London and Pelagea Wlassowa in Paris. Quite simply, the SED did not dare to challenge the heroine of the GDR's *Staatsfeststück*.

The SED's attempts to resolve the BE's internal crises show how far it had, even by the mid-1960s, moved from the doctrinaire interventionism of 1951. These attempts also reveal that cultural politicians were surprisingly weak when it came to dealing with Brecht's heirs. Even in the GDR, private property rights were such that Weigel could have dissolved the BE and refused to license Brecht's plays for performance. Since these steps would have seriously damaged the GDR's image as the protector of the German cultural heritage, Hager and Hoffmann shied away from addressing the fundamental conflict between the BE's functions. Whilst they eventually curbed the heirs' powers in 1976, this attempt at damage limitation occurred only after years of further negotiations had failed. So, overall, the SED's dealings with Brecht's heirs show how its increased concern for the GDR's international image restricted its room for manœuvre: by the mid-1960s, even cultural ideologues had reluctantly acknowledged the importance of public relations.

4. POST-BRECHTIAN APPROACHES

Productions of *Die Mutter* suggest that a decisive shift towards post-Brechtian theatre occurred around 1970, when a new generation of directors departed from the model and began to use Brecht's methods selectively and subversively. Styles and techniques soon proliferated as practitioners drew inspiration from diverse sources, including dance, film, and television. In some cases directors even dispensed with the epic features in the text: for instance, Frank and Peymann cut the captions, and Havergal replaced the report of Pawel's death with an on-stage execution. But whilst directors no longer felt compelled to use Brecht's methods when staging *Die Mutter*, they all continued to work with—or against—his *cachet* as a political dramatist: Apprich, for example, drew attention to Brecht's ideology and didacticism in order to criticize them from a right-wing perspective.

Even the few theatres that used Brecht's methods did so creatively, without replicating his productions. In Manchester and London, for instance, Christie hung the captions from a washing-line—a resourceful, humorous way of showing that politics begins at home. In West Berlin, meanwhile, Stein blocked the Schaubühne's production according to Brecht's principles, used captions, and eliminated superfluous details, but developed the actor/character split in accordance with his own preoccupation with anti-authoritarian theatre. Indeed, all three stagings were closely tailored to their own context: whilst Stein stimulated quiet reflection on the position of the West German Left in 1970, Christie and Trevis articulated the British Left's outspoken opposition to Thatcherism in 1986.

Die Mutter was a seminal text in the repertoires of Western alternative companies in the mid-1970s and 1980s, particularly in England and Scandinavia. Since alternative companies were attracted by a constellation of features specific to this text—its confrontational politics, independent heroine, and learning narrative—most of them had no qualms about dispensing with Brecht's staging methods.[14] In San Francisco, the Mime Troupe used circus tricks and folk-songs to make its production more entertaining, while militant English companies rewrote *Die Mutter* and rejected most of Brecht's dramatic techniques too. Indeed, McGrath and Red Ladder dispensed entirely with Brecht's *Historisierung*, depicted scenes from modern English working-class life, and created an aesthetic that was strongly influenced by television and pop music. But because Arden and D'Arcy espoused similarly revolutionary aims to Brecht, they used *Historisierung* to promote their radical agenda: by comparing Northern Ireland explicitly with Tsarist Russia, they argued that the IRA might eventually end British rule in Northern Ireland.

During the 1970s, other European directors reacted against traditional models of political theatre. In the GDR, for instance, Berghaus challenged affirmative Socialist Realist theatre, and in France Heymann rejected agitation in favour of a dialectical, non-prescriptive approach. In pursuit of these broad aims, they developed Brecht's separation of the elements in new, contrasting ways, under the influence of other

---

[14] e.g. McGrath acknowledged Brecht's theatrical influence only grudgingly: 'My main gurus are Joan Littlewood, Alan Dossor, Colette King, George Devine, Anthony Page, Lindsay Anderson, Ariane Mnouchkine, Tumanashvili and the Film Actors Studio of Tbilisi, Richard Eyre and, I suppose, Bertolt Brecht (critically).' McGrath, *Naked Thoughts*, p. xi.

early avant-garde practitioners like Palucca and Eisenstein. At the BE, Berghaus used the lighting, line delivery, and set to interpret situations in the text and create a shocking, intense staging that rejected both Brecht's model and the SED's idealized version of history. In contrast, Heymann used the set and props to create clear contradictions between the dramatic action, its historical context and stage history, and present reality. By these means, he challenged his spectators to re-evaluate *Die Mutter* and search for new solutions to the socio-economic problems that it depicts. Significantly, though, he offered no assurances that any such solutions existed—an approach that contrasted completely with the faith that the alternative companies still placed in political change.

More recently, postmodern performance has moved beyond the 'Trennung der Elemente'. In 1997, for instance, New York's Irondale Ensemble Project rejected Brecht's metanarrative in favour of wholesale fragmentation, eclecticism, and irony. But because this approach gave the impression that the actors were just making fun of *Die Mutter*, the spectators had little incentive to construct their own interpretations. Indeed, the difficulties of preserving political meaning while pursuing technical subversion may explain why Frank and Peymann re-asserted the *Fabel* and *Grundgestus* when they each staged *Die Mutter* in the reunified Berlin. Unlike Irondale's production, these stagings clearly communicated their directors' political concerns: Frank's desire to reflect on the failure of the Socialist Utopia and Peymann's determination to oppose a second Gulf War. Even though their approaches were theatrically more conservative than those of Berghaus, Heymann, and Irondale, they still provided fresh perspectives on the text, its history, and the contemporary context.

5. FUTURE PERSPECTIVES

Now that so many theatres preserve detailed records of their stagings, production history has the potential to become a significant sub-discipline of theatre studies. Indeed, far from posing an insuperable obstacle to analysis, transience constitutes the chief interest of performance, because it licenses theatre practitioners to create provisional, imaginative, context-specific interpretations of dramatic texts. So, by comparing how theatres have responded to the same text in the light of their different experiences and concerns, a production history can chart social, cultural and theatrical change. It can also provide a resource for future practitioners, who already creatively incorporate ideas from earlier productions. Equally importantly, production history can complement literary criticism by offering fresh perspectives on plays and taking full account of the historical and aesthetic contingency of dramatic meaning. By these means, it may even encourage more literary critics to approach plays as texts that are designed primarily for the stage.

This book indicates that a greater reciprocity between the study of dramatic texts and theatrical practice is essential if scholars are to do justice to Brecht's work as a writer-director. At present, the academic separation of drama and performance means that most literary critics approach Brecht exclusively through his plays and theoretical writings, even though he intended these theoretical writings to complement his theatrical practice as a director. This problem has been exacerbated by the disproportionate attention that is still devoted to Brecht's polemical contrasts between Aristotelian and epic theatre—contrasts that oversimplify the textual and performance strategies even in *Die Mutter*, which is usually considered one of his most 'epic' works. Consequently, whilst the view that Brecht completely opposed identification and emotion now lacks credibility, it still dominates public perceptions of his work.[15] By paying more attention to Brecht's theatrical practice in different contexts, scholars and teachers can develop a better understanding of how his plays and stagings worked, of how his aesthetic approach changed over time, and of how he became far more flexible and pragmatic than his theories often suggest.

While Brecht was writing *Der gute Mensch von Sezuan* in exile, without recourse to the theatre, he complained that it was impossible to finish a play without the stage.[16] Although any dramatic text is incomplete without the stage, this production history indicates that plays are actually continued, not finished, in performance. Both as a dramatist and as a director, Brecht exploited the potential of drama by rewriting and re-interpreting texts for new audiences. His plays, his productions, and the performance history of *Die Mutter* are a powerful demonstration of the possibilities that such an approach creates. *Die*

---

[15] e.g. *The Oxford Concise Companion to the Theatre* states that epic theatre is 'designed to appeal more to the audience's reason than to its emotions, *thus excluding sympathy and identification*' (my italics). Phyllis Hartnoll and Peter Found, *The Oxford Concise Companion to the Theatre*, 2nd edn (Oxford: Oxford University Press, 1996), 147.

[16] *BFA*, xxvi. 395.

Mutter is now much more than it was in 1932 because it has acquired so many new associations through its productions, historical change, and theatrical innovation. Indeed, far from rendering the play obsolete, the demise of the GDR and the USSR has actually re-invigorated its performance history by creating new problems and opportunities for theatre practitioners. As long as this continues, *Die Mutter* will still satisfy Brecht's definition of a long-lasting work: one which invites and rewards effort.[17]

---

[17] *BFA*, xiv. 34.

Glossary

Abendbericht evening performance report.

blocking the movement and configuration of the actors on stage.

Brechtpflege caring for Brecht, i.e. for his legacy.

dialectics Hegel's method of logical disputation: the contradiction between a thesis and an antithesis is resolved into a synthesis of the two. This is treated as a new thesis, so that the clash of arguments continues.

epic theatre Brecht's term for his form of theatre, in which the dramatic action is interrupted by narrative captions, songs, direct addresses to the audience, projected photographs, and/or film sequences. By introducing these narrative elements into performance, Brecht contravened the traditional separation of the epic and the dramatic, which Aristotle presented as entirely separate genres in his *Poetics*. For this reason, Brecht also called epic theatre 'non-Aristotelian'.

Fabel not simply the plot of a play, but the sociopolitical story which the director wants to tell through its staging. When preparing a production, Brecht would set out the *Fabel*, then identify the key points in each scene and relate them to it.

Gesamtgestus the overall purpose, point, and character of a production: agitation in the 1932 production of *Die Mutter*, winning over the audience in the 1951 production.

Gestus in relation to acting, this is best understood as a physical action or spatial configuration which reveals the ideological, social and economic relations between two or more characters.

Historisierung historicization. Brecht uses this term to indicate that familiar phenomena are not eternal: 'what is, was not always so, and will not remain so forever'.

Intendantentheater hierarchical form of theatre led by a manager, opposed after 1968 by theatre reformers like Peter Stein, who sought to establish more democratic, collectively led institutions.

Lehrstück a form of 'learning play' that Brecht developed as a pedagogical exercise for performers. It was revolutionary because it fulfilled its purpose simply by being rehearsed; Brecht saw its performance before an audience only as a possible by-product, not a necessary end-product, of the rehearsals.

Mitbestimmung collective decision making, as opposed to hierarchical management.

Modellbuch documentary record of a production, consisting of several hundred photographs with captions. Ruth Berlau invented the *Modellbuch*, and Brecht used it to document his postwar productions.

Nicht, Sondern Prinzip 'not, but principle'. In addition to showing what a character does, the actor should also show what the character does not do.

Staatsfeststück play used to mark state anniversaries and celebrations.

Trennung der Elemente 'separation of the elements'. Brecht argued that the different elements of performance (e.g. text, line delivery, music, costume) should comment on and even contradict each other, rather than consistently providing the same information.

Verfremdung best translated as 'estrangement'. It aims to make spectators see familiar phenomena and people from fresh angles so that they can question them, instead of taking them for granted.

Wende a term that means 'change' or 'turn' and refers to the fall of the Berlin Wall, the collapse of the GDR, and the period leading up to reunification on 3 October 1990.

Werktreue fidelity to the original work, often cited by conservatives in defence of dominant literary interpretations and traditional modes of performance.

Bibliography

For reasons of space, this bibliography does not include entries for archival sources, newspaper articles (except interviews), and theatre reviews. Full bibliographic details for these sources are given in the footnotes.

1. ARCHIVES CONSULTED

Berliner Ensemble Archive, Berlin.
Bertolt-Brecht-Archiv, Berlin.
Billy Rose Collection, New York Public Library.
Deutsches Literaturarchiv, Marbach.
Institut für Zeitungsforschung, Dortmund.
Landesarchiv Berlin.
National Theatre Archive, London.
Schaubühne am Lehniner Platz Archive, Berlin.
Schloß Wahn Theatersammlung, Cologne.
Scottish Theatre Archive, Glasgow University Library, Department of Special Collections.
Stadtgeschichtliches Museum Leipzig.
Stadtmuseum Berlin.
Stiftung Archiv der Akademie der Künste am Robert-Koch-Platz, Berlin.
Stiftung Archiv der Parteien und Massenorganisationen der DDR im Bundesarchiv, Berlin.
University of Davis at California.

2. AUDIO RECORDINGS

Brecht, Bertolt, *Die Mutter*, dir. Manfred Wekwerth, 1988, Wekwerth's personal copy.
—— *Die Mutter*, dir. Ruth Berghaus, 1974 (BEA).
—— and Hanns Eisler, *Die Mutter*, Coro della Radio Svizzera, cond. Diego Fasolis, 1995, CHAN 9820.
—— —— *Die Mutter*, Ernst Busch and the BE, cond. Adolf Fritz Guhl, *c.* 1951, on *Historische Aufnahmen*, 0092302BC.
—— —— *Die Mutter: Kantate op. 25*, Chor der Hochschule für Musik 'Hanns Eisler', cond. Fritz Höft, 1969/70, EdBa 01315-2.

3. VIDEO RECORDINGS

Brecht, Bertolt, *La Mère*, dir. Jacques Delcuvellerie Groupov, film dir. Michel Jakar, Wallonie Image Production, 1997 (AdK RKP).

—— *Die Mutter*, dir. Brecht, film dir. Manfred Wekwerth, DEFA, 1958 (Goethe-Institut, London).

—— *Die Mutter*, dir. Hans-Joachim Frank, 1998 (CPR).

—— *Die Mutter*, dir. Wolfgang Schwiedrzik, Patrick Steckel, Peter Stein, film dir. Uwe Reuter, 1970 (AdK RKP).

—— *Die Mutter* [excerpts], dir. Brecht, on *Syberberg filmt bei Brecht*, film dir. Hans Jürgen Syberberg, 1953, ISBN 3-923854-80-3.

Gorky, Maxim, *Mother*, dir. Vsevolod Pudovkin, 1926, re-released by Tartan Video, 1997, TVT 1275.

Mihan, Jörg, talk on theater 89's production of *Die Mutter* at the CPR, 27–9 Nov. 1998 (CPR).

4. PRINTED SOURCES

4.1 Primary

4.1.1 Literary texts

Brecht, Bertolt, *Gesammelte Werke*, 2 vols (London: Malik, 1938), ii.

—— *Große kommentierte Berliner und Frankfurter Ausgabe*, ed. Werner Hecht *et al.*, 30 vols (Frankfurt/Main and Berlin: Suhrkamp and Aufbau, 1988–2000).

—— 'The Mother', trans. Lee Baxandall and adapted by the San Francisco Mime Troupe, *Ramparts*, 13.1 (Aug. 1974), 41–4.

—— *The Mother*, trans. Steve Gooch (London: Eyre Methuen, 1978).

—— *Die Mutter* (East Berlin: Henschel, [1951]), BEA, box file 132.

—— 'Die Mutter', adapted by the Schaubühne am Halleschen Ufer, in *Die Mutter: Regiebuch der Schaubühnen-Inszenierung*, ed. Volker Canaris (Frankfurt/Main: Suhrkamp, 1971), 7–97.

—— *Die Mutter: Bühnenfassung des Berliner Ensembles*, ed. Joachim Tenschert (East Berlin: Henschel, 1970).

—— *Die Mutter; Geschichten aus der Revolution*, Versuche 15–16 (Berlin: Kiepenheuer, 1933).

—— *Stücke*, ed. Elisabeth Hauptmann, 14 vols (Frankfurt/Main: Suhrkamp, 1953–67), v (1957).

Brook, Peter, *et al.*, *US: The Book of Royal Shakespeare Theatre Production US* (London: Calder and Boyars, 1968).

Gorky, Maxim, *Die Mutter*, trans. Adolf Hess (Berlin: Malik, 1927).

—— *Sommergäste*, trans. August Scholz (Berlin: Ladyschnikow, 1906).

Hauptmann, Elisabeth, *Julia ohne Romeo: Geschichten, Stücke, Aufsätze, Erinnerungen*, ed. Rosemarie Eggert and Rosemarie Hill (East Berlin: Aufbau, 1977).

Hochhuth, Rolf, *Der Stellvertreter: Ein christliches Trauerspiel* (Reinbek bei Hamburg: Rowohlt, 1963).

McGrath, John, *Little Red Hen* (London: Pluto, 1977).

—— *Yobbo Nowt* (London: Pluto, 1978).

Maltz, Albert, *The Black Pit* (New York: G. P. Putnam, 1935).

—— and George Sklar, *Peace on Earth: An Anti-War Play* (New York: Samuel French, 1934).

Müller, Heiner, 'Lessings Schlaf Traum Schrei', in *Herzstück* (West Berlin: Rotbuch, 1983), 34–7.

Peters, Paul, and George Sklar, *Stevedore* (New York: Covici Friede, 1934).

Red Ladder, 'Strike while the Iron Is Hot: A Woman's Work Is Never Done', in *Strike while the Iron Is Hot: Three Plays on Sexual Politics*, ed. Michelene Wandor (London: Journeyman, 1980), 17–62.

Richards, Gavin, *England Expects: A Musical Entertainment for All Those Sick with Sacrifice* (London: Journeyman and Belt & Braces Roadshow, 1977).

Stark, Günther, and Günther Weisenborn, 'Die Mutter', ed. Emma Lewis Thomas, *Brecht heute*, 3 (1973), 64–105.

Weiss, Peter, *Diskurs über die Vorgeschichte und den Verlauf des lang andauernden Befreiungskampfes in Viet Nam als Beispiel für die Notwendigkeit des bewaffneten Kampfes der Unterdrückten gegen ihre Unterdrücker sowie über die Versuche der Vereinigten Staaten von Amerika die Grundlagen der Revolution zu vernichten* (Frankfurt/Main: Suhrkamp, 1968).

—— *Die Ermittlung: Oratorium in 11 Gesängen* (Frankfurt/Main: Suhrkamp, 1965).

4.1.2 Other primary sources

Aufricht, Ernst Josef, *Erzähle, damit du dein Recht erweist* (West Berlin: Propyläen, 1966).

Baedeker, Karl, *Berlin und Umgebung*, 20th edn (Leipzig: Karl Baedeker, 1927).

Bienert, Gerhard, *Ein Leben in tausend Rollen*, ed. Dieter Reimer (East Berlin: Henschel, 1989).

Bömelburg, Wolfgang, *Hobellied für Bertolt Brecht: Ein Theatertischler erzählt* (Berlin: Eulenspiegel, 1997).

Braun, Matthias, 'Gespräch mit Ekkehard Schall über Helene Weigel', *Sinn und Form*, 36 (1984), 1039–51.

Brecht, Bertolt, *et al.*, *Theaterarbeit: Sechs Aufführungen des Berliner Ensembles*, ed. Berliner Ensemble and Helene Weigel, 3rd rev. edn (East Berlin: Henschel, [1966]).

Brown, John Vere, *The Citizens Company 1979–1985* (Glasgow: Citizens Theatre, 1985).

Buchmann, Ditte (ed.), '*Eine Begabung muß man entmutigen* … ': *Wera und Claus Küchenmeister erinnern sich an Brecht* (East Berlin: Henschel, 1986).

Bunge, Hans (ed.), *Brechts Lai-Tu: Erinnerungen und Notate von Ruth Berlau*, 2nd edn (Darmstadt: Hermann Luchterhand, 1985).

——— (ed.), *Gespräche mit Hans Bunge: Fragen Sie mehr über Brecht: Hanns Eisler im Gespräch* (Leipzig: Deutscher Verlag für Musik, 1975).

Dieckmann, Friedrich, 'Meine Schleef-Mappe: Einar Schleefs Berliner Bühnenbildner-Jahre', in *Einar Schleef*, ed. Gabriele Gerecke, Harald Müller, and Hans-Ulrich Müller-Schwefe, Theater der Zeit Arbeitsbuch, 11 (Berlin: Podewil, 2002), 20–7.

———and Karl-Heinz Drescher (eds), *Die Plakate des Berliner Ensembles 1949–1989* (Hamburg: Europäische Verlagsanstalt, 1992).

Dreifuß, Alfred, *Ensemblespiel des Lebens: Erinnerungen eines Theatermannes* (East Berlin: Der Morgen, 1985).

Eisler, Hanns, 'Briefe an Nathan Notowicz', in *Sinn und Form* (*Sonderheft Hanns Eisler*), ed. Deutsche Akademie der Künste (East Berlin: Rütten & Loening, 1964), 278–81.

———*Materialien zu einer Dialektik der Musik* (Leipzig: Reclam, 1976).

———*Neun Balladen aus 'Die Mutter'*, ed. Manfred Grabs (Leipzig: Deutscher Verlag für Musik, 1977).

———*Neun Lieder aus 'Die Mutter'*, 2nd edn (Leipzig: Deutscher Verlag für Musik, 1997).

Fetting, Hugo (ed.), *Von der Freien Bühne zum Politischen Theater: Drama und Theater im Spiegel der Kritik*, 2 vols (Leipzig: Philipp Reclam jun., 1987).

Fischer, Hannelore, 'Neuinszenierung *Die Mutter*: Vor der BE-Premiere. Interview mit Karl Mickel', *Sonntag* (East Berlin), 20 Oct. 1974.

Frank, Reinhard (ed.), *Das Strafgesetzbuch für das Deutsche Reich*, 18th edn (Tübingen: J. C. B. Mohr, 1931).

Geschonneck, Erwin, *Meine unruhigen Jahre*, ed. Günter Agde (Berlin: Aufbau, 1997).

Gronius, Jörg W., and Wend Kässens, *Theatermacher: Gespräche mit Luc Bondy, Jürgen Flimm, Hansgünther Heyme, Hans Neuenfels, Peter Palitzsch, Claus Peymann, Frank-Patrick Steckel, George Tabori und Peter Zadek* (Frankfurt/Main: Hain, 1990).

Hager, Kurt, 'Kurt Hager beantwortete Fragen der Illustrierten *Stern*', *Neues Deutschland* (East Berlin), 10 Apr. 1987.

Heymann, Pierre-Etienne, *Regards sur les mutations du théâtre public (1968–1998): La Mémoire et le désir* (Paris: L'Harmattan, 2000).

Hildebrandt, Dieter, *et al.*, 'Was kann man machen? Ein Gespräch über Theater und Theatermachen in diesem Jahr 1968 mit den Regisseuren Peter Stein und Peter Zadek', *Theater heute Jahresheft*, 9 (1968), 26–9.

Hoffmann, Ludwig, and Klaus Pfützner (eds), *Theater der Kollektive: Proletarisch-revolutionäres Berufstheater in Deutschland 1928–1933: Stücke, Dokumente, Studien*, 2 vols (East Berlin: Henschel, 1980), i.

Honecker, Erich, '[Schlußwort Erich Honeckers auf der 4. Tagung des ZK der SED Dezember 1971, Auszug]', in *Dokumente zur Kunst-, Literatur- und Kulturpolitik der SED 1971–1974*, ed. Gisela Rüß (Stuttgart: Seewald, 1976), 287–8.

Kaufmann, Hans, 'Wie er nicht im Buche steht: Erinnerungen an Brecht', *Juni-Magazin für Literatur und Politik*, 24 (1996), 77–90.

Kokkos, Yannis, [designs for *La Mère*], *Obliques*, 20–1 (1979), 152, 159, 216, 222, 242–7.

Kommunistische Partei Deutschlands, *Die Rote Fahne* (Berlin), 1 Mar. 1929–31 Mar. 1932.

Kreuzer, Helmut, and Karl-Wilhelm Schmidt (eds), *Dramaturgie in der DDR (1945–1990)*, 2 vols (Heidelberg: C. Winter, 1998).

Lang, Joachim, and Jürgen Hillesheim (eds), *'Denken heißt verändern… ': Erinnerungen an Brecht* (Augsburg: Maro, 1998).

Lauter, Hans (ed.), *Der Kampf gegen den Formalismus in Kunst und Literatur, für eine fortschrittliche deutsche Kultur* (East Berlin: Dietz, 1951).

Lyon, James K. (ed.), 'Der Briefwechsel zwischen Bertolt Brecht und der New Yorker Theatre Union von 1935', *Brecht Yearbook*, 5 (1975), 136–55.

Mahlke, Stefan (ed.), *'Wir sind zu berühmt, um überall hinzugehen': Helene Weigel: Briefwechsel 1935–1971* (Berlin: Theater der Zeit, 2000).

Mainusch, Herbert (ed.), *Regie und Interpretation: Gespräche mit Regisseuren* (Munich: Wilhelm Fink, 1989).

Marx, Karl, and Friedrich Engels, *Über Kunst und Literatur*, ed. Manfred Kliem, 2 vols (East Berlin: Dietz, 1967), i.

May, Gisela, *Mit meinen Augen* (East Berlin: Der Morgen, 1976).

Mickel, Karl, 'Das Berliner Ensemble der Ruth Berghaus', *Theater der Zeit*, Mar./Apr. 1996, 50–1.

Müller, Heiner, 'Brecht gebrauchen, ohne ihn zu kritisieren, ist Verrat', *Theater 1980*, Jahrbuch der Zeitschrift *Theater heute*, 134–6.

—— *Gesammelte Irrtümer 2: Interviews und Gespräche*, ed. Gregor Edelmann and Renate Ziemer (Frankfurt/Main: Verlag der Autoren, 1990).

—— *Krieg ohne Schlacht: Leben in zwei Diktaturen* (Cologne: Kiepenheuer & Witsch, 1992).

Nagel, Ivan, *Streitschriften: Politik Kulturpolitik Theaterpolitik 1957–2001* (Berlin: Siedler, 2001).

Notowicz, Nathan, *Gespräche mit Hanns Eisler und Gerhart Eisler: Wir reden hier nicht von Napoleon: Wir reden von Ihnen!*, ed. Jürgen Elsner (East Berlin: Neue Musik, 1971).

Peymann, Claus, 'Hier herrscht der Kannibalismus', interview with Henryk M. Broder and Wolfgang Höbel, *Der Spiegel*, 25 Feb. 2002, 210–12.

—— 'Im Unruhestand', interview with Volker Corsten, *Die Welt am Sonntag* (Hamburg), 4 Aug. 2002.

—— 'Nichts ist, wie es bleibt', interview with Christine Dössel, *Süddeutsche Zeitung* (Munich), 31 July 2002.

—— 'Wir leben im Übergang', interview with Wolfgang Höbel and Joachim Kronsbein, *Der Spiegel*, 8 Jan. 2001, 161–3.

Piscator, Erwin, *Das politische Theater* (Berlin: Adalbert Schultz, 1929).

Rühle, Günther, *Theater für die Republik im Spiegel der Kritik*, 2 vols, rev. edn (Frankfurt/Main: Fischer, 1988).

Rülicke, Käthe, 'Dreizehn Bühnentechniker erzählen', *Sinn und Form (Sonderheft Bertolt Brecht)*, ed. Deutsche Akademie der Künste (East Berlin: Rütten & Loening, 1957), 465–77.

Sauter, Josef-Hermann, 'Gespräch mit Günther Weisenborn, *Sinn und Form*, 20 (1968), 714–25.

Schaubühne am Halleschen Ufer, '*Peer Gynt*: Protokolle', in *Kreativität und Dialog: Theaterversuche der 70er Jahre in Westeuropa*, ed. Joachim Fiebach and Helmar Schramm (East Berlin: Henschel, 1983), 153–77.

Schroeder, Max, *Von hier und heute aus* (East Berlin: Aufbau, 1957).

Schubbe, Elimar (ed.), *Dokumente zur Kunst-, Literatur- und Kulturpolitik der SED* (Stuttgart: Seewald, 1972).

Senda, Koreya, 'Meine Brecht-Rezeption', *Brecht Yearbook*, 19 (1994), 323–45.

Sozialdemokratische Partei Deutschlands, *Protokoll über die Verhandlungen des Parteitages* (Berlin: J. H. W. Dietz Nachfolger, 1931).

Sternberg, Fritz, *Der Dichter und die Ratio: Erinnerungen an Bertolt Brecht* (Göttingen: Sachse & Pohl, 1963).

Storch, Wolfgang (ed.), *Material Brecht—Kontradiktionen 1968–1976: Erfahrungen bei der Arbeit mit den Stücken von Bertolt Brecht*, Ausstellung und Broschüre aus Anlaß des 4. Kongresses der Internationalen Brecht Gesellschaft (West Berlin: Albert Hentrich, 1976).

Tretyakov, Sergey, 'Bert Brecht', in *Brecht: A Collection of Critical Essays*, ed. Peter Demetz (Englewood Cliffs, NJ: Prentice-Hall, 1962), 16–29.

Verband der Theaterschaffenden der DDR (ed.), *Regisseure der DDR inszenieren Brecht: Materialien und Fotos zu zwölf Inszenierungen* (East Berlin: Verband der Theaterschaffenden, 1977).

Weber, Carl, 'Brecht as Director', *TDR*, 12 (1967), 101–7.

Weisenborn, Günther, 'Hanns Eisler', *Sonntag* (East Berlin), 10 Jan. 1965.

—— *Memorial: Der gespaltene Horizont: Niederschriften eines Außenseiters* (East Berlin: Aufbau, 1982).

Wekwerth, Manfred, 'Brechts Theater mit Brecht selbst verändern', interview with Gerhard Haase, *Deutsche Volkszeitung* (Düsseldorf), 5 May 1977.

—— 'Der Durst nach Sinn', interview with Dieter Kranz, *notate*, 1/87, 10.

—— *Erinnern ist Leben: Eine dramatische Autobiographie* (Leipzig: Faber & Faber, 2000).

—— '*Die Mutter* 1988: Gedanken während der Arbeit', in *Theater nach Brecht: Baukasten für eine Theorie und Praxis des Berliner Ensembles in den neunziger Jahren*, ed. Wekwerth (East Berlin: Sonderausgabe der Theater Arbeit, 1989), 124–9.

—— *Notate: Zur Arbeit des Berliner Ensembles 1956–1966* (East Berlin: Aufbau, 1967).

—— *Schriften: Arbeit mit Brecht* (East Berlin: Henschel, 1973).

—— 'Sieg der Vernunft—Sieg der Vernünftigen', interview with Joachim Maaß, *Neue Berliner Illustrierte* (East Berlin), 29 Sept. 1989.

—— 'Zum Grundverständnis des Berliner Ensembles in unserer Zeit', *Brecht Yearbook*, 16 (1991), 141–51.

Zipes, Jack, 'Interview with Peter Stein', *Brecht heute*, 3 (1973), 210–20.

4.2 Secondary

4.2.1 Die Mutter *and its productions*

Barthes, Roland, 'Sur *La Mère* de Brecht', in *Essais Critiques*, rev. edn (Paris: Editions du Seuil, 1981), 143–6.

Bawey, Petermichael von, 'Dramatic Structure of Revolutionary Language: Tragicomedy in Brecht's *The Mother*', in *Critical Essays on Bertolt Brecht*, ed. Siegfried Mews (Boston: G. K. Hall, 1989), 96–106.

Baxandall, Lee, 'Brecht in America, 1935', *TDR*, 12.1 (Fall 1967), 68–87.

Benjamin, Walter, 'Ein Familiendrama auf dem epischen Theater', in *Versuche über Brecht*, ed. Rolf Tiedemann (Frankfurt/Main: Suhrkamp, 1967), 39–43.

Bradley, Laura, 'Collaboration and Cultural Practice: The "Brecht" Version of *Die Mutter*', *Brecht Yearbook*, 28 (2003), 189–208.

—— ' "A Struggle of Two Styles": Brecht's *Mother* at the New York Theatre Union, 1935', in *Drama Translation and Theatre Practice*, ed. Sabine Coelsch-Foisner and Holger Klein (Frankfurt/Main: Peter Lang, 2004), 399–413.

Canaris, Volker, 'Bertolt Brechts *Mutter* an der Schaubühne—ein Lehrstück', in *Die Mutter: Regiebuch der Schaubühnen-Inszenierung*, ed. Volker Canaris (Frankfurt/Main: Suhrkamp, 1971), 103–18.

Case, Sue-Ellen, 'Brecht and Women: Homosexuality and the Mother', *Brecht Yearbook*, 12 (1983), 65–74.

Dial, Joseph, 'Brecht in den USA', *Weimarer Beiträge*, 24.2 (1978), 160–72.

Dümling, Albrecht, ' "Im Stil der Lehrstücke": Zu Entstehung und Edition von Eislers Musik für Brechts Gorki-Bearbeitung *Die Mutter*', in *Der Text im musikalischen Werk: Editionsprobleme aus musikwissenschaftlicher und literaturwissenschaftlicher Sicht*, ed. Walther Dürr *et al.* (Berlin: Erich Schmidt, 1998), 361–81.

—— 'Die Mutter', in *Brecht Handbuch*, ed. Jan Knopf, 5 vols (Stuttgart: J. B. Metzler, 2001), i. 294–309.

Frey, Daniel, '*La Mère*: De Gorki à Brecht à travers trente ans d'histoire', *Etudes de lettres*, n.s. 6 (1963), 125–51.

Goldhahn, Johannes, 'Brecht und Gorki—eingreifendes Lernen', *notate*, 5/87, 6–8.

Gordon, Mel, 'The San Francisco Mime Troupe's *The Mother*', *TDR*, 19.2 (June 1975), 94–101.

Hecht, Werner (ed.), *Materialien zu Bertolt Brechts 'Die Mutter'* (Frankfurt/Main: Suhrkamp, 1976).

Himelstein, Morgan Y., 'The Pioneers of Bertolt Brecht in America', *Modern Drama*, 9 (1966), 178–89.

Kepka, Ania, 'The Relationship of Brecht's *Die Mutter* to its Sources: A Reassessment', *GLL*, 38 (1985), 233–48.

Klatt, Gudrun, 'Brechts *Mutter*: Zur Geschichte eines Theatermodells', *Connaissance de la RDA*, 9 (1979), 187–200.

Piens, Margot, 'Über Gesetzmäßigkeiten bei der Anwendung von Modellen am Beispiel der Inszenierungen von Bertolt Brechts Stück *Die Mutter* am Berliner Ensemble unter Berücksichtigung des besonderen Charakters des Lehrstücks' (unpublished *Diplomarbeit*, Theaterwissenschaftliche Abteilung der Theaterhochschule 'Hanns Otto' in Leipzig, 1968).

Reus, Günther, 'Die historisierende Neuinszenierung von Brechts *Mutter* 1951', in *Oktoberrevolution und Sowjetrußland auf dem deutschen Theater: Zur Verwendung eines geschichtlichen Motivs im deutschen Schauspiel von 1918 bis zur Gegenwart*, 2 vols (Bonn: Bouvier, 1978), ii. 254–8.

Ritterhof, Teresa, 'Ver/Ratlosigkeit: Benjamin, Brecht, and *Die Mutter*', *Brecht Yearbook*, 24 (1999), 247–62.

Schumacher, Claude, 'The Glasgow Citizens Company Production of Brecht's *The Mother* (Nov.–Dec. 1982)', in *Das Drama und seine Inszenierung*, ed. Erika Fischer-Lichte, Medien in Forschung + Unterricht, series A, 16 (Tübingen: Niemeyer, 1985), 173–85.

Thomas, Emma Lewis, 'Bertolt Brecht's Drama *Die Mutter*: A Case of Double Adaptation' (unpublished doctoral thesis, Indiana University, 1972).

——— 'The Stark–Weisenborn Adaptation of Gorky's *Mutter*: Its Influence on Brecht's Version', *Brecht heute*, 3 (1973), 57–63.

Tschörtner, Heinz-Dieter, '*Die Mutter* für das Theater', *Neue Deutsche Literatur*, 34 (1986), 168–72.

4.2.2 Theories of performance, reception, and translation

Bassnett, Susan, and André Lefevere (eds), *Constructing Cultures: Essays on Literary Translation*, Topics in Translation, 11 (Clevedon: Multilingual Matters, 1998).

——— ——— (eds), *Translation, History and Culture*, rev. edn (London: Cassell, 1995).

Bennett, Susan, *Theatre Audiences: A Theory of Production and Reception*, 2nd edn (London: Routledge, 1999).

Carlson, Marvin, 'Invisible Presences: Performance Intertextuality', *Theatre Research International*, 19/2 (1994), 111–16.

Gooch, Steve, *All Together Now: An Alternative View of Theatre and the Community* (London: Methuen, 1984).

Harris, Geraldine, *Staging Femininities: Performance and Performativity* (Manchester: Manchester University Press, 1999).

Hiß, Guido, *Der theatralische Blick: Einführung in die Aufführungsanalyse* (Berlin: Dietrich Reimer, 1993).

Iser, Wolfgang, *Der Akt des Lesens: Theorie ästhetischer Wirkung* (Munich: Wilhelm Fink, 1976).

Jauß, Hans Robert, *Ästhetische Erfahrung und literarische Hermeneutik* (Frankfurt/Main: Suhrkamp, 1982).

—— *Literaturgeschichte als Provokation der Literaturwissenschaft* (Konstanz: Universitätsverlag, 1967).

Kohlmayer, Rainer, *Oscar Wilde in Deutschland und Österreich: Untersuchungen zur Rezeption der Komödien und zur Theorie der Bühnenübersetzung* (Tübingen: Niemeyer, 1996).

McGrath, John, *The Bone Won't Break: On Theatre and Hope in Hard Times* (London: Methuen, 1990).

—— *A Good Night Out: Popular Theatre: Audience, Class and Form*, 2nd edn (London: Nick Hern, 1996).

—— *Naked Thoughts that Roam About: Reflections on Theatre 1958–2001*, ed. Nadine Holdsworth (London: Nick Hern, 2002).

Marinis, Marco de, ' "A Faithful Betrayal of Performance": Notes on the Use of Video in Theatre', *New Theatre Quarterly*, 1.4 (Nov. 1985), 383–9.

Pavis, Patrice, *Languages of the Stage: Essays in the Semiology of the Theatre* (New York: Performing Arts Journal, 1982).

—— *Theatre at the Crossroads of Culture*, trans. Loren Kruger (London: Routledge, 1992).

Rabkin, Gerald, 'Is There a Text on This Stage?', *Performing Arts Journal*, 26/7 (1985), 142–59.

Rubidge, Sarah, 'Does Authenticity Matter? The Case for and against Authenticity in the Performing Arts', in *Analysing Performance: A Critical Reader*, ed. Patrick Campbell (Manchester: Manchester University Press, 1996), 219–33.

Schleiermacher, Friedrich, 'Über die verschiedenen Methoden des Übersetzens', in *Das Problem des Übersetzens*, ed. Hans Joachim Störig, Wege der Forschung, 8 (Stuttgart: Henry Goverts, 1963), 38–70.

Scolnicov, Hanna, and Peter Holland (eds), *Transferring Plays from Culture to Culture* (Cambridge: Cambridge University Press, 1989).

Toro, Fernando de, *Theatre Semiotics: Text and Staging in Modern Theatre*, trans. John Lewis, rev. and ed. Carole Hubbard (Toronto: University of Toronto Press, 1995).

Venuti, Laurence, *The Translator's Invisibility: A History of Translation* (London: Routledge, 1995).

Warning, Rainer (ed.), *Rezeptionsästhetik: Theorie und Praxis* (Munich: Wilhelm Fink, 1975).

Wekwerth, Manfred, *Theater und Wissenschaft* (Munich: Hanser, 1974).

Wolff, Janet, *The Social Production of Art* (London: Macmillan, 1981).

4.2.3 Other secondary sources

Anon., 'Le Répertoire du Berliner Ensemble de 1949 à 1986', *Théâtre en Europe*, 12 (Oct. 1986), 70–1.

Ansorge, Peter, *Disrupting the Spectacle: Five Years of Experimental and Fringe Theatre in Britain* (London: Pitman, 1975).

Beil, Hermann, *et al.* (eds), *Bertolt Brecht on Stage: Exhibition by Inter Nationes* (Frankfurt/Main: Erich Imbescheidt, 1968).

Bertisch, Klaus, *Ruth Berghaus* (Frankfurt/Main: Fischer, 1989).

Betz, Albrecht, *Hanns Eisler: Musik einer Zeit, die sich eben bildet*, ed. Heinz Ludwig Arnold (Munich: edition text + kritik, 1976).

Bodek, Richard, *Proletarian Performance in Weimar Berlin: Agitprop, Chorus, and Brecht* (Columbia, SC: Camden House, 1997).

Bryant-Bertail, Sarah, *Space and Time in Epic Theater: The Brechtian Legacy* (Rochester, NY: Camden House, 2000).

Burns, Rob, and Wilfried van der Will, *Protest and Democracy in West Germany: Extra-Parliamentary Opposition and the Democratic Agenda* (London: Macmillan, 1988).

Champagne, Lenora, *French Theatre Experiment since 1968*, Theater and Dramatic Studies, 18 (Michigan: UMI, 1984).

Coveney, Michael, *The Citz: 21 Years of the Glasgow Citizens Theatre* (London: Nick Hern, 1990).

Cronin, Mary J., 'The Politics of Brecht's Women Characters' (unpublished doctoral thesis, Brown University, 1974).

Dümling, Albrecht, *Laßt euch nicht verführen: Brecht und die Musik* (Munich: Kindler, 1985).

Durrani, Osman, Colin Good, and Kevin Hilliard (eds), *The New Germany: Literature and Society after Unification* (Sheffield: Sheffield Academic Press, 1995).

Eckert, Nora, *Das Bühnenbild im 20. Jahrhundert* (Berlin: Henschel, 1998).

Eddershaw, Margaret, *Performing Brecht: Forty Years of British Performances* (London: Routledge, 1996).

Einem, Gottfried von, and Siegfried Melchinger (eds), *Caspar Neher* (Velber bei Hannover: Friedrich, 1966).

Ekmann, Bjørn, *Gesellschaft und Gewissen: Die sozialen und moralischen Anschauungen Bertolt Brechts und ihre Bedeutung für seine Dichtung* (Copenhagen: Munksgaard, 1969).

Emmerich, Wolfgang, *Kleine Literaturgeschichte der DDR*, rev. edn (Leipzig: Kiepenheuer, 1996).

Erbe, Günter, *Die verfemte Moderne: Die Auseinandersetzung mit dem 'Modernismus' in Kulturpolitik, Literaturwissenschaft und Literatur der DDR* (Opladen: Westdeutscher Verlag, 1993).

Erdmann-Rajski, Katja, *Gret Palucca: Tanz und Tanzerfahrung in Deutschland im 20. Jahrhundert: Weimarer Republik, Nationalsozialismus, Deutsche Demokratische Republik* (Hildesheim: Georg Olms, 2000).

Esslin, Martin, *Brecht: A Choice of Evils* (London: Mercury, 1965).

Fehervary, Helen, 'Enlightenment or Entanglement: History and Aesthetics in Bertolt Brecht and Heiner Müller', *New German Critique*, 8 (Spring 1976), 80–109.

Fetting, Hugo, 'Caspar Neher: *Die Mutter*, Berliner Ensemble, 1951', *Theater der Zeit*, Nov. 1979, 1.

Fiebach, Joachim, ' "Das entscheidende [*sic*] für uns ... ist das Theater in Paradoxis": Zur Schaubühne am Halleschen Ufer von 1970 bis 1980', in *Theater seit den 60er Jahren: Grenzgänge der Neo-Avantgarde*, ed. Erika Fischer-Lichte, Friedemann Kreuder, and Isabel Pflug (Tübingen: Franke, 1998), 235–315.

——Christa Hasche, and Traute Schölling, *Theater in der DDR: Chronik und Positionen* (Berlin: Henschel, 1994).

Fischbach, Fred, 'Brecht, Eisler et les pièces didactiques', in *Bertolt Brecht: Actes du Colloque franco-allemand tenu en Sorbonne (15–19 novembre 1988)*, ed. Jean-Marie Vallentin and Theo Buck (Bern: Peter Lang, 1990), 139–62.

——'Pour une nouvelle lecture des pièces de Brecht à la lumière de la musique de scène de Hanns Eisler', *Recherches germaniques*, 13 (1983), 137–66.

Fuegi, John, *Bertolt Brecht: Chaos According to Plan* (Cambridge: Cambridge University Press, 1987).

——*Brecht & Co.: Sex, Politics, and the Making of the Modern Drama* (New York: Grove, 1994).

——*The Essential Brecht* (Los Angeles: Hennessey & Ingalls, 1972).

Garde, Ulrike, ' "Never in Body and Seldom in Spirit": Australian Productions of Brecht's Plays and their Reviews from 1945 to 1998', *Brecht Yearbook*, 26 (2001), 101–25.

Gersch, Wolfgang, *Film bei Brecht: Bertolt Brechts praktische und theoretische Auseinandersetzung mit dem Film* (East Berlin: Henschel, 1975).

Geyer, Dietrich, 'Sowjetrußland und die deutsche Arbeiterbewegung 1918–1932', *Vierteljahresheft für Zeitgeschichte*, 24 (1976), 2–37.

Glaser, Hermann, *Kleine Kulturgeschichte der Bundesrepublik Deutschland 1945–1989* (Munich: Hanser, 1991).

Godard, Colette, *Le Théâtre depuis 1968* (Paris: J.-C. Lattès, 1980).

Goldstein, Malcolm, *The Political Stage: American Drama and Theater of the Great Depression* (New York: Oxford University Press, 1974).

Goodbody, Axel, Dennis Tate, and Ian Wallace, 'The Failed Socialist Experiment: Culture in the GDR', in *German Cultural Studies: An Introduction*, ed. Rob Burns (Oxford: Oxford University Press, 1995), 147–207.

Gorelik, Mordecai, *New Theatres for Old* (New York: Samuel French, 1947).

Grabs, Manfred, *Hanns Eisler: Kompositionen—Schriften—Literatur: Ein Handbuch* (Leipzig: Deutscher Verlag für Musik, 1984).

—— *Hanns Eisler: Werk und Edition*, Arbeitsheft 28 (East Berlin: AdK, 1978).

Hahn, Hans J., ' "Es geht nicht um Literatur": Some Observations on the 1990 "Literaturstreit" and its Recent Anti-Intellectual Implications', *GLL*, 50 (1997), 65–81.

Hahn, Karl-Claus (ed.), *Brecht 81: Brecht in sozialistischen Ländern*, Brecht-Zentrum der DDR, 3 (East Berlin: Henschel, 1981).

Hanssen, Paula, *Elisabeth Hauptmann: Brecht's Silent Collaborator* (Frankfurt/Main: Peter Lang, 1994).

Hartnoll, Phyllis, and Peter Found, *The Oxford Concise Companion to the Theatre*, 2nd edn (Oxford: Oxford University Press, 1996).

Hecht, Werner, *Brecht Chronik* (Frankfurt/Main: Suhrkamp, 1997).

—— *Brecht: Vielseitige Betrachtungen* (East Berlin: Henschel, 1978).

—— 'Farewell to her Audience: Helene Weigel's Triumph and Final Exit', *Brecht Yearbook*, 25 (2000), 317–27.

—— *Helene Weigel: Eine große Frau des zwanzigsten Jahrhunderts* (Frankfurt/Main: Suhrkamp, 2000).

—— *Sieben Studien über Brecht* (Frankfurt/Main: Suhrkamp, 1972).

Henneberg, Fritz (ed.), *Das große Brecht-Liederbuch*, 3 vols (Frankfurt/Main: Suhrkamp, 1984), iii: *Kommentare*.

—— 'Zur Dialektik des Schließens in Liedern von Hanns Eisler', in *Sammelbände zur Musikgeschichte der DDR*, ed. Heinz Alfred Brockhaus and Konrad Niemann (East Berlin: Neue Musik, 1971).

Herlinghaus, Hermann, *Slatan Dudow* (East Berlin: Henschel, 1965).

Herold, Christine, *Mutter des Ensembles: Helene Weigel—ein Leben mit Bertolt Brecht* (Cadolzburg: ars vivendi, 2001).

Heukenkamp, Ursula and Rudolf, *Karl Mickel* (East Berlin: Volk & Wissen, 1985).

Himelstein, Morgan Y., *Drama Was a Weapon: The Left-Wing Theatre in New York 1929–1941* (New Brunswick, NJ: Rutgers University Press, 1963).

Hoffmann, Dieter, Helmut Müller-Enbergs, and Jan Wielgohs (eds), *Wer war wer in der DDR? Ein biographisches Lexikon*, 2nd rev. edn (Berlin: Ch. Links, 2001).

Horst, Astrid, *Prima inter pares: Elisabeth Hauptmann: Die Mitarbeiterin Bertolt Brechts* (Würzburg: Königshausen & Neumann, 1992).

Hubert, Martin, *Politisierung der Literatur—Ästhetisierung der Politik: Eine Studie zur literaturgeschichtlichen Bedeutung der 68er Bewegung in der Bundesrepublik Deutschland* (Frankfurt/Main: Peter Lang, 1992).

Iden, Peter, *Die Schaubühne am Halleschen Ufer 1970–1979* (Munich: Hanser, 1979).

Itzin, Catherine, *Stages in the Revolution: Political Theatre in Britain since 1968* (London: Eyre Methuen, 1980).

Jacobs, Nicholas, and Prudence Ohlsen (eds), *Bertolt Brecht in Britain* (London: Irat/TQ, 1997).

Jäger, Andreas, *John McGrath und die 7:84 Company Schottland: Politik, Popularität und Regionalismus im Theater der siebziger Jahre in Schottland*, Münchener Studien zur neueren englischen Literatur, 1 (Amsterdam: B. R. Grüner, 1986).

Jäger, Manfred, *Kultur und Politik in der DDR 1945–1990* (Cologne: Nottbeck, 1995).

Jameson, Fredric, *Brecht and Method* (London: Verso, 1998).

Jelavich, Peter, *Berlin Cabaret* (Cambridge, Mass.: Harvard University Press, 1993).

Jones, David Richard, *Great Directors at Work: Stanislavsky, Brecht, Kazan, Brook* (Berkeley: University of California Press, 1986).

Joyce, Douglas A., *Hugo von Hofmannsthal's 'Der Schwierige': A Fifty-Year Theater History* (Columbia, SC: Camden House, 1993).

Kändler, Klaus, *Drama und Klassenkampf: Beziehungen zwischen Epochen-problematik und dramatischem Konflikt in der sozialistischen Dramatik der Weimarer Republik*, Beiträge zur Geschichte der deutschen sozialistischen Literatur im 20. Jahrhundert, 4 (East Berlin: Aufbau, 1970).

Karasek, Helmuth, *Bertolt Brecht: Vom Bürgerschreck zum Klassiker* (Hamburg: Hoffmann & Campe, 1995).

Kebir, Sabine, *Ein akzeptabler Mann? Streit um Brechts Partnerbeziehungen* (East Berlin: Der Morgen, 1987).

——*Ich fragte nicht nach meinem Anteil: Elisabeth Hauptmanns Arbeit mit Bertolt Brecht* (Berlin: Aufbau, 1997).

Kleber, Pia, and Colin Visser (eds), *Re-interpreting Brecht: His Influence on Contemporary Drama and Film* (Cambridge: Cambridge University Press, 1990).

Klunker, Heinz, *Zeitstücke und Zeitgenossen: Gegenwartstheater in der DDR* (Munich: DTV, 1975).

Knellessen, Friedrich Wolfgang, *Agitation auf der Bühne: Das politische Theater der Weimarer Republik* (Emsdetten: Lechte, 1970).

Knepler, Georg, 'Was des Eislers ist …', *Beiträge zur Musikwissenschaft*, 15 (1973), 29–47.

Knopf, Jan, *Brecht-Handbuch: Theater* (Stuttgart: J. B. Metzler, 1980).

——'Verfremdung', in *Brechts Theorie des Theaters*, ed. Werner Hecht (Frankfurt/Main: Suhrkamp, 1986), 93–141.

Koberg, Roland, *Claus Peymann: Aller Tage Abenteuer* (Berlin: Henschel, 1999).

Kuhn, Tom, 'Bertolt Brecht and Notions of Collaboration', in *Bertolt Brecht: Centenary Essays*, ed. Steve Giles and Rodney Livingstone (Amsterdam: Rodopi, 1998).

Kurz, Thomas, *'Blutmai': Sozialdemokraten und Kommunisten im Brennpunkt der Berliner Ereignisse von 1929* (Bonn: J. H. W. Dietz Nachfolger, 1988).

Lennox, Sara, 'Women in Brecht's Works', *New German Critique*, 14 (1978), 83–96.

Lucchesi, Joachim, and Ronald K. Shull, *Musik bei Brecht* (Frankfurt/Main: Suhrkamp, 1988).

Lyon, James K., *Bertolt Brecht in America* (Princeton: Princeton University Press, 1980).

—— 'Brecht in Postwar Germany: Dissident Conformist, Cultural Icon, Literary Dictator', in *Brecht Unbound*, ed. James K. Lyon and Hans-Peter Breuer (London: Associated University Presses, 1995), 76–88.

—— 'Collective Productivity: Brecht and his Collaborators', *Brecht Yearbook*, 21 (1996), 1–18.

Mittenzwei, Werner, *Bertolt Brecht: Von der 'Maßnahme' zu 'Leben des Galilei'*, 4th edn (East Berlin: Aufbau, 1977).

—— (ed.), *Wer war Brecht? Der Realismusstreit um Brecht: Grundriß zu einer Brecht-Rezeption der DDR 1945–1976* (West Berlin: Verlag das europäische Buch, 1977).

Mumford, Meg, 'Showing the Gestus: A Study of Acting in Brecht's Theatre' (unpublished doctoral thesis, University of Bristol, 1997).

Needle, Jan, and Peter Thomson, *Brecht* (Oxford: Blackwell, 1981).

Neef, Sigrid, *Das Theater der Ruth Berghaus* (East Berlin: Henschel, 1989).

Nössig, Manfred, Johanna Rosenberg, and Bärbel Schrader, *Literaturdebatten in der Weimarer Republik: Zur Entwicklung des marxistischen literaturtheoretischen Denkens 1918–1933* (East Berlin: Aufbau, 1980).

Nussbaum, Laureen, 'The Evolution of the Feminine Principle in Brecht's Work: Beyond the Feminist Critique', *German Studies Review*, 8.2 (May 1985), 217–44.

—— 'The Image of Woman in the Work of Bertolt Brecht' (unpublished doctoral thesis, University of Washington, 1977).

Paffrath, Elifius (ed.), *Brecht 80: Brecht in Afrika, Asien und Lateinamerika: Dokumentation*, Brecht-Zentrum der DDR, 2 (East Berlin: Henschel, 1980).

Palm, Kurt, *Vom Boykott zur Anerkennung: Brecht und Österreich*, rev. edn (Vienna: Löcker, 1984).

Parker, Stephen, Matthew Philpotts, and Peter Davies, 'Introduction to Part Five', in *Brecht on Art and Politics*, ed. Steve Giles and Tom Kuhn (London: Methuen, 2003).

Patterson, Michael, *Peter Stein: Germany's Leading Theatre Director* (Cambridge: Cambridge University Press, 1981).

——— *The Revolution in German Theatre 1900–1933* (London: Routledge and Kegan Paul, 1981).

Philpotts, Matthew, *The Margins of Dictatorship: Assent and Dissent in the Work of Günter Eich and Bertolt Brecht*, British and Irish Studies in German Language and Literature, 34 (Bern: Peter Lang, 2003).

Pianca, Marina, 'Brecht in Latin America: Theater Bearing Witness', in *A Bertolt Brecht Reference Companion*, ed. Siegfried Mews (Westport, Conn.: Greenwood Press, 1997), 356–78.

Rabkin, Gerald, *Drama and Commitment: Politics in the American Theatre of the Thirties* (Bloomington: Indiana University Press, 1964).

Raddatz, Fritz J., 'Ent-weiblichte Eschatologie: Bertolt Brechts revolutionärer Gegenmythos', in *Text & Kritik Sonderband Bertolt Brecht II*, ed. Heinz Ludwig Arnold (Munich: Richard Boorberg, 1973), 152–9.

Rischbieter, Henning, *Brecht*, 2 vols (Velber: Friedrich, 1966), i.

Ritchie, Gisela F., 'Erst Opfer—dann Trägerin der Handlung: Die Aufgabe der Frau bei Brecht', in *Der Dichter und die Frau: Literarische Frauengestalten durch drei Jahrhunderte* (Bonn: Bouvier, 1989), 213–50.

Rouse, John, *Brecht and the West German Theatre: The Practice and Politics of Interpretation*, Theater and Dramatic Studies, 62 (London: UMI, 1989).

Rülicke-Weiler, Käthe, *Die Dramaturgie Brechts: Theater als Mittel der Veränderung* (East Berlin: Henschel, 1968).

Schebera, Jürgen, *Hanns Eisler: Eine Bildbiografie* (East Berlin: Henschel, 1981).

Schlenker, Wolfram, 'Brecht hinter der Großen Mauer: Zu seiner Rezeption in der Volksrepublik China', *Brecht Yearbook*, 9 (1980), 43–137.

Schoeps, Karl-Heinz, 'Brechts *Lehrstücke*: A Laboratory for Epic and Dialectic Theatre', in *A Bertolt Brecht Reference Companion*, ed. Siegfried Mews (Westport, Conn.: Greenwood Press, 1997), 70–87.

Schumacher, Ernst, *Die dramatischen Versuche Bertolt Brechts 1918–1933* (East Berlin: Rütten & Loening, 1955).

Schwarz, Roswita, *Vom expressionistischen Aufbruch zur Inneren Emigration: Günther Weisenborns weltanschauliche und künstlerische Entwicklung in der Weimarer Republik und im Dritten Reich* (Frankfurt/Main: Peter Lang, 1995).

Shellard, Dominic, *British Theatre since the War* (New Haven: Yale University Press, 1999).

Sheppard, Richard, *Tankred Dorst's Toller: A Case-Study in Reception* (New Alyth: Lochee, 1989).

Smeliansky, Anatoly, *The Russian Theatre after Stalin*, trans. Patrick Miles (Cambridge: Cambridge University Press, 1999).

Smith, Patricia J. (ed.), *After the Wall: Eastern Germany since 1989* (Boulder, Colo.: Westview Press, 1999).

Speirs, Ronald, *Bertolt Brecht* (London: Macmillan, 1987).

Sperr, Monika (ed.), *Therese Giehse: 'Ich hab nichts zum Sagen'* (East Berlin: Henschel, 1977).

Stuber, Petra, 'Helene Weigel und ihre Rolle als Intendantin zwischen 1949 und 1954', *Brecht Yearbook*, 25 (2000), 252–75.

—— *Spielräume und Grenzen: Studien zum DDR-Theater* (Berlin: Ch. Links, 1998).

Suvin, Darko, 'A Brief Introduction to Senda Koreya [*sic*]: Theater Director and Brechtian', *Brecht Yearbook*, 19 (1994), 291–5.

Tatsuji, Iwabuchi, 'Die Brecht-Rezeption in Japan aus dem Aspekt der Theaterpraxis', *Brecht Yearbook*, 14 (1989), 87–99.

Thomson, Peter, *Brecht: Mother Courage and her Children* (Cambridge: Cambridge University Press, 1997).

Törnqvist, Egil, *Ibsen: A Doll's House* (Cambridge: Cambridge University Press, 1995).

Völker, Klaus, *Bertolt Brecht: Eine Biografie* (Munich: DTV, 1978).

Wandor, Michelene, *Look Back in Gender: Sexuality and the Family in Post-War British Drama* (London: Methuen, 1987).

—— 'Women Playwrights and the Challenge of Feminism in the 1970s', in *The Cambridge Companion to Modern British Women Playwrights*, ed. Elaine Aston and Janelle Reinelt (Cambridge: Cambridge University Press, 2000), 53–68.

Weber, Carl, 'Brecht and the Berliner Ensemble: The Making of a Model', in *The Cambridge Companion to Brecht*, ed. Peter Thomson and Glendyr Sacks (Cambridge: Cambridge University Press, 1994), 167–84.

—— 'Brecht is at Home in Asia', *Brecht Yearbook*, 14 (1989), 30–43.

Weisstuch, Mark W., 'The Theatre Union, 1933–1937: A History' (unpublished doctoral thesis, City University of New York, 1982).

Wekwerth, Manfred, 'Was spricht eigentlich gegen Brecht?', *Das Argument*, 226 (1998), 531–42.

White, John J., *Bertolt Brecht's Dramatic Theory* (Rochester, NY: Camden House, 2004).

Whitton, David, *Stage Directors in Modern France* (Manchester: Manchester University Press, 1987).

Willett, John, 'Bacon ohne Shakespeare? The Problem of Mitarbeit', *Brecht Yearbook*, 12 (1983), 121–37.

—— *Caspar Neher: Brecht's Designer* (London: Methuen, 1986).

Williams, Jay, *Stage Left* (New York: Charles Scribner's Sons, 1974).

Worrall, Nick, *Modernism to Realism on the Soviet Stage: Tairov—Vakhtangov—Okhlopkov* (Cambridge: Cambridge University Press, 1989).

Wright, Elizabeth, *Postmodern Brecht: A Re-Presentation* (London: Routledge, 1989).

Zipes, Jack, 'The Irresistible Rise of the Schaubühne am halleschen [*sic*] Ufer: A Retrospective of the West Berlin Theater Collective', *Theater*, 7 (1977), 7–45.

5. INTERNET RESOURCES

Berliner Ensemble repertoire, <http://www.berliner-ensemble.de/index_repertoire.htm> [accessed 24 Feb. 2005].

Companhia Ensaio Aberto, <http://www.ensaioaberto.com/a_mae_imagens.htm> [accessed 21 Feb. 2005].

European Industrial Relations Observatory Online, 'Nationwide Protests As Unemployment Reaches New Record High', <http://www.eiro.eurofound.ie/print/1998/02/feature/DE9802148F.html> [accessed 10 Jan. 2003].

German general election results 1949–2002, <http://www.election.de> [accessed 24 Feb. 2005].

German unemployment statistics 2002, <http://www.arbeitsamt.de/hst/statistik/200210/iiia4/s0341.pdf> [accessed 11 Jan. 2003].

Irondale Ensemble Project, <http://www.irondale.org> [accessed 21 Feb. 2005].

——newsletter for *The Mother*, <http://www.irondale.org/newsletters/FALL97.PDF> [accessed 21 Feb. 2005].

Klee, Paul, 'Brückenbögen treten aus der Reihe', <http://www.guggenheimcollection.org/site/artist_work_md_75_7.html> [accessed 24 Feb. 2005].

—— 'Revolution des Viaduktes', <http://www.architetturamoderna.com/klee/Immagini/Viaduct%20Revolution,%20193.jpg> [accessed 24 Feb. 2005].

Stadttheater Konstanz, 'Die Spielzeit 2002/2003 im Einzelnen', <http://stadt.konstanz.de/kultur_freizeit/theater/stadttheater_kn/vorschau/inhalt/index.htm> [accessed 24 Feb. 2005].

Index of Works by Brecht

Titles of the works quoted or mentioned in this book are listed below in both German and English.

Index of Names and Subjects

Italic numbers denote reference to illustrations.